patient care ®
PROCEDURES
FOR YOUR
PRACTICE

patient care®

PROCEDURES FOR YOUR PRACTICE

Edited by

Charles E. Driscoll, MD
Professor and Head
Department of Family Practice
The University of Iowa
Iowa City, Iowa

Robert E. Rakel, MD
Associate Dean for Academic and Clinical Affairs
Professor and Chairman
Department of Family Medicine
Baylor College of Medicine
Houston, Texas

Medical Economics Books
Oradell, New Jersey 07649

Designer: Brianne Carey Wright

Illustrator: Paul Singh-Roy

Library of Congress Cataloging-in-Publication Data

Driscoll, Charles E.
  Patient care procedures for your practice.

  Articles reprinted from Patient care.
  Includes bibliographies.
  1. Family medicine. I. Rakel, Robert E.
II. Patient care. III. Title. [DNLM: 1. Family Practice—methods—collected
works. WB 110 D781p]
RC46.D75 1987   616   87-18571
ISBN 0-87489-444-1

ISBN 0-87489-444-1

Medical Economics Company Inc.
Oradell, New Jersey 07649

Printed in the United States of America

The authors and publisher have exerted every effort to ensure that drug selection,
dosage, and therapeutic modalities set forth in this text are in accord with current
recommendations and practice at the time of publication. However, in view of ongoing
research, changes in government regulations, and the constant flow of information
relating to drug therapy and drug reactions, the reader is urged to check the package
insert for each drug for any change in indications and dosage and for added warnings
and precautions. This is particularly important when the recommended agent is a new
or infrequently employed drug.

Contents

Contributors

Timothy Appenheimer, MD
Family Physician
Department of Family Practice
Medical Arts Clinic
Dixon, Illinois

Martin M. Bartolac, MD
Family Physician
Columbus, Wisconsin

Elizabeth A. Burns, MD, MA
Associate Professor and
Associate Residency Director
Department of Family Practice
The University of Iowa
Iowa City, Iowa

Carol Buss, RD, LD
Private Practitioner and Owner
Nutrition Associates of Iowa City
Iowa City, Iowa

R.J. Coble, MD
Director of Patient Care
Department of Family Practice
The University of Iowa
Iowa City, Iowa

Phillip Couchman, MD
Family Physician
Rockport, Massachusetts

Keith E. Davis, MD
Family Physician
Shoshone Family Medical Center
Shoshone, Idaho

Richard C. Dobyns, MD
Family Physician
Family Practice Medical Center
   of Willmar, Minnesota
Willmar, Minnesota

Dan Heslinga, MD
Resident Physician
Department of Family Practice
The University of Iowa
Iowa City, Iowa

Charles D. Huss, MD
Director
Emergency Care Unit
Mercy Hospital
Iowa City, Iowa

Rafael Ivan Iriarte, MD
Associate Professor
Department of Family Medicine
Ponce School of Medicine
Ponce, Puerto Rico

Ralph Knudson, MD
Associate
Department of Family Practice
The University of Iowa
Iowa City, Iowa

Elizabeth Loeb, MS, MD
Assistant Professor
Department of Family Practice
The University of Iowa
Iowa City, Iowa

Gerald J. McGowan, MD
Program Director
Family Practice Residency
  Program
Siouxland Medical Education
  Foundation Inc.
Sioux City, Iowa

Richard E. Munns, MD
Clinical Associate Professor
Department of Family Practice
The University of Iowa
Director
Family Practice Residency
St. Joseph Mercy Hospital
Mason City, Iowa

Timothy Nagel, MD
Family Physician
Community Family Practice Clinic
Clarion, Iowa

Gayle Nelson, RN
Program Associate and Coordinator
Family Physician Learning Lab
Department of Family Practice
The University of Iowa
Iowa City, Iowa

Richard W. Niska, MD
Emergency Physician
Department of Emergency Services
Kennebec Valley Medical Center
Augusta, Maine

Darrell Randle, MD
Department of Family Practice
US Army Hospital
Wurzburg, Germany

Leroy R. Schlesselman, MD
Resident
Department of Family Practice
The University of Iowa
Iowa City, Iowa

Elliott D. Schmerler, MD
Family Physician
Incline Village, Nevada

Lawrence W. Steinkraus, MD
Associate
Department of Family Practice
The University of Iowa
Iowa City, Iowa

Bev L. True, Pharm.D
Medical Student
The University of Iowa
College of Medicine
Iowa City, Iowa

Leslie E. Weber, MD
Associate
Department of Family Practice
The University of Iowa
Iowa City, Iowa

Glenys O. Williams, MD
Associate Professor
Department of Family Practice
The University of Iowa
College of Medicine
Iowa City, Iowa

Paul S. Williamson, MD
Associate Professor
Department of Family Practice
The University of Iowa
Iowa City, Iowa

Steve A. Wilson, MD
Family Physician
Department of Family Practice
Fairview Ridges Hospital
Burnsville, Minnesota

Foreword

Since family practice is a relatively new specialty, most books used are written by physicians in other fields. Consequently, much of what is printed misses the mark, either by including details that are not relevant to family medicine, or by omitting problems that are frequently seen.

This book hits the mark. It is written by family physicians for family and primary care physicians. I doubt that there is a procedure commonly performed in primary care that is not in this volume. Even if you are comfortable with a particular procedure, you should be reassured to review the technique, especially if you have not performed it for awhile.

While other procedural volumes have been written, none has been so carefully planned to aid the busy practitioner. Careful selection of appropriate procedures is combined with clear separation of the various phases necessary for successful performance. Other procedural guides provide less step-by-step, descriptive procedural detail—a point of particular relevance to primary care.

In your office, you often need to perform a simple, relatively noninvasive procedure, but the details of the technique are too vague in your mind to feel comfortable proceeding. This book should provide the necessary refresher to enable you to go ahead and complete each procedure accurately and safely.

Drs. Driscoll, Rakel, and colleagues have provided other important information for performing these procedures, including indications, contraindications, complications, and suggestions for further reading. Clear, helpful illustrations complete the requirements for a well-written procedural handbook that will help you provide the highest quality patient care.

Charles W. Smith, Jr, MD
Professor of Family Medicine and Dean,
School of Primary Medical Care
University of Alabama in Huntsville

Preface

On numerous occasions in a busy medical practice, particularly in an ambulatory setting, a technical procedure will aid in diagnosis or management of a patient's condition. These procedures are familiar, but perhaps not practiced frequently. You may ask: What are the anatomic landmarks for exact placement of the needle? What are the contraindications to performing this procedure? These and other common questions prompted us to prepare this book as an instruction guide for performing a new procedure and as a refresher on proper technique.

These "Procedures for Your Practice" have appeared in the journal, *Patient Care*. We have rewritten and updated each procedure. Current references and tables are provided for interpretation of diagnostic tests (e.g., synovial fluid analysis and percent body fat).

This book should serve as a quick, ready, and clear reference to appropriate indications, contraindications, and methods for performing the most common procedures you will encounter in your practice. We hope you will find it an easy to use and helpful guide.

Charles E. Driscoll, MD

Publisher's Notes

These procedures for your practice are drawn from *Patient Care* magazine. The authors are hands-on practitioners who know and do what they are talking about, and show you how to do it simply and safely. The coeditors of the book have been the coordinators of the magazine series: Dr. Rakel introduced the first procedure in 1983; Dr. Driscoll began in 1985 and continues to produce the series.

Charles E. Driscoll, MD, is professor and head of the Department of Family Practice at the University of Iowa College of Medicine in Iowa City, coauthor of *The Handbook of Family Practice,* and associate editor of *Year Book of Family Practice.*

Robert E. Rakel, MD, is associate dean for academic and clinical affairs and professor and chairman of the Department of Family Medicine at the Baylor College of Medicine in Houston, author of *Principles of Family Medicine,* and editor of *Textbook of Family Practice, Conn's Current Therapy,* and *Year Book of Family Practice.*

Paul Singh-Roy drew the illustrations for the magazine series and book.

Richard F. Graber edited the original manuscripts.

Robert L. Edsall, editor of *Patient Care,* was there at each step from conception to completion of the book.

Caroline Mast was an invaluable assistant to Drs. Driscoll and Rakel and all of us in pulling and keeping all the contributions together.

ROUTINE
PROCEDURES

Starting an IV Line in an Adult

Phillip Couchman, MD
Keith Davis, MD

An IV infusion serves numerous purposes, from administering medication and anesthesia, to parenteral nutrition, restoration of blood volume, and measurement of central venous pressure and blood gases. Peripheral venipuncture is the most common infusion technique, and the cannula-over-needle IV catheter procedure described here is preferable to the conventional rigid needle for an adult. The catheter, when inserted and secured, is much more trouble free than a rigid needle, and usually allows the patient some movement at the site.

Materials

- IV stand
- IV solution
- IV tubing, connected to the bottle or bag of solution and flushed with solution to remove air bubbles
- Antiseptic for skin prep: povidone-iodine solution (Betadine) and/or alcohol
- Gauze pads
- Lidocaine HCl (Xylocaine) (optional)
- 26- or 30-gauge intradermal needle (optional)
- 19- or 20-gauge venipuncture needle (optional)
- Adhesive tape (cloth or paper)
- Sterile gauze dressing
- Tourniquet or blood pressure cuff
- IV catheter of appropriate size (may come in kit also containing tourniquet, prepping swabs, and tape)
- Cotton or gauze
- Padded arm board or splint

Site selection

The choice of site for an IV insertion should be based on several factors: the general condition of the patient's veins, the existence of inflammation and tenderness at previous sites of infusion, and the anticipated amount of patient activity and movement after the catheter is in place. One general rule is to choose a site that is as distal as possible. In the event that an optimum site is ruined, possibly from a previous infusion, you may still be able to use the more proximal part of the vein. (In a life-threatening situation, however, use the most accessible vein.)

An important consideration is the amount of time that the catheter must remain in place.

SHORT-TERM IV ACCESS   is associated with quick surgical procedures and diagnostic tests. In patients whose veins are difficult to visualize, the dorsum of the hand is a good insertion site. Look for a vein that branches distally, and enter the vein at the junction of the branches. This minimizes rolling of the vein being entered—a problem often encountered in patients with tough vein walls. Other major insertion sites include the large vein on the radial side of the wrist (or as distal on the forearm as possible), and, when clearly visible, a vein on the volar aspect of the forearm.

LONG-TERM IV ACCESS,   for the purpose of such things as parenteral nutrition or delivery of medication, has different site requirements than short-term IVs. In this case, it is advisable to avoid placement at the wrist or elbow, as these sites often require the addition of an uncomfortable splint or arm board, to prevent displacement of the catheter and infiltration of the IV solution upon movement.

Keeping these facts in mind will facilitate preparation for the procedure and ensure a more calm and comfortable experience for the patient.

Preparation

1.   Hang the bottle or bag of IV solution from the IV stand, ready for use.
2.   Tear or cut off sections of adhesive tape and place them within convenient reach.
3.   Thoroughly wash your hands.
4.   Apply a tourniquet or blood pressure cuff proximal to the site selected. If you use a blood pressure cuff, set the pressure midway between the patient's diastolic and systolic pressures. In an emergency, 100 mmHg is a reasonable estimate for the patient with a palpable pulse. If cuff pressure is too high, blood will not enter the extremity, the patient will become uncomfortable, and veins will not

distend. If cuff pressure is too low, blood flow will not be obstructed, and venous distention will not occur.

5. If you have difficulty locating a favorable point of entry, let the patient's arm hang over the edge of the bed briefly to improve venous distention, place a heating pad or warm towel over the site for a few minutes, or gently tap the skin over the vein. If you must palpate for a deep vein, apply antiseptic to your fingertips first.

6. Cleanse the site thoroughly with povidone-iodine solution or alcohol on gauze pads.

Note: A local anesthetic such as lidocaine can facilitate painless venipuncture, especially with larger cannula insertion. Use a 26- or 30-gauge intradermal needle and infiltrate carefully and slowly to avoid distortion of the venous structure.

PROCEDURE

1. With your nondominant hand, apply traction to the skin distal to the entry site.

2. With your dominant hand, hold the catheter, with the needle bevel side up, at a 20-degree angle to the vein (see Figure 1-1).

3. Insert the needle with steady pressure until you see a blood return in the needle hub. If you are introducing a large cannula, consider first puncturing the dermis with a sharp, 19- or 20-gauge venipuncture needle to facilitate entry. Elevate the skin with the needle to avoid injury to the vein you will subsequently cannulate.

Figure 1-1: Proper angle for needle insertion.

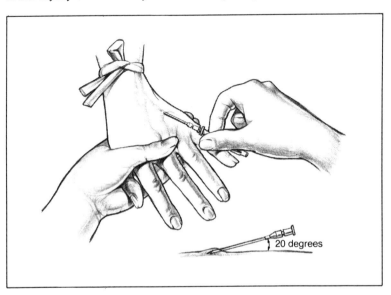

Figure 1-2: Immobilize needle while advancing catheter into the vein.

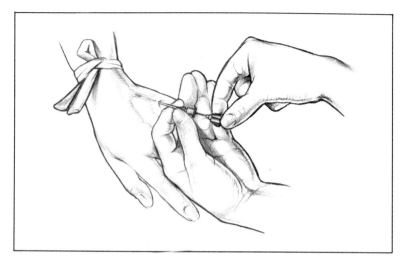

Figure 1-3: Secure catheter in place with tape.

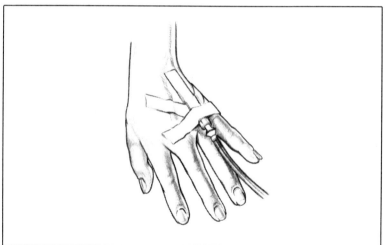

4. With your nondominant hand, advance the catheter alone into the vein while holding the needle immobile with your dominant hand (see Figure 1-2). Once the catheter is in the vein, remove the needle and advance the catheter to the desired position. (If advancement is difficult, attaching the IV tubing to the catheter hub and running the infusion at a slow rate may facilitate advancement.)

5. Remove the tourniquet or blood pressure cuff, attach the IV tubing to the catheter hub, and start the infusion. Should a valve in a large vein obstruct flow, withdraw the catheter slightly or advance it to a different position until the solution flows. If a hematoma or swelling occurs at the entry site, remove the catheter and apply pressure over the site of bleeding, using a gauze pad. Select a new site and enter the vein without applying a tourniquet or blood pressure cuff.

6. If the infusion flows smoothly, use cotton or gauze to remove any blood or spilled solution; then apply a sterile gauze dressing over the site. Secure the catheter to the skin with tape (see Figure 1-3); also secure the patient's arm to a board, if necessary.

Complications

Local complications, largely avoidable with careful site selection and technique, include, in order of frequency:

- Hematoma
- Phlebitis
- Thrombosis
- Cellulitis

Systemic complications include:

- Air embolism
- Pulmonary thromboembolism
- Sepsis

An uncommon complication in cannula-over-needle IV catheter placement is catheter fragment embolism. This will not happen if you do not attempt to reintroduce the needle into the catheter. If you need to try a second site, for example, use a new catheter set rather than run the risk of this complication.

Suggested Readings

Kaye W: Intravenous techniques, in McIntyre KM, Lewis AJ (eds): *Textbook of Advanced Cardiac Life Support.* Dallas, American Heart Association, 1981, pp. xii-1-xii-12.

Ludbrook J, Jamieson GG: Disorders of veins, in Sabiston DC Jr (ed): *Davis-Christopher Textbook of Surgery: The Biological Basis of Modern Surgical Practice,* ed 12. Philadelphia, WB Saunders Co, 1981, pp. 1808-1827.

Starting an IV Line in a Newborn Infant

Paul S. Williamson, MD
Richard Dobyns, MD

Successful insertion of peripheral IV lines in the neonate is a psychomotor skill that improves only with practice. Once a successful technique is mastered, it must be performed frequently in order to maintain a competent level of skill. The procedure for inserting an IV line in a newborn infant can be modified and adapted for implementation in the older infant, 12-18 months of age. The older, stronger infant does require more postinsertion restraint.

Indications for an IV insertion include infusion of fluids or delivery of intravenous medications through an indwelling line, though this same basic cannulation technique is also recommended for rapid entry and removal, such as obtaining blood samples with a steel needle on a syringe.

The average duration of peripheral IV access at one site is approximately 24-48 hours in the neonate receiving antibiotic therapy, and 48-72 hours in the neonate receiving only crystalloid infusion.

Materials

- A worktable—preferably a neonatal intensive care bed with movable side rails, overhead light, and radiant warmer
- IV tubing set, IV pole, heparin lock, and bottle of intravenous fluid
- IV catheter—22-gauge Abbocath[1] or 24-gauge Jelco[2]; catheter should be preflushed with sterile saline; a 23- or 25-gauge butterfly may be used as a temporary line
- 4″ × 4″ gauze pad and clear adhesive tape (½″ wide, 1½″ long) to cover and protect needle site after insertion
- Four ½″ × 3″ strips of tape and four 1″ × 3″ strips of double-backed tape to secure the catheter and arm board, precut and stuck within easy reach; double-backed tape prevents skin damage, especially in premature infants; to prepare a strip of double-backed tape, stick together two pieces of adhesive tape, one shorter than the other, so that the only adhesive exposed is at the ends of the longer piece

- Alcohol prep pads
- Arm board, which can be fashioned from a tongue blade covered with gauze padding
- Antibiotic ointment

Site selection

The choices of location for an IV insertion in an infant are very different from those of an adult. The best site for venous access in a neonate are the superficial veins on the dorsum of the hand. Also accessible is the greater saphenous vein at the medial aspect of the ankle, just anterior to the medial malleolus. Less desirable are the veins in the antecubital area, which are occasionally visible, but more often need to be located by palpation. The least desirable site of infusion is the scalp. Scalp veins are very cleary visible after shaving off a patch of the infant's hair, but this extra requirement is unpopular with parents.

POSITIONING THE INFANT.   Place the infant supine on the work surface and have your assistant immobilize the access site and control all other extremities by wrapping the infant in a towel, papoose style, if need be. Careful restraint is essential: A kicking foot can quickly undo a lot of work.

For insertion into veins on the dorsum of the hand, have your assistant grasp the upper arm so that his or her thumb and index finger serve as a tourniquet. With one hand, palmar flex the infant's wrist, applying skin traction with your thumb to facilitate needle insertion (see Figure 2-1). *Warning:* Too much flexion of the wrist can flatten the vein you are trying to cannulate.

For insertion into the saphenous vein, hold the infant's foot in extension with a slight varus angle. Have your assistant's hand proximal on the leg, out of your way, grasping the calf as a tourniquet. Have him use his other hand and forearm to restrain the infant's arms and body.

For insertion into veins in the antecubital area, have your assistant stabilize the infant's shoulder with the palm of one hand, which also serves as a tourniqet around the upper arm. Have him use the other hand to hold the infant's elbow in extension. *Note:* Once cannulated, the antecubital vein works well, but insertion is sometimes difficult because the vein traverses a joint, valves hinder the return of blood, and the vein is difficult to see.

For insertion into a scalp vein, place the infant with his head at the edge of the table and have your assistant stabilize the body and all four extremities. Place a large rubber band around the circumference

Figure 2-1: Palmar flex of infant's wrist, with thumb applying skin traction.

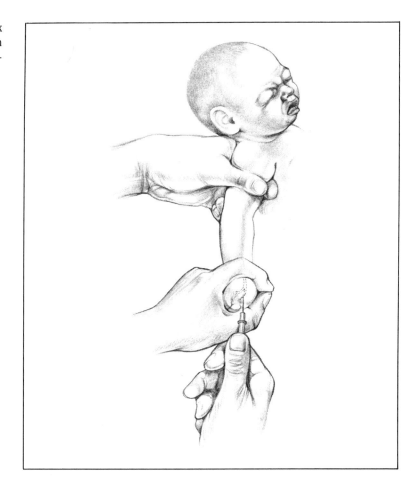

of the head just above the ears as a tourniquet. Stabilize the infant's head with one hand (see Figure 2-2).

PROCEDURE

1. Locate a vein junction as you would in an adult and prep the skin with an alcohol pad. Lidocaine HCI (Xylocaine) and other local anesthetics are of little use in the newborn; they only obscure the vein.
2. Prefill the catheter with sterile saline to maximize visualization of blood return when you enter the vein: Blood return is minimal in the low-pressure veins used for cannulation, and trying to tell when an infant's vein is cannulated by the feel of the catheter is difficult. If you use a butterfly, facilitate back flow by removing the tubing plug and leaving it open at a level lower than the point of insertion.
3. With the obturator in the cannula, pierce the skin about 1 cm (⅜

Figure 2-2: Positioning for scalp vein infiltration. Assistant gently immobilizes limbs while rubber band tourniquet is applied around circumference of head. Note that the infant's head is stabilized with the nondominant hand.

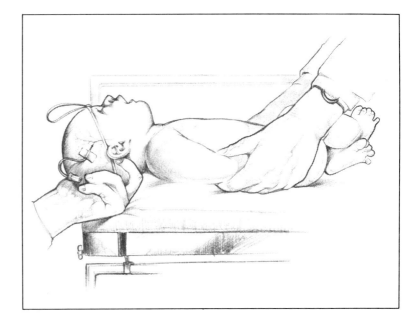

in) distal to where you plan to pierce the vein for better anchoring of the catheter by the skin. Enter the vein in the direction of venous blood flow and remove the obturator. You don't need to insert the cannula more than 5-10 mm ($\frac{3}{16}$-$\frac{3}{8}$ in) into the lumen of the vein.
4.   Once blood return is visible, have your assistant release his tourniquet grasp. If you are using a butterfly, proceed to step 5. If you are using a catheter, slowly advance it 2-3 mm ($\frac{1}{16}$ in) while flushing it with saline. (As an alternative to flushing, rotate the catheter slightly as you advance it.)
5.   Test the position of the catheter tip by flushing a small amount of saline into the catheter with a syringe. A subcutaneous bleb at the vein entrance site indicates infiltration: Withdraw and begin the whole procedure at a different site. If no bleb appears, insert the catheter into IV tubing that has been preconnected via a rate-limiting device to a bottle of fluid and prefilled with solution.
6.   If you are using a cannula and tubing, secure them as you would in an adult patient. Tape the cannula in position, wrapping ½" tape around the extremity at the insertion site or, if you are cannulating a scalp vein, crisscrossing strips of tape over the insertion site. Then tape a loop of IV tubing next to the cannula. If you are using a butterfly, place a piece of gauze between wings and skin to maintain the angle of the cannula as inserted, then apply tape over the wings to

fix them to the skin. Cover the catheter where it enters the skin with a dressing of antibiotic ointment and gauze. If you cannulated an extremity, secure the arm or leg to the tongue-blade board with double-backed tape to prevent flexion of the joints near the insertion site.

Suggested Readings

Archibald ME: Intravenous technique, in Roberts PW (ed): *Useful Procedures in Medical Practice.* Philadelphia, Lea & Febiger, 1986, pp. 547-565.

DeLorimier AA, Harrison MR: Special procedures: Intravenous cannulation, in Pascoe DJ, Grossman M (eds): *Quick Reference to Pediatric Emergencies,* ed 3. Philadelphia, JB Lippincott Co, 1984, pp. 560-561.

Hughes WT, Buescher ES: *Pediatric Procedures,* ed 2. Philadelphia, WB Saunders Co, 1980, pp. 87-115.

Administering Local Anesthesia

Darrell Randle, MD
Charles E. Driscoll, MD

Surgical procedures performed in an office setting can usually be accomplished using local anesthesia. Such anesthesia is available in three basic forms: local infiltration, regional nerve block, and IV regional nerve block (Bier's block). Choosing the type that is most appropriate in any given situation is dependent on several factors: the nature of the surgical procedure, the area to be anesthetized, the physician's experience with administering the various types, and the status of the patient.

The six agents commonly used in local anesthesia are lidocaine HCL (Xylocaine), mepivacaine HCL (Carbocaine), bupivacaine HCL (Marcaine, Sensorcaine), cocaine HCL, procaine HCL (Novocaine), and chloroprocaine HCL (Nesacaine). The first three agents are amide compounds and the last three agents are ester compounds. Since there is little cross-reactivity between these two groups, a patient who is hypersensitive to an ester compound can usually be given an amide compound with no difficulty. Lidocaine is the most commonly used agent because of its prompt, long-lasting, intense effect. If a more rapid onset of action is desired, mepivacaine is the agent to use. If anesthetic effect of longer duration is required, use bupivacaine. Cocaine, procaine, and chloroprocaine are seldom the drugs of choice.

As is true with the administration of any medication, precautions must be taken to avoid adverse reactions. The toxic manifestations of anesthetics involve both the central nervous system and the cardiovascular system. The common initial signs of toxicity to watch for are anxiety, restlessness, garrulousness, and tremor. Classic treatment of toxic reactions is to halt administration of the agent, give cardiovascular support, and administer diazepam (Valium), 5-10 mg IV, to control convulsions. Epinephrine, frequently given concurrently to decrease capillary oozing and prolong the action of a local anesthetic, also may produce anxiety and dysrhythmia. In order to avoid possible toxicity problems, observe the following precautions:

TABLE 3-1

Maximum recommended doses of commonly used local anesthetics		
Agent	Without epinephrine	With epinephrine
Lidocaine HCl (Xylocaine)	3-5 mg/kg	7 mg/kg
Mepivacaine HCl (Carbocaine)	8 mg/kg	
Bupivacaine HCl* (Marcaine, Sensorcaine)	2.5 mg/kg	3.0 mg/kg
In young, old, and very ill patients, the maximum recommended dose is roughly 25% less.		
*Not recommended for use in children under age 12.		

- Do not exceed the maximum dose recommended for each anesthetic agent. Note that for the very old, the very young, and seriously ill patients, the maximum dose is 25% less than the maximum dose allowable for a healthy adult (see Table 3-1).
- If the patient has a history of allergic reaction to a particular anesthetic agent, select an agent from the other basic group (i.e., amide versus ester compound, or vice versa). It may be helpful to inject 0.25 mL of the suspect agent subcutaneously as a test, and observe the patient for 15 minutes to detect any adverse reactions.
- Do not use epinephrine with an anesthetic in fingers, toes, nose, ears, or penis. The vasoconstriction it induces may significantly compromise circulation.
- Do not use epinephrine in patients who have hypertension, cardiac rhythm disturbances, or other heart disease.
- Any setting where anesthetics are used should be equipped to handle adverse reactions. This includes a staff that is trained in resuscitative and life support technique, and materials and equipment for dealing with cardiopulmonary stress and anaphylactic shock.

Local infiltration

Local infiltration anesthesia is indicated when the area to be anesthetized is small, when it is not amenable to a regional block, or when you want to supplement a regional block. This includes repair of a simple laceration on a limb, where nerve blockage of the entire limb is not feasible, when it is apparent that an administered regional block has not taken suitable effect, or areas such as the head and abdomen, which are not amenable to regional blocks.

Materials

- 1% lidocaine HCI (Xylocaine) with or without epinephrine, or other anesthetic as appropriate
- 18-gauge, 1½-in needle
- 25- or 30-gauge, 1½-in needle
- Syringe
- Skin prep such as povidone-iodine (Betadine)

PROCEDURE

1. Prep the injection site. Withdraw lidocaine from the vial with an 18-gauge needle to avoid dulling the fine needle used for injection.

2. Using a 25- or 30-gauge needle, slowly inject 0.1 mL of lidocaine intradermally to create a small wheal.

3. Wait 30 seconds, then very slowly inject the target area of skin, working from the anesthetized area outward. Aspirate before each bolus injection to confirm that the needle is not in a vein.

4. Wait at least three minutes after you complete injection, and test for absence of pinprick sensation before beginning the procedure.

5. In anesthetizing for wound closure, you can minimize iatrogenic pain by dripping lidocaine into the wound, waiting three minutes, then injecting the required amount through the wound edges.

Regional nerve block

When a particular procedure calls for a great amount of anesthetic to effectively prevent pain, or if local infiltration of anesthesia would distort the anatomy to the extent that it would inhibit good closure, a regional nerve block should be used.

Materials

- 25-gauge, 2½-in needle (for tibial nerve block only)
- 1% lidocaine HCL (Xylocaine), with or without epinephrine, or other anesthetic as appropriate
- 18-gauge, 1½-in needle
- 25- or 30-gauge, 1½-in needle
- Syringe
- Skin prep such as povidone-iodine (Betadine)

PROCEDURE

1. Prep the injection site and withdraw lidocaine HCL (Xylocaine) from the vial with an 18-gauge needle.

2. Familiarize yourself with the appropriate landmarks (see discussions of individual blocks). Using a 25-gauge needle, slowly inject 0.1 mL of lidocaine intradermally to create a small wheal.

3. Wait 30 seconds before inserting the needle slowly into the target area through the wheal. The patient's report of a momentary paresthesia indicates correct placement.

Note: Persistent paresthesia indicates nerve penetration; withdraw the needle until the paresthesia clears.

4. Slowly inject the anesthetic in small boluses, withdrawing the needle almost completely and redirecting it several times to leave a fanlike distribution. Always alternate aspiration with injection to avoid intravenous administration.

Digital (finger or toe) nerve block. This nerve block provides pain-free nail removal, closure of digital lacerations, manipulation of phalangeal fractures and dislocations, and digital incision and drainage.

1. Raise a wheal on the dorsal aspect of the digit at the base, using lidocaine without epinephrine.

2. Slowly inject 1-2 mL of anesthetic along the lateral aspect of the digit, staying as close to the bone as possible without touching it. Advance the needle to the volar skin as you inject.

3. Withdraw and repeat on the medial side of the digit.

Metacarpal/metatarsal nerve block. This block can be used for the same indications as the digital block, when digital block could compromise blood flow to the digit or area of procedure, or when a wound interferes with placing an adequate digital block.

1. Using lidocaine without epinephrine, raise two small skin wheals, one on the dorsomedial and one on the dorsolateral aspect of the metacarpal near the MCP joint.*

2. Inject continuously as you advance the needle alongside the metacarpal until it is palpable on the volar surface of the hand (see Figure 3-1). Inject a total of 2 mL of lidocaine.

3. Withdraw and repeat on the other side.

---

*For clarity, only metacarpal block is described; technique for metatarsal block is virtually identical.

Figure 3-1: Placement of needle alongside the metacarpal for injection of lidocaine.

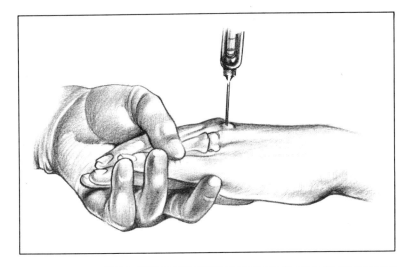

Figure 3-2: Fields anesthetized by blocks placed at three nerve innervations.

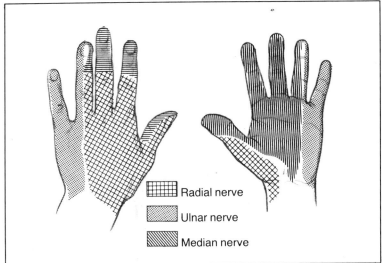

Radial nerve

Ulnar nerve

Median nerve

Wrist blocks are indicated for minor procedures done in the area innervated by the ulnar, median, or radial nerve (see Figure 3-2).

Ulnar nerve
1. Locate the palmar branch of the nerve by having the patient flex and ulnarly deviate his or her wrist against resistance, which should identify the flexor carpi ulnaris tendon. Palpate the ulnar artery and raise a skin wheal between the tendon and artery at the level of the ulnar styloid (see Figure 3-3). The ulnar nerve lies above the flexor retinaculum.

Figure 3-3: Site of needle insertion for ulnar nerve block. Determine location by palpating the ulnar artery, and raising a skin wheal midway between the artery and the flexor carpi ulnaris tendon.

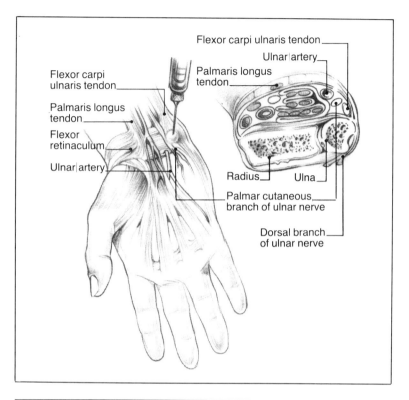

Figure 3-4: Site of needle insertion for median nerve block. Raise a small wheal immediately radial to the palmaris longus tendon.

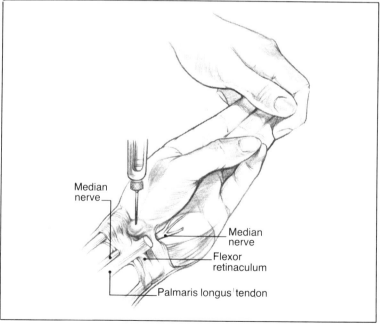

2. Advance the needle through the wheal approximately 1 cm (⅜ in) until you elicit paresthesia. Inject 5-10 mL of 1% lidocaine without epinephrine.

3. Block the dorsal branch of the ulnar nerve by infiltrating 5-10 mL of 1% lidocaine without epinephrine subcutaneously in a linear array of subcutaneous injections that extends from the flexor carpi ulnaris around the ulnar aspect of the wrist to the middorsal aspect.

Median nerve

1. Have the patient flex his wrist against resistance and oppose his thumb and fifth finger to make apparent the tendon of the palmaris longus in the volar aspect of the wrist. Raise a small wheal immediately radial to the tendon at the level of a line connecting radial and ulnar styloid processes (see Figure 3-4).

2. Advance the needle 1.5-2.0 cm (½-¾ in) through the skin wheal until paresthesia occurs, then inject 3-5 mL of 1% lidocaine without epinephrine. You may feel a faint pop as the needle passes through the flexor retinaculum; the median nerve lies 1 cm dorsal to this.

Radial nerve

1. Palpate for the radial artery and raise a skin wheal immediately lateral to it at the level of a line connecting the radial and ulnar styloid processes (see Figure 3-5).

2. Inject 2 mL of 1% lidocaine without epinephrine subcutaneously through the wheal.

3. Extend infiltration laterally to the middorsal aspect of the wrist in a series of separate subcutaneous injections, for a total of 10 mL of 1% lidocaine.

Supraorbital nerve block provides anesthesia of forehead, upper eyelid, and scalp to the lambdoid suture.

1. Palpate the superior orbital rim to identify the supraorbital notch. With the patient gazing straight ahead, it should be palpable directly over the pupil. Raise a skin wheal over the notch.

2. Insert the needle through the wheal, advancing it until you elicit paresthesia. Inject 2 mL of 1% lidocaine as you apply pressure to the upper eyelid to avoid migration of the anesthetic into the lid (see Figure 3-6).

Infraorbital nerve block provides anesthesia of the upper lip, nose, lower eyelid, and maxillary portion of the face.

1. Palpate along the inferior border of the infraorbital ridge to locate

Figure 3-5: Site of needle insertion for radial nerve block. Skin wheal positioned lateral to the radial artery at the level of the radial styloid process.

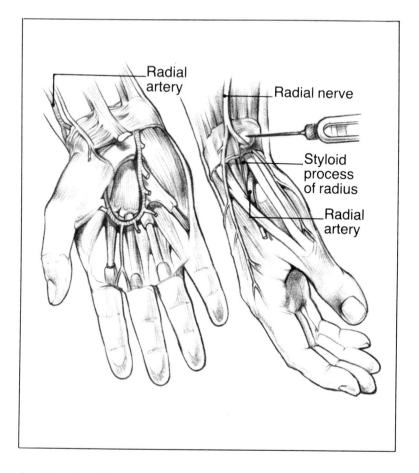

Radial artery

Radial nerve

Styloid process of radius

Radial artery

the infraorbital foramen, which should lie directly below the pupil, with the patient gazing straight ahead.

2. Placing one finger over the foramen, retract the upper lip, and raise a small wheal in the oral mucosa opposite the second maxillary bicuspid.

3. Advance the needle through the wheal until the tip is palpable at the foramen, and inject 2 mL of 1% lidocaine without epinephrine (see Figure 3-7). Apply pressure over the infraorbital rim to prevent migration of the anesthetic into the lower lid.

Intercostal nerve block will relieve chest and abdominal pain caused by rib fractures.

1. Have the patient sit and lean forward, arms drawn up. Identify the affected rib and the angle described by that rib and the lateral border of the sacrospinalis muscle (see Figure 3-8). Place moderate cephalad-directed tension on the skin overlying this angle.

Figure 3-6: To place a supraorbital nerve block, the needle is advanced through a skin wheal raised directly over the supraorbital notch. When paresthesia occurs, begin injecting lidocaine. Note that the first finger of the nondominant hand is applying pressure to the upper eyelid. This prevents infiltration of anesthetic into the lid.

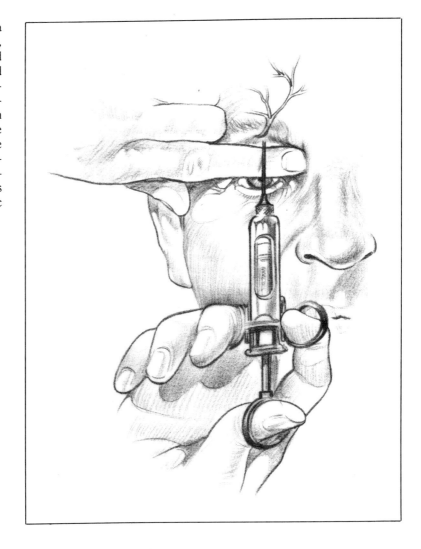

2. Raise a skin wheal over the inferior border of the rib at the apex of the angle.

3. Introduce the needle into the skin wheal until it meets bone. Withdraw slightly, tip the needle slightly caudally, and carefully advance it just under the inferior rib border for 2-3 mm (approximately ⅛ in).

4. Aspirate, then inject 5 mL of 1% lidocaine with epinephrine.

Ankle blocks are indicated for minor procedures performed in the area innervated by the deep peroneal, superficial peroneal, sural, or tibial nerve (see Figure 3-9).

Figure 3-7: For placement of an infraorbital nerve block, place one finger over the infraorbital foramen, while retracting the upper lip. Advance the needle alongside the second maxillary bicuspid until the needle tip is felt at the foramen.

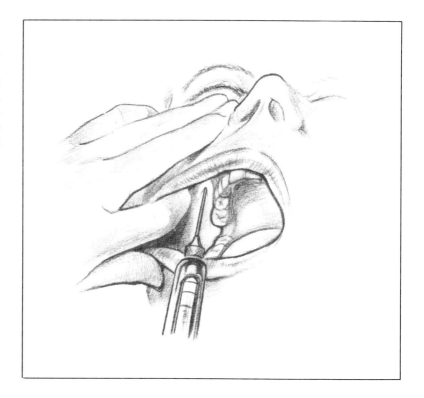

Deep peroneal nerve

1. Identify the anterior tibial tendon by having the patient dorsiflex his foot against resistance. Raise a skin wheal lateral to the tendon at the level of a line connecting the superior borders of the medial and lateral malleoli (see Figure 3-10, a).

2. Insert the needle into the wheal and advance it slightly medially. When you elicit paresthesia, inject 5 mL of 1% lidocaine without epinephrine in a fan pattern.

Superficial peroneal nerve

Infiltrate 5-10 mL of 1% lidocaine in a series of separate subcutaneous injections along a line extending from the anterior tibia to the lateral malleolus at the level of the malleoli (see Figure 3-10, b).

Sural nerve

Infiltrate 10 mL of 1% lidocaine in a series of separate subcutaneous injections along a line extending from the lateral border of the Achilles

Figure 3-8: Patient is leaning forward to receive an intercostal nerve block. Arrow indicates the direction in which to apply pressure while advancing needle under the inferior border of the affected rib.

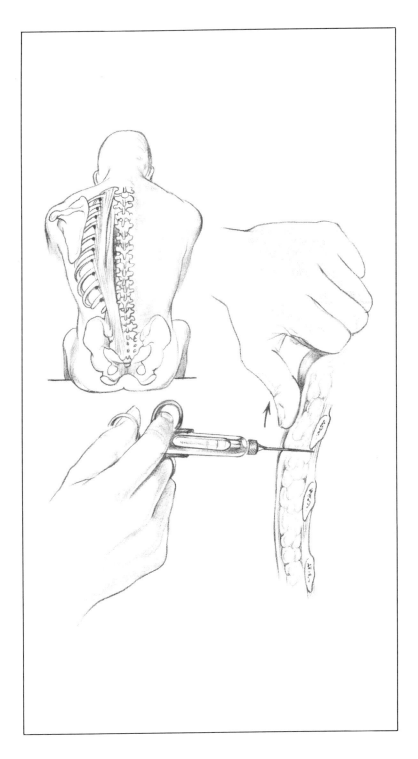

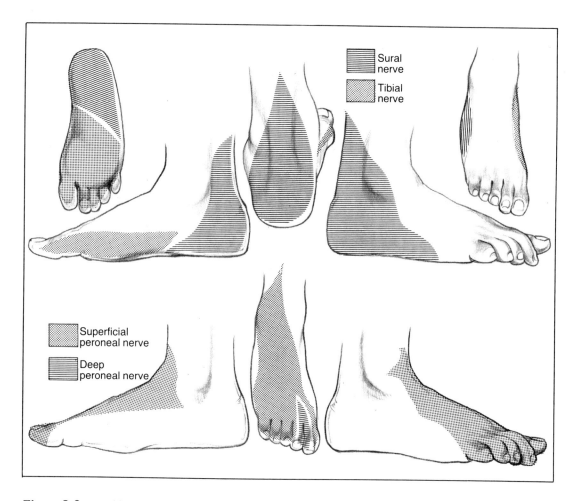

Figure 3-9: Fields anesthetized by blocks placed at different nerve innervations.

tendon to the lateral malleolus at the level of the malleoli (see Figure 3-10, c).

Tibial nerve
1. With the patient prone, identify the Achilles tendon and posterior tibial artery by palpation.
2. Insert a 25-gauge, 2½-in needle lateral to the artery at the level of the superior border of the medial malleolus (see Figure 3-10, d). If the artery is not palpable, insert the needle immediately lateral to the border of the Achilles tendon.
3. Advance the needle until you elicit paresthesia, then inject 5-10 mL of 1% lidocaine without epinephrine.
4. If you do not elicit paresthesia, advance the needle to the tibia, withdraw 1 cm, and inject 10 mL of 1% lidocaine in a fan pattern.

Figure 3-10: a) Deep peroneal nerve block, b) Superficial peroneal nerve block, c) Sural nerve block, d) Tibial nerve block.

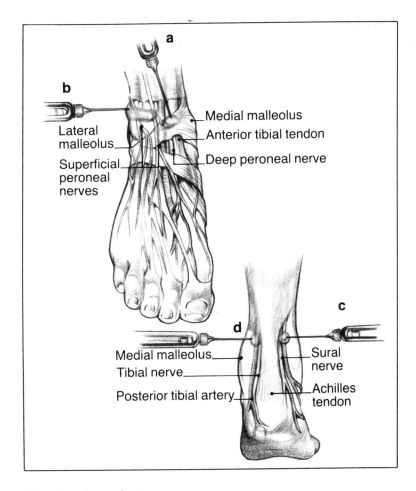

IV regional anesthesia

IV regional anesthesia is indicated for more lengthy, complicated procedures, such as reduction of long bone fractures, extensive wound closure or wound debridement, and tendon repair in upper and lower extremities.

Materials

- 0.5% lidocaine HCI (Xylocaine) *without* epinephrine
- 18-gauge, 1½-in needle
- 22-gauge IV catheter
- Double tourniquet with inflator
- Elastic bandage

- 60-mL syringe
- IV setup
- Skin prep such as povidone-iodine (Betadine)

PROCEDURE

1. Determine the amount of anesthetic needed: 2-3 mg/kg of lidocaine for an upper extremity block, 5 mg/kg for a lower extremity block. In an average-size adult, this is about 40-60 mL of 0.5% lidocaine. Draw the desired amount of lidocaine (without epinephrine) into the syringe.
2. Establish an IV line in an uninvolved limb as a precautionary measure.
3. Preset the tourniquet pressure to twice the patient's systolic pressure and place the uninflated tourniquet on the affected limb.
4. Insert the 22-gauge cannula into a vein distal to the tourniquet in the affected limb.
5. Elevate the limb and wrap it firmly in elastic bandage, working toward the tourniquet. When the entire limb distal to the tourniquet is compressed by the wrap, inflate the distal cuff, then the proximal cuff of the tourniquet. After inflating the proximal cuff, deflate the distal cuff and remove the bandage.
6. Inject the anesthetic via the cannula. Remove or cap the cannula, and wait 10 minutes for adequate anesthesia to be established.
7. If the procedure lasts beyond 15 minutes, you may reinflate the distal cuff and deflate the proximal cuff to avoid tourniquet pain.
Note: Leave the tourniquet inflated for at least 30 minutes after injection of the anesthetic. Earlier deflation does not allow enough time for the anesthetic to diffuse out of the vasculature of the limb; it may release a systemic bolus of the agent.

Suggested Readings

Hill GJ II (ed): *Outpatient Surgery,* ed 2. Philadelphia, WB Saunders Co, 1980.

Posies WJ, Thomas FT (eds): *Office Surgery for the Family Physician.* Stoneham, Mass, Butterworth's, 1984.

Ramamurti CC: *Orthopaedics in Primary Care.* Baltimore, Williams & Wilkins Co, 1979.

Laryngoscopy

Charles E. Driscoll, MD

You can make laryngoscopy work for you routinely. All you need are the right tools, the right technique, and practice.

Visual examination of the nasopharynx, especially the larynx, is both universally recommended and almost universally ignored in primary care practice. One reason physicians tend to avoid the procedure is that the traditional method, using headlamp and angled visualizing mirrors, is difficult to learn. Two relatively new techniques—indirect viewing with a laryngeal telescope and direct viewing with a flexible fiberoptic nasopharyngolaryngoscope—enable you to view the larynx more easily in children as well as adults. Most primary care physicians who try the fiberoptic instrument find they succeed in viewing the larynx on the first try in 9 out of 10 patients, even in uncooperative children or semicomatose patients. Primary care physicians usually have best results with the flexible fiberoptic scope, next best with the laryngeal telescope, and worst with mirrors. Cost may influence your choice of technique: A flexible nasopharyngolaryngoscope can cost more than $3,500-6,900, while a laryngeal telescope may cost $500, and the cost of laryngeal mirrors is negligible by comparison. If you can become skillful in any of the methods by using it routinely, you'll not only gain obvious advantages in examining symptomatic patients, but also be more able to spot the early lesions or other pathology present in 10-15 percent of asymptomatic patients.

In addition to routine use in physical examinations, indications for laryngoscopy include:

- Persistent hoarseness
- Pain in the throat or neck with stridor
- Recurrent pneumonia, bronchitis, or sinusitis
- Dysphagia
- A foreign body in the throat
- Persistent nasal drainage
- Unilateral serous otitis media
- Cervical lymphadenopathy
- Earache with normal examination results

PROCEDURE

Using the flexible nasopharyngolaryngoscope

Materials

- Comfortable chair for patient and stool for physician
- 5% cocaine solution or tetracaine HCI (Pontocaine) and an adrenalin solution
- Flexible fiberoptic nasopharyngolaryngoscope with light source (Figure 4-1)[1]

1. Direct your viewing during laryngoscopy by means of the landmarks of the nasal chamber and nasopharynx (Figure 4-2).

2. Anesthetize and decongest the patient's nose by spraying with 5% cocaine solution or tetracaine in an atomizer or by inserting cotton-tipped applicators soaked in either of these anesthetics, gradually advancing them to the rear of the nasal cavity. Have adrenalin ready in case a rare allergic reaction to the solution occurs. Alternatively, one may use 0.5-1.0% neosinephrine and 4% lidocaine topical spray in a dose less than 4.5 mg/kg (in general, below 300 mg), when cocaine allergy exists.

Figure 4-1: Flexible fiberoptic nasopharyngolaryngoscope.

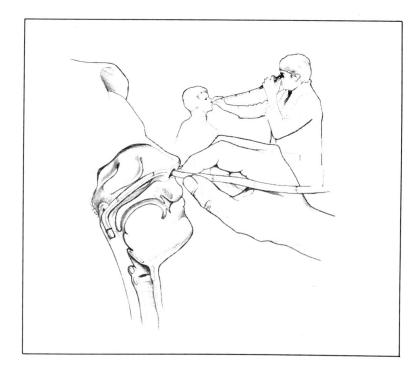

Figure 4-2: As you advance the scope through the nose, check the accuracy of your progress by looking for these landmarks.

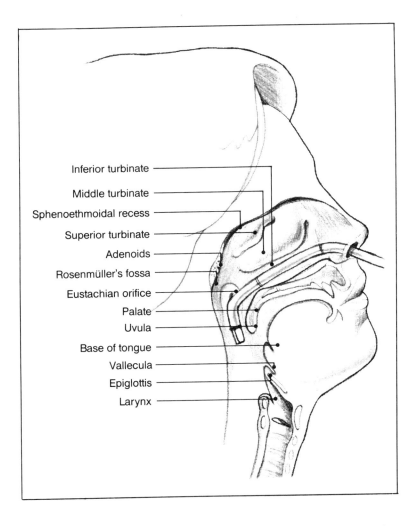

Inferior turbinate
Middle turbinate
Sphenoethmoidal recess
Superior turbinate
Adenoids
Rosenmüller's fossa
Eustachian orifice
Palate
Uvula
Base of tongue
Vallecula
Epiglottis
Larynx

3. Have the patient breathe through his or her mouth. Introduce the scope through a naris and slide it along the floor of the nose. When you reach the end of the septum, note the ipsilateral eustachian tube orifice (Figure 4-3).

4. Rotate the instrument 90 degrees and angle the tip of the tube to inspect the contralateral eustachian tube orifice.

5. Rotate the scope back to its upright position and have the patient breathe through his nose. This causes the soft palate to fall away from the posterior pharyngeal wall. Angle the scope 90 degrees downward to view the larynx (Figure 4-4) and advance the scope to the epiglottis, exercising care not to transcend the glottis. If mucus accumulation occludes the lens, have the patient swallow, sniff, or blow air through his nose.

Figure 4-3: Appearance of the ipsilateral eustachian tube orifice at the end of the septum.

Figure 4-4: Appearance of the larynx. a) Inter-arytenoid fold, b) vestibular fold, c) epiglottis, d) vocal cord, e) cuneiform tubercle.

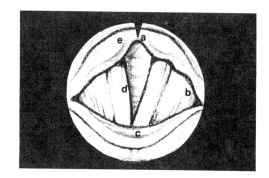

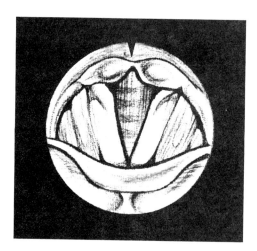

Figure 4-5: Appearance of larynx at rest.

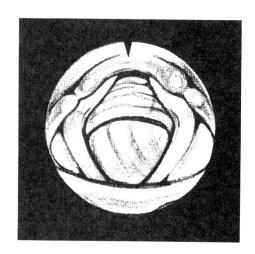

Figure 4-6: Appearance of larynx while patient is inhaling.

Figure 4-7: Appearance of larynx while patient is phonating.

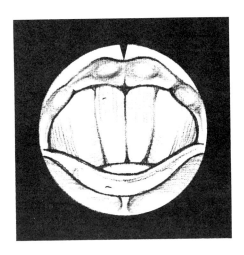

6. At this position, being careful to avoid the vocal cords with the scope, take time to visualize the larynx. Have the patient phonate so you can view the laryngeal mechanism in action (Figures 4-5, 4-6, 4-7). The procedure is comfortable for the patient, and the scope is narrow enough not to occlude the airway. You will be able to view the larynx clearly in almost every attempt.

Caution: Avoid transcending the larynx, which causes laryngospasm.

Using the laryngeal telescope

Materials

- Comfortable chair for patient and stool for physician
- Laryngeal telescope[2] (Figure 4-8)
- Thumb guide for steadying the advancing scope (optional)
- $4'' \times 4''$ gauze pads for grasping tongue
- Benzocaine spray (Hurricane) (optional)

1. Grasp the patient's extended tongue with a gauze pad. If he needs distraction, have him hold his own tongue. Gagging is not common with this procedure, so you seldom need anesthesia; for some patients, however, you may find benzocaine spray helpful. *Note:* If you do spray with benzocaine or other topical anesthetic, tell the patient to eat nothing for the next two hours; the anesthetic prevents him from feeling heat or cold on the palate as well as inhibits the gag reflex.

2. Insert the scope transorally and watch the insertion directly until the tip enters the throat. Then—and only then—look through the eyepiece. Direct visualization of the insertion helps you avoid striking

Figure 4-8: Laryngeal telescope.

Figure 4-9: Positioning of long-angled laryngeal mirror. Insert illustrates the approximate area of visualization.

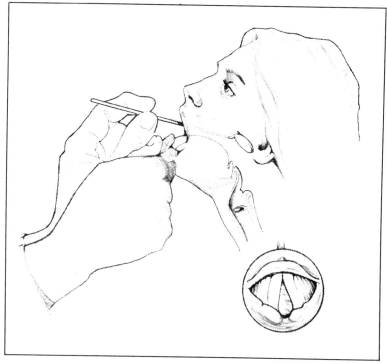

the uvula, the posterior pharyngeal wall, or the back of the tongue, all of which can cause gagging.

3. With the scope in place, ask the patient to "pant like a puppy." This opens the airway for better visualization.

4. To view the nasopharynx, rotate the scope 180 degrees. Do your viewing quickly and repeat the process if necessary; patients undergoing this procedure tire quickly.

Using mirrors

Materials

- Comfortable chair with high back for the patient and movable stool for the physician
- 4" × 4" gauze pads for grasping tongue
- Tongue blades for depressing tongue
- Long-angled laryngeal mirror (Figure 4-9) and smaller pharyngeal mirror
- Headlamp or head mirror with illumination from behind the patient
- Benzocaine spray (Hurricaine)

1. Try the procedure without anesthesia, but don't hesitate to spray the nasopharynx with benzocaine if gagging is a problem. Sometimes having the patient supine prevents gagging.

2. Use a gauze pad to grasp the patient's extended tongue. Protect the tongue from front-teeth laceration by positioning the middle finger of the hand grasping the tongue between teeth and tongue and pulling the tongue forward.

3. Keep the tongue extended as you insert the angled mirror. If the patient begins to gag as you advance the mirror, tell the patient to pant like a puppy; this drops the tongue base down and elevates the uvula— also providing easier passage for the mirror to the back of the throat. Remember to lift the uvula rather than push it back.

4. With the angled mirror in position, have the patient phonate a high pitched "E" to relax the glottis, improve visualization of the larynx, and demonstrate movement of the cords.

5. Take a brief look and return once or twice more if necessary, allowing the patient to rest between examinations. Many patients fatigue quickly during this procedure.

6. To examine the nasopharynx, use a tongue depressor to keep the tongue against the floor of the mouth. Asking the patient to breathe through his nose, insert the small pharyngeal mirror, angling it to reflect the nasopharynx. Thorough examination of the area with this technique requires considerable practice.

Note: If your mirror fogs, wipe it with hexachlorophene (pHiso-Hex) or hold it over a light bulb for heat. If you do warm the mirror, test it on your cheek before reintroducing it to prevent patient burns.

Suggested Readings

Grossan M: Indirect laryngoscopy and nasopharyngoscopy. *Ear Nose Throat J* 1978; 57:430-3.

Klein HC: Why can't physicians examine the larynx? *JAMA* 1982; 247:2111.

Silberman HD: Advances in the optical examination of the upper airway. *Otolaryngol Clin North Am* 1978; 11:355-63.

Silberman HD: The use of the flexible fiberoptic nasopharyngolaryngoscope in the pediatric upper airway. *Otolaryngol Clin North Am* 1978; 11:365-70.

Vanderstock L, Vermeersch H: A new flexible fiberoptic nasopharyngolaryngoscope. *Endoscopy* 1981; 13:243-5.

Skinfold Measurements

Carol Buss, RD
Charles E. Driscoll, MD

Anthropometry is the science which deals with the measurement of the size, weight, and proportions of the human body. Such anthropometric measurements are valuable for assessing growth rate, diagnosing undernutrition and obesity, and detecting changes in body composition that reveal underlying disease states.

In adults, anthropometric assessment includes height, weight, and upper arm circumference, as well as skinfold measurements. In children, head circumference is also recorded.

Skinfold measurements, when properly done, can prove valuable in determining the percentage of overall body fat. It should be noted, however, that multiple skinfold measurements represent only an *approximation* of the percentage of overall body fat, and actually serve better as an evaluation of *changes* in body composition.

Skinfold measurements are indicated when there is a need to monitor change in body composition, such as at the start of a diet regimen in the undernourished or the obese patient, and throughout the course of therapy to assess progress.

There are no contraindications for the taking of skinfold measurements, but be aware that they are difficult to obtain in the extremely obese patient, and the results in these cases may be unreliable. Results may also prove unreliable in geriatric patients, who tend to have significant skin atrophy and marked loss of subcutaneous fat.

Materials

- Skinfold caliper[1]
- Measuring tape of flexible steel or nonstretchable fiberglass
- Reference tables for estimating percentage of body fat (Table 5-1)

PROCEDURE

1. Select the body sites for skinfold measurements by following the requirements in the reference tables you are using. The tables given

37

TABLE 5-1

Guidelines for evaluating percent body fat		
BODY FAT NORMS*		
	Women	Men
Very low	14-17%	7-10%
Low	17-20%	10-13%
Average	20-24%	13-17%
Above Normal	24-27%	17-20%
Very high	27-30%	20-25%
Obese	Above 30%	Above 25%

*Norms for female athletes are 13-20% with an absolute minimum of 10%; for male athletes, norms are 4-12%, with an absolute minimum of 3%.

here (Tables 5-2 and 5-3) call for three measurement sites—chest, abdomen, and thigh for men, and triceps, suprailiac area, and thigh for women.

Note: Always take measurements from the right side of the patient's body unless otherwise indicated by the reference source you are using. If it is possible, measurements should be taken while the patient is standing.

2. At each site, grasp the appropriate skinfold between thumb and forefinger, taking care to pick up only skin and immediate subcutaneous fat, not muscle.

TRICEPS: With measuring tape, locate the midpoint between the acromion and olecranon over the triceps. With the patient's arm extended and relaxed, take a vertical skinfold measurement (see Figure 5-1).

SUBSCAPULAR AREA: Take an oblique skinfold along the inferior angle of the scapula (see Figure 5-1).

CHEST: Take a diagonal skinfold at an angle medial to the anterior axillary line, midway between the nipple and the axillary line (see Figure 5-2).

ABDOMEN: Take a vertical skinfold approximately 2 cm (¾ in) lateral to the umbilicus (see Figure 5-2).

THIGH: With the patient's weight shifted to the left leg, and the right leg slightly flexed, take a vertical skinfold on the anterior aspect of the thigh midway between the patella and the inguinal fold (see Figure 5-2).

TABLE 5-2

Percent Fat Estimates for Women: Sum Triceps, Suprailium and Thigh Skinfolds

	AGE TO THE LAST YEAR								
Sum of skinfolds (mm)	Under 22	to 27	23 to 32	28 to 37	33 to 42	38 to 47	48 to 52	53 to 57	Over 58
8-10	1.3	1.8	2.3	2.9	3.4	3.9	4.5	5.0	5.5
11-13	2.2	2.8	3.3	3.9	4.4	4.9	5.5	6.0	6.5
14-16	3.2	3.8	4.3	4.8	5.4	5.9	6.4	7.0	7.5
17-19	4.2	4.7	5.3	5.8	6.3	6.9	7.4	8.0	8.5
20-22	5.1	5.7	6.2	6.8	7.3	7.9	8.4	8.9	9.5
23-25	6.1	6.6	7.2	7.7	8.3	8.8	9.4	9.9	10.5
26-28	7.0	7.6	8.1	8.7	9.2	9.8	10.3	10.9	11.4
29-31	8.0	8.5	9.1	9.6	10.2	10.7	11.3	11.8	12.4
32-34	8.9	9.4	10.0	10.5	11.1	11.6	12.2	12.8	13.3
35-37	9.8	10.4	10.9	11.5	12.0	12.6	13.1	13.7	14.3
38-40	10.7	11.3	11.8	12.4	12.9	13.5	14.1	14.6	15.2
41-43	11.6	12.2	12.7	13.3	13.8	14.4	15.0	15.5	16.1
44-46	12.5	13.1	13.6	14.2	14.7	15.3	15.9	16.4	17.0
47-49	13.4	13.9	14.5	15.1	15.6	16.2	16.8	17.3	17.9
50-52	14.3	14.8	15.4	15.9	16.5	17.1	17.6	18.2	18.8
53-55	15.1	15.7	16.2	16.8	17.4	17.9	18.5	18.1	19.7
56-58	16.0	16.5	17.1	17.7	18.2	18.8	19.4	20.0	20.5
59-61	16.9	17.4	17.9	18.5	19.1	19.7	20.2	20.8	21.4
62-64	17.6	18.2	18.8	19.4	19.9	20.5	21.1	21.7	22.2
65-67	18.5	19.0	19.6	20.2	20.8	21.3	21.9	22.5	23.1
68-70	19.3	19.9	20.4	21.0	21.6	22.2	22.7	23.3	23.9
71-73	20.1	20.7	21.2	21.8	22.4	23.0	23.6	24.1	24.7
74-76	20.9	21.5	22.0	22.6	23.2	23.8	24.4	25.0	25.5
77-79	21.7	22.2	22.8	23.4	24.0	24.6	25.2	25.8	26.3
80-82	22.4	23.0	23.6	24.2	24.8	25.4	25.9	26.5	27.1
83-85	23.2	23.8	24.4	25.0	25.5	26.1	26.7	27.3	27.9
86-88	24.0	24.5	25.1	25.7	26.3	26.9	27.5	28.1	28.7
89-91	24.7	25.3	25.9	26.5	27.1	27.6	28.2	28.8	29.4
92-94	25.4	26.0	26.6	27.2	27.8	28.4	29.0	29.6	30.2
95-97	26.1	26.7	27.3	27.9	28.5	29.1	29.7	30.3	30.9
98-100	26.9	27.4	28.0	28.6	29.2	29.8	30.4	31.0	31.6
101-103	27.5	28.1	28.7	29.3	29.9	30.5	31.1	31.7	32.3
104-106	28.2	28.8	29.4	30.0	30.6	31.2	31.8	32.4	33.0
107-109	28.9	29.5	30.1	30.7	31.3	31.9	32.5	33.1	33.7
110-112	29.6	30.2	30.8	31.4	32.0	32.6	33.2	33.8	34.4
113-115	30.2	30.8	31.4	32.0	32.6	33.2	33.8	34.5	35.1
116-118	30.9	31.5	32.1	32.7	33.3	33.9	34.5	35.1	35.7
119-121	31.5	32.1	32.7	33.3	33.9	34.5	35.1	35.7	36.4
122-124	32.1	32.7	33.3	33.9	34.5	35.1	35.8	36.4	37.0
125-127	32.7	33.3	33.9	34.5	35.1	35.8	36.4	37.0	37.6

$BD = 1.1093800 - 0.0008267(X_1) + 0.0000016(X_1)^2 - 0.0002574(X_2)$, where X_1 is sum of chest, abdominal and thigh skinfolds and X_2 is age in years. Percent fat $= (495/BD) - 450$.

From Baumgartner, T.A., and Jackson, A.S. Measurement for Evaluation in Physical Education. W.C. Brown, Dubuque, 1982, 2nd Ed., p. 295. Reprinted by permission of W.C. Brown Co., Dubuque.

TABLE 5-3

Percent Fat Estimates for Men: Sum of Chest, Abdominal and Thigh Skinfolds

Sum of skinfolds (mm)	AGE TO THE LAST YEAR								
	Under 22	23 to 27	28 to 32	33 to 37	38 to 42	43 to 47	48 to 52	53 to 57	Over 58
23-25	9.7	9.9	10.2	10.4	10.7	10.9	11.2	11.4	11.7
26-28	11.0	11.2	11.5	11.7	12.0	12.3	12.5	12.7	13.0
29-31	12.3	12.5	12.8	13.0	13.3	13.5	13.8	14.0	14.3
32-34	13.6	13.8	14.0	14.3	14.5	14.8	15.0	15.3	15.5
35-37	14.8	15.0	15.3	15.5	15.8	16.0	16.3	16.5	16.8
38-40	16.0	16.3	16.5	16.7	17.0	17.2	17.5	17.7	18.0
41-43	17.2	17.4	17.7	17.9	18.2	18.4	18.7	18.9	19.2
44-46	18.3	18.6	18.8	19.1	19.3	19.6	19.8	20.1	20.3
47-49	19.5	19.7	20.0	20.2	20.5	20.7	21.0	21.2	21.5
50-52	20.6	20.8	21.1	21.3	21.6	21.8	22.1	22.3	22.6
53-55	21.7	21.9	22.1	22.4	22.6	22.9	23.1	23.4	23.6
56-58	22.7	23.0	23.2	23.4	23.7	23.9	24.2	24.4	24.7
59-61	23.7	24.0	24.2	24.5	24.7	25.0	25.2	25.5	25.7
62-64	24.7	25.0	25.2	25.5	25.7	26.0	26.7	26.4	26.7
65-67	25.7	25.9	26.2	26.4	26.7	26.9	27.2	27.4	27.7
68-70	26.6	26.9	27.1	27.4	27.6	27.9	28.1	28.4	28.6
71-73	27.5	27.8	28.0	28.3	28.5	28.8	28.0	29.3	29.5
74-76	28.4	28.7	28.9	29.2	29.4	29.7	29.9	30.2	30.4
77-79	29.3	29.5	29.8	30.0	30.3	30.5	30.8	31.0	31.3
80-82	30.1	30.4	30.6	30.9	31.1	31.4	31.6	31.9	32.1
83-85	30.9	31.2	31.4	31.7	31.9	32.2	32.4	32.7	32.9
86-88	31.7	32.0	32.2	32.5	32.7	32.9	33.2	33.4	33.7
89-91	32.5	32.7	33.0	33.2	33.5	33.7	33.9	34.2	34.4
92-94	33.2	33.4	33.7	33.9	34.2	34.4	34.7	34.9	35.2
95-97	33.9	34.1	34.4	34.6	34.9	35.1	35.4	35.6	35.9
98-100	34.6	34.8	35.1	35.3	35.5	35.8	36.0	36.3	36.5
101-103	35.3	35.4	35.7	35.9	36.2	36.4	36.7	36.9	37.2
104-106	35.8	36.1	36.3	36.6	36.8	37.1	37.3	37.5	37.8
107-109	36.4	36.7	36.9	37.1	37.4	37.6	37.9	38.1	38.4
110-112	37.0	37.2	37.5	37.7	38.0	38.2	38.5	38.7	38.9
113-115	37.5	37.8	38.0	38.2	38.5	38.7	39.0	39.2	39.5
116-118	38.0	38.3	38.5	38.8	39.0	39.3	39.5	39.7	40.0
119-121	38.5	38.7	39.0	39.2	39.5	39.7	40.0	40.2	40.5
122-124	39.0	39.2	39.4	39.7	39.9	40.2	40.4	40.7	40.9
125-127	39.4	39.6	39.9	40.1	40.4	40.6	40.9	41.1	41.4
128-130	39.8	40.0	40.3	40.5	40.8	41.0	41.3	41.5	41.8

BD = 1.0994921 − 0.0009929(X$_1$) + 0.0000023(X$_1$) − 0.0001392(X$_2$), where X$_1$ is the sum of triceps, suprailium and thigh skinfolds and X$_2$ is age in years.
From Baumgartner, T.A., and Jackson, A.S. *Measurement for Evaluation in Physical Education*. W.C. Brown, Dubuque, 1982, 2nd Ed., p. 296. Reprinted by permission of W.C. Brown Co., Dubuque.

Figure 5-1: Vertical measurement of triceps taken at midpoint between acromion and olecranon. Subscapular area measured at inferior angle of the scapula.

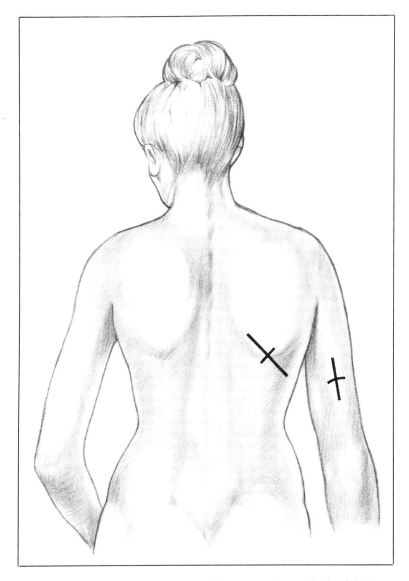

SUPRAILIAC AREA: Take an oblique or diagonal skinfold just superior to the crest of the ilium where an imaginary line would descend from the anterior axillary line (see Figure 5-3).

3. Maintaining your grasp, place the calipers around the skinfold approximately 5 mm (¼ in) below your fingers (Figure 5-4). Place the calipers as deep as possible without pinching the muscle.

4. Wait one or two seconds after placing the calipers, and then read the dial to the nearest 0.5 mm.

Figure 5-2: Chest: Diagonal skinfold taken medial to anterior axillary line, midway between nipple and axillary line. Abdomen: Vertical skinfold 2 cm lateral to umbilicus. Thigh: Vertical skinfold on anterior aspect of thigh midway between patella and inguinal fold.

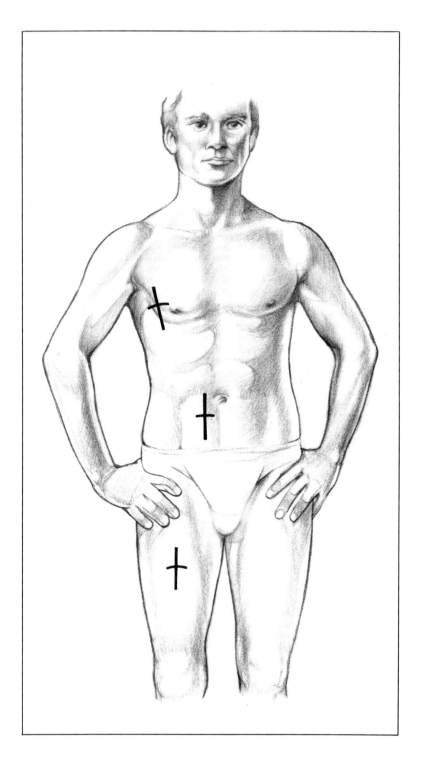

Figure 5-3: Suprailiac area: Oblique or diagonal skinfold just superior to crest of ilium where an imaginary line would descend from anterior axillary line.

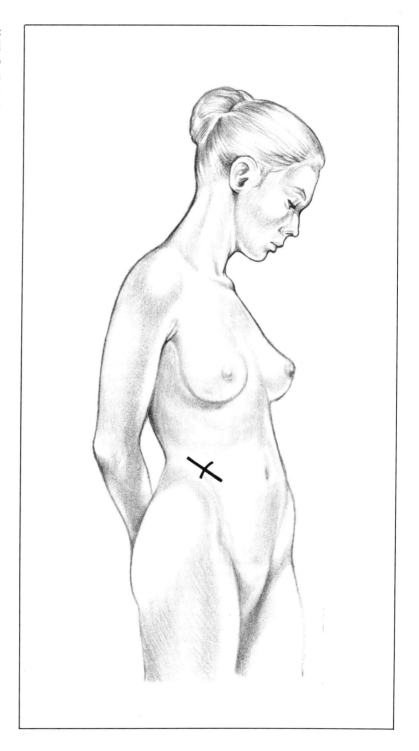

Figure 5-4: Place calipers approximately 5 cm
below fingers around
skinfold.

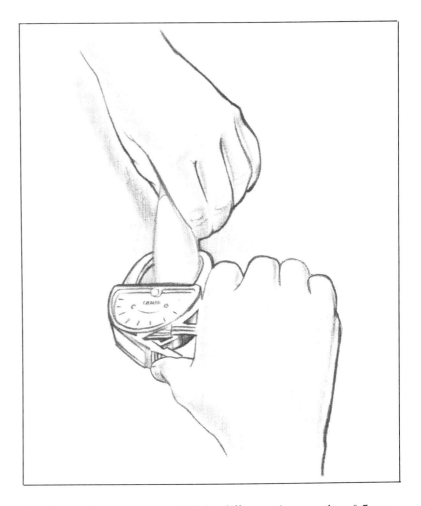

5. Repeat the measurement. If the difference is more than 0.5 mm,
take a third measurement, and average the two readings closest to one
another in value. *Note:* If consecutive measurements at a given site
become smaller with each successive reading, the fat is being
compressed. This situation is common in "fleshy" patients. Move on to
the next site, and return to remeasure after all other measurements
are recorded. The final value at the problem spot should be the average
of the two numbers that appear to best represent the proportion of fat
at the skinfold site relative to the other results.

6. Proceed with skinfold measurements at the remaining sites.

7. Derive an estimate of percent body fat from the sum of all the
skinfold measurements by consulting the appropriate table.

Suggested Readings

Grant A, Dehoog S: *Nutritional Assessment and Support,* ed 3. Seattle, Ann Grant and Susan Dehoog, 1985.

Linder P, Linder D: *How to Assess Degrees of Fatness: A Working Manual.* Maryland, Cambridge Scientific Industries, 1973.

Simko MD, Cowell C, Gilbride JA: *Nutrition Assessment: A Comprehensive Guide for Planning Intervention.* Rockville, Maryland, Aspen Systems Corp, 1984.

Storlie J, Jordan HA: *Evaluation and Treatment of Obesity.* New York, SP Medical and Scientific Books, 1984.

6

Suprapubic Bladder Tap in Infants and Children

Elizabeth A. Burns, MD

An easy way to obtain an uncontaminated urine specimen from an infant or child under age 4 who is not a candidate for urethral catheterization, and who cannot void on command, is to perform a suprapubic bladder tap. It provides accurate information on the presence of organisms in the urine and is a helpful adjunct to the physical examination. It is also an integral part of the workup for sepsis in a newborn, or fever of unknown origin or suspected urinary tract infection in young children.

Some physicians administer a local anesthesia before performing the tap, but this is hardly necessary as the injection of anesthesia is just as discomforting as the procedure itself.

Materials

- 5- or 10-mL syringe
- 23-gauge, 1½-in needle
- Alcohol or povidone-iodine (Betadine) swabs
- Adhesive strip

PROCEDURE

Caution: Postpone the bladder tap for an hour or so if the child has recently voided or if preparation of the skin for the tap initiates reflex voiding.

1. Place the child in a supine position; have an assistant ready to control the extremities if necessary during the procedure. (Some

47

Figure 6-1: To determine the site of needle insertion, place the child in supine position and palpate the symphysis pubis.

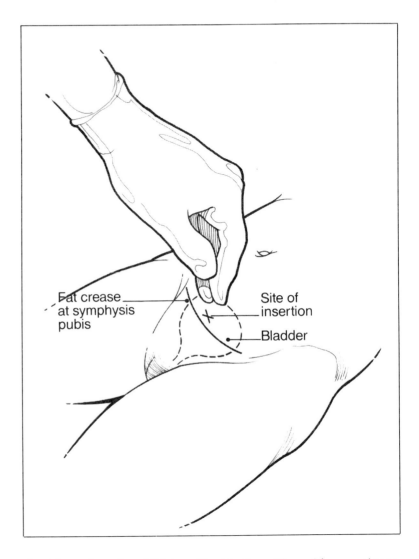

physicians place the child in a "frog leg" position with an assistant providing gentle restraint.)

2. Prepare the suprapubic skin using either alcohol or povidone-iodine solution. If you use alcohol, cleanse with an alcohol swab, allow the area to air dry, then recleanse with another alcohol swab, and let that dry.

3. Palpate the symphysis pubis. Often a small child will have a crease in this area conveniently located for use as a landmark (Figure 6-1).

4. Attach a 23-gauge × 1½-in needle to a 5- or 10-mL syringe and insert it in the midline above the superior pubic border, pointing the needle approximately toward the infant's coccyx (Figure 6-2).

Figure 6-2: Insert the needle in the direction of the coccyx to a depth of 3 cm.

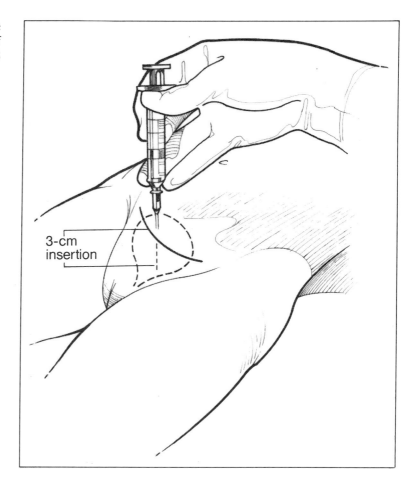

3-cm insertion

5. Withdraw the plunger slightly to provide slight negative pressure and advance the needle slowly until urine appears in the syringe. *Note:* If you advance the needle 3 cm (about 1 ⅕ inch) with no evidence of urine, assume that you have a dry tap and *withdraw the needle.*

6. When urine enters the syringe, collect the amount needed for culture and tests, then withdraw the needle.

7. Apply an adhesive strip over the insertion site if needed.

Suggested Readings

Cloherty JP, Stark AB (eds): *Manual of Neonatal Care.* Boston, Little Brown & Co, 1980, p. 368.

Reece RM (ed): *Manual of Emergency Pediatrics,* ed 2. Philadelphia, WB Saunders Co., 1978, p. 664.

Passing a Urinary Catheter

Elizabeth Loeb, MS, MD
Robert E. Rakel, MD

Urinary catheterization is a procedure not without complications. For this reason, the decision to order the procedure should be made only after giving careful consideration to alternatives.

Because the catheter can introduce bacteria into the bladder, it is absolutely mandatory that insertion be carried out under aseptic technique. Bacterial invasion of the bladder can cause cystitis or sepsis in any patient, and more specifically, epididymitis in males. The possibility of such infection increases in elderly patients, debilitated patients, patients with large volumes of residual urine, diabetes, and women in the puerperium. Long-term indwelling catheters can cause formation of urinary calculi as well as changes in the urinary bladder as a result of inflammation. Excessive pressure at the penoscrotal angle from an indwelling catheter can cause urethral fistulas in the male patient.

Other reasons to consider the patient's situation carefully before ordering urinary catheterization include the pain it can cause in patients with degenerative hip disease, and the possibility that a demented or delirious patient will cause him or herself urethral trauma by inadvertently pulling out an indwelling catheter with the balloon still inflated.

TEMPORARY CATHETERIZATION   is useful in relieving temporary urethral obstruction, or in patients who are unable to void. It can also be used to obtain a sterile urine specimen from patients who cannot perform a clean-catch void because of weakness, obesity, or other medical complications. In asymptomatic women with pyuria or bacteriuria on clean-catch specimens, it can be used to collect sterile urine. Diagnostically, temporary catheterization can determine residual urine volume, or serve as an access route for the injection of contrast medium or normal saline for urologic studies such as cystometrography, cystoscopy, or delineation of the urethral anatomy.

INDWELLING CATHETERS   serve as monitors of urine output in critical care or comatose patients, relieve anatomic or physiologic obstruction following urethral or prostatic surgery, and alleviate persistent incontinence, which is especially beneficial in patients experiencing tissue breakdown or decubitus ulcers in the perineal and anal areas.

The insertion of a urinary catheter is contraindicated in patients with partial or complete rupture of the prostatic urethra, or presence of acute urethral or prostatic infection. The procedure should be stopped if it is not possible to pass the catheter without using force.

Materials

- Adequate lighting
- 3-in adhesive tape
- Povidone-iodine solution (Betadine)
- Safety pin
- Urine collection basin
- Kelly clamp
- Sterile catheterization tray or kit containing:
- Straight catheter or retention (Foley) catheter with 10-mL balloon (usually No. 14 or No. 16 French catheter)
- Drapes, including waterproof underpad and fenestrated drape
- Gloves
- Cotton balls (at least five)
- Forceps
- Water-soluble lubricant
- Specimen container with lid
- 10-mL syringe filled with sterile water (Foley set)
- Flat drainage bag, tubing, and puncture port (Foley set)

Preparation

Note: Having an assistant often facilitates the procedure and helps to maintain aseptic technique, especially when patients are uncooperative, restless, or weak.

1. If the patient is conscious, explain the procedure to him or her. If you are determining residual volume, have the patient void.
2. Provide privacy. Position the patient supine with knees bent, hips abducted, and feet resting 60 cm (2 ft) apart. (Consider Sims' position for the patient with contractures of the hips or knees.)
3. Drape the patient. Place the sterile catheterization tray in easy reach, generally between the patient's feet, and adjust the light.
4. If you are inserting an indwelling catheter and the drainage set is

in a separate package, open it and attach the set to the bed frame near the bottom of the bed.

5. Wash your hands thoroughly, open the tray, and put on sterile gloves.

6. If you are inserting an indwelling catheter, test the integrity of the balloon, using the 10-mL syringe and sterile water.

7. Place a waterproof drape under the patient's buttocks. Place the fenestrated drape (hole in the center) over the perineum, with the labia or penis exposed.

8. Saturate cotton balls with povidone-iodine solution, prepare the specimen container if one is needed, and squeeze lubricant onto the sterile field in an accessible location.

PROCEDURE

Female patient

1. With your nondominant hand, approach the genitalia proximally and expose the meatus by placing your thumb and forefinger between

Figure 7-1: Passing a urinary catheter in a female patient. The nondominant hand retracts the labia minora outward and upward toward the symphysis. The dominant hand holds the lubricated tubing approximately 8 cm from the tip and gently inserts it into the urethra until urine return is seen. Be sure to check that the other end of the catheter is in a basin.

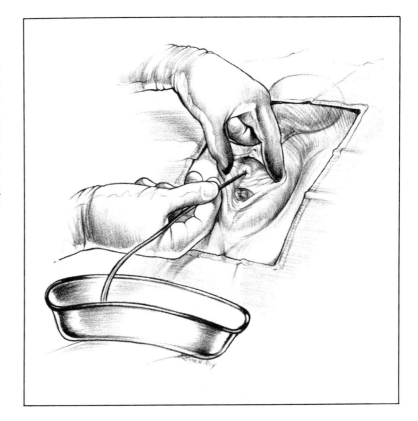

the labia minora, retracting them outward and upward toward the symphysis. *Caution:* Consider this hand now contaminated; if it slips during or after cleansing the genital area, reprep the area.

2. Clean the area of the meatus with cotton balls soaked in povidone-iodine solution: Manipulating forceps with your dominant hand, pick up the cotton balls one at a time. Use each ball to wipe from front to back with a downward pull, and discard each ball outside the sterile field.

3. With your dominant hand, pick up the catheter 8 cm (3 in) from the tip. Use a Kelly clamp to handle the catheter, if you prefer. Lubricate the first 5 cm (2 in), being careful not to clog the drainage hole. Check to be sure the other end of the catheter is in the collection basin.

4. With gentle pressure, insert the cather into the urethra. You may be able to facilitate insertion by having the patient inhale to open the meatus as you advance the catheter. Direct the catheter superiorly and posteriorly into the bladder (about 8 cm) until you obtain urinary return (see Figure 7-1). If there is no urinary flow, rotate the catheter. Lack of urine could also indicate misdirection of the catheter into the vagina. If this has occurred, remove the catheter and recatheterize, using a new sterile catheter. If you are using a retention catheter, insert it 5 cm beyond the point where you obtain urinary return. Release the labia.

Male patient

Note: If the patient has an enlarged prostate, consider using a No. 12 French or a coudé-tip Foley catheter.

1. With your nondominant hand, grasp the penis firmly, directly behind the glans—a light grasp may cause an erection.

2. Holding cotton balls soaked in povidone-iodine solution with forceps manipulated by your dominant hand, start at the glans to cleanse the penis with spiral motion around the circumference of the shaft and 5-7 cm (2-3 in) down the shaft. In an uncircumcised man, start by retracting the foreskin and wiping off all smegma. Discard cotton balls away from the sterile field.

3. With your nondominant hand, hold the penis at an angle of 60-90 degrees to the patient's body with the meatus toward the patient's head (see Figure 7-2).

4. With your dominant hand, pick up the catheter 8 cm (3 in) from the tip. Use a Kelly clamp to handle the catheter, if you prefer. Lubricate the first 5 cm, being careful not to clog the drainage hole, and lubricate the urethral orifice. Check to be sure the other end of the catheter is in the collection basin.

Figure 7-2: Catheter insertion in a male patient. The nondominant hand firmly grasps the penis behind the glans and holds the penis at a 60-90 degree angle to the patient's body. With the dominant hand, gently insert the well-lubricated catheter along the anterior wall of the urethra to a depth of approximately 15-18 cm, or until urine return is achieved.

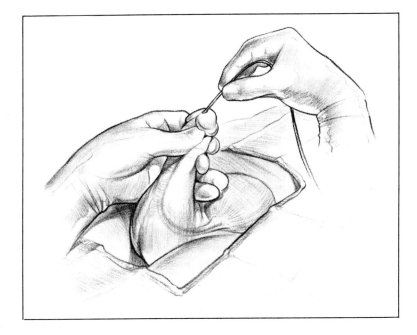

5. Gently insert the catheter along the anterior wall of the urethra and advance it 15-18 cm (6-7 in) until urine begins flowing. If you are using a retention catheter, insert it 2.5-5.0 cm (1-2 in) further.

Caution: Never force the catheter. If you meet substantial resistance, remove the catheter and squeeze 2-3 mL of lubricant from a sterile, newly opened tube into the urethra before again inserting the catheter.

6. If the patient is uncircumcised, return the foreskin over the glans to prevent phimosis.

Postinsertion technique

Male or female patient

1. Holding the catheter in place with your dominant hand, collect a urine sample in the specimen container, if needed. Let the rest of the urine drain into the basin.

2. If the bladder contains a large volume of urine, consider clamping the catheter tubing for 30 minutes after the patient has passed the first 1,000 mL. (A controversial theory unsubstantiated by research holds that rapid decompression of the bladder can lead to shock secondary to release of the pressure on pelvic vessels.)

3. If you've used a straight catheter, remove it when the urine stops flowing. If you've inserted an indwelling catheter, start to inflate the balloon once you think you've inserted the catheter far enough to get

Figure 7-3: Indwelling catheters in the male patient should be taped to the dorsum of the thigh to prevent compression at the penoscrotal angle.

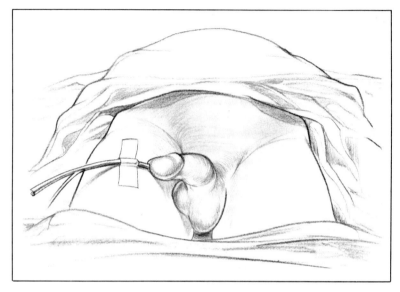

the balloon into the bladder. Inject sterile water through the catheter side arm, observing the patient for pain that would indicate the balloon is still in the urethra. In the absence of pain, complete inflation using 10 mL of sterile water, then gently pull on the catheter to check that the balloon is anchored against the bladder neck. Connect the drainage system to the catheter.

4. Tape the indwelling catheter in place—to the inner thigh, if the patient is female, and laterally, to the dorsum of the thigh, if male. This arrangement in the male patient prevents compression at the penoscrotal angle, which can lead to pressure sores, abscesses, and fistulas (see Figure 7-3).

5. Dry the perineum, return the patient to a comfortable position, and remove your gloves. Attach the catheter to the patient's gown with a safety pin.

Most complications associated with insertion of a urinary catheter, such as false passage, sepsis, and urethral stricture, are uncommon and may be avoided by strict adherence to aseptic technique and by inserting the catheter gently.

Suggested Readings

Implementing Urologic Procedures. Horsham, Pennsylvania, Intermed Communications, Inc., 1982.

Slade N, Gillespie WA: *Urinary Tract and the Catheter.* New York, John Wiley & Sons, 1985.

Smith DR: *General Urology,* ed 11. Los Altos, California, Lange Medical Publications, 1984.

8

Inserting an Intrauterine Device

Elizabeth A. Burns, MD
Martin Bartolac, MD

There is only one type of intrauterine device (IUD) currently available as a contraceptive in the United States. This is an IUD that contains progesterone. The inert devices (Lippes Loop and Saf-T-Coil), and the copper devices (Cu-7 and Tatum-T) are no longer marketed here, but many are still in use. The inert devices can remain in place indefinitely, but the copper IUD's should be removed and replaced three years after insertion.

Progesterone is the mechanism of action in the Progestasert[1] IUD, as it is gradually released into the urinary cavity. This infiltration of progesterone creates a pseudodecidual uterine environment not suitable for embryo implantation.

The theoretic effectiveness of IUDs is 97-99%; their use-effectiveness is 90-96%, depending on such variables as age and frequency of intercourse. Some 50% of pregnancies among IUD users result in spontaneous abortion, prematurity, amnionitis, or gestational bleeding. It has been determined that ectopic pregnancies are more likely to occur in women with an IUD in place than in women who are not using one.

Insertion of an IUD is absolutely contraindicated in women with acute pelvic infection, or those discovered to be pregnant. Careful consideration should be given in cases where the woman has a history of recurrent pelvic infection (gonococcal or chlamydial), multiple sexual partners, any occurrence of abnormal uterine bleeding, history of ectopic pregnancy, impaired coagulation from either therapy or a clotting defect, postpartum endometriosis, or has had an abortion within three months. Of relative concern in an IUD candidate are:

- Valvular heart disease predisposing to subacute bacterial endocarditis (assess need for prophylactic antibiotics)
- Abnormal pap smear or cervical neoplasm
- Cervical stenosis

- Small uterus
- Endometriosis
- Leiomyomata or polyps
- Bicornuate uterus
- Dysmenorrhea or menorrhagia
- Anemia
- Inability to check presence/location of IUD thread

Materials

- Examining table
- Intrauterine device
- Povidone-iodine solution (Betadine)
- Local anesthetic such as 0.5% lidocaine HCI (Xylocaine)
- Syringe
- 22-gauge spinal needle
- Gloves
- Vaginal speculum
- Drapes
- Bowl for povidone-iodine solution
- Sponges or cotton balls
- Uterine sound
- Cotton swab
- Tenaculum
- Scissors
- Ring forceps or long Kelly clamp
- Silver nitrate sticks

THE IUD CANDIDATE.   Let the uterine depth, determined by sounding at the time of initial counseling, guide the choice of an IUD as a contraceptive. Insertion is not recommended unless the uterus sounds between 6 and 10 cm (2 ⅜-3 ¹⁵/₁₅ in).

Progestasert is a good therapeutic choice for the patient with dysmenorrhea or heavy menses.

TIMING OF IUD INSERTION.   It is optimal to insert the IUD during the patient's menstrual period when the cervix is soft and dilated. The bleeding that sometimes follows IUD insertion for about one week is not alarming if it is masked by menses. This bleeding, along with the continuing menses, can actually help reassure the patient that she is not pregnant.

Insert an IUD during the remainder of the patient's menstrual cycle only if she has not had intercourse since her last period, was protected during intercourse, or has just finished her period.

Preinsertion Procedure

1. Become thoroughly familiar with the manufacturer's instructions for insertion of the IUD chosen.

2. Explain the concept and the procedure to the patient. Show her the device. Allow sufficient time for her to read the patient information material provided and ask questions.

3. With the draped patient in the lithotomy position on the examining table, don sterile gloves and perform a bimanual examination to determine whether the uterus is anteflexed or retroflexed, to rule out pregnancy, and to detect infection.

4. Reglove with sterile gloves and insert a vaginal speculum to aid in visual examination of the cervix.

5. With sterile materials and sterilized equipment laid out, cleanse the cervix with an antiseptic solution—povidone-iodine solution (Betadine), if the patient is not allergic to it—using a sterile sponge or a cotton ball held by a ring forceps or long Kelly clamp.

6. Administer a paracervical block, if necessary, using a 22-gauge spinal needle and 5-10 mL 0.5% lidocaine HCL (Xylocaine) without epinephrine. *Note:* Candidates for local anesthesia are nulliparous

Figure 8-1: Measure depth of uterus by placing swab alongside sound at the cervix and removing them together.

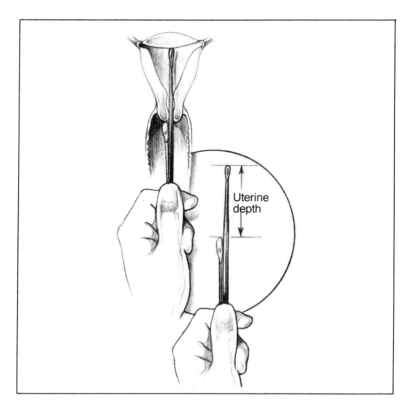

Uterine depth

women, who generally have narrow cervical canals and small uterine cavities, and patients prone to vasovagal activity when experiencing pain. Nonsteroidal anti-inflammatory drugs (such as 250-375 mg naproxen [Naprosyn], or two 275-mg tablets naproxen sodium [Anaprox]) given 30 minutes before IUD insertion may diminish discomfort in these patients.

7. Be prepared to manage syncope, bradycardia, or other neurovascular episodes that can occur during IUD insertion.

PROCEDURE

1. Continuing aseptic technique, gently grasp the anterior lip of the cervix with a tenaculum about 1.5 cm (⁹⁄₁₆ in) above the external os.

2. Sound the uterus for direction and depth. With the sound inserted to maximum depth, place a cotton swab at the cervix and remove it with the sound to get an accurate measurement (Figure 8-1).

Figure 8-2: Introduce inserter slowly through cervical canal into the uterus, checking to be sure it is in the horizontal plane.

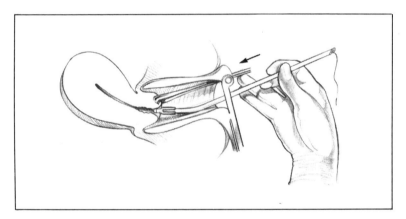

3. Just before insertion (1-2 minutes, depending on the device), load the IUD into the inserter according to manufacturer's directions.

4. Apply gentle traction of the cervical lip with the tenaculum. If necessary, apply sufficient downward traction to straighten the uterine axis.

5. Introduce the inserter into the cervical canal and then the uterus, advancing it slowly and gently, checking any indicators provided on the inserter to be sure the device is inserted in the horizontal plane. The arm cocker will slide along the inserter shaft. The number at the base of the arm cocker approximates the uterine depth (in centimeters) and will assist in determining when the fundus is reached (Figures 8-2 and 8-3).

6. To situate the IUD in the fundus, the thread-retaining plug is released. This frees the thread and the IUD from the inserter as the

Figure 8-3: Numbers at the base of the arm cocker approximate uterine depth and help determine when the fundus is reached.

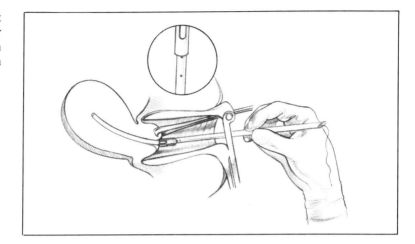

Figure 8-4: Release plug to situate the IUD in the fundus.

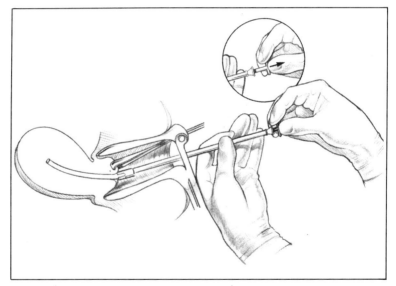

inserter is slowly withdrawn (Figure 8-4). To check the position, measure the length of the short "indicator" thread (Figure 8-5). The depth of the uterus plus the length of the indicator thread should approximate 9 cm for correct placement.

7.   Trim the thread of the device at least 5 cm (2 in) from the cervix; it can always be cut shorter later if desired. Have the patient feel the piece of thread you trim off to familiarize herself with its texture.

8.   Observe tenaculum insertion sites. If bleeding persists, use silver nitrate sticks to cauterize the area.

9.   After the patient has rested following the procedure, have her feel the thread in her vagina.

Figure 8-5: To check position of device, measure the length of exposed indicator thread—depth of the uterus plus length of thread should equal approximately 9 cm.

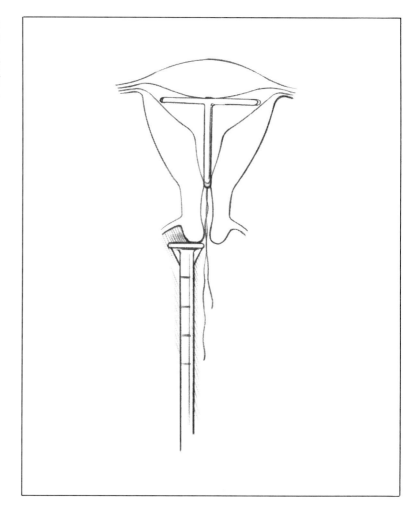

Complications

INFECTION   causes more hospitalization than any other complication of IUD use. Symptoms include pain, fever, and chills. Remove the IUD before treating the patient with antibiotics; an IUD left in place can be a continuing medium for the infecting organism, seeding the endometrium. Treat pelvic inflammatory disease with broad-spectrum antibiotics for 10-14 days. Rule out ectopic pregnancy. Wait 3-12 months before considering reinsertion of an IUD after infection, or recommend another method of contraception if the patient plans future pregnancies. Though a tailless IUD is less apt to cause infection, its status cannot be as easily determined as that of an IUD with a thread.

UTERINE PERFORATION   occurs in about 1 per 1,000 IUD users, and is often asymptomatic. Lowest rates of perforation are reported for the Lippes Loop and the Cu-7. When they occur, symptoms may include pain, bleeding, gradual apparent shortening of the thread, and symptoms of pregnancy. Ultrasound can detect both metallic and nonmetallic devices effectively. Should the IUD perforate the cervix, you can push the device back in toward the fundus and then remove it through the cervical os. If the device has penetrated the peritoneal sac, laparoscopy or laparotomy is needed to retrieve it.

PREGNANCY,   uterine or ectopic, is possible with an IUD in place. If uterine pregnancy occurs, remove the IUD if possible. If you can't remove the device, consult with the patient on the option of terminating the pregnancy. Continuing the pregnancy with an IUD in place involves increased risk of spontaneous abortion and increased risk of sepsis. If ectopic pregnancy occurs, treat as you would in a patient not using an IUD.

EXPULSION   occurs most often in the first two months following IUD insertion and is more common in nulliparous women. The overall rate of expulsion is 5%-20% per year. Symptoms include discharge, cramping or pain, spotting, dyspareunia in the patient or difficulty in coitus in the partner, and apparent lengthening of the thread. The patient may be able to feel the device when she checks for the thread. You may notice partial expulsion on direct examination or on ultrasonography or radiography. Remove any partially expelled IUD. After determining the probable cause for expulsion, consider changing to a different size or model if indicated.

BLEEDING   following IUD insertion is common, particularly in the form of heavier menstrual periods, periods of longer duration, or spotting between periods. Fifteen percent of women discontinue IUD use because of this. When a patient presents with these complaints, always consider other causes, such as expulsion of the device, perforation, infection, and causes not related to use, including polyps, neoplasm, and fibroadenoma.

Follow-up

Instruct the patient to check for the thread weekly until she feels comfortable with the checking procedure; then have her check routinely after each menstrual period.

Recommend that she use an additional method of contraception for the first three months.

Alert the patient to common side effects of IUD insertion such as pain, bleeding or spotting, and cramps with periods. Ask her to report a late or missed period, abdominal pain, fever, chills, foul smelling discharge, or bleeding with clots (see "Complications").

Replace a progesterone-containing device every year. Be sure to sound the patient's uterus before inserting a new IUD.

Removal

Remove the IUD at the patient's request, if you note endometriosis, if the hematocrit drops five points, or below 30%, if the device is partially expelled, or if the device is due for replacement because its stores of copper or progesterone are depleted.

Removing an IUD usually involves minimal pain. If the device has been in place more than five years, however, narrowing of the cervical canal or embedding of the device in the uterine wall can cause discomfort.

It's best to remove the IUD during menses, when the os is open. Using aseptic technique, apply slow, gentle, steady traction on the thread with a ring forceps or a long Kelly clamp. If difficulties arise, don't risk breaking the thread. Instead, sound the uterus for 30 seconds, then rotate the sound 90 degrees to dislodge the device. You may want to use a paracervical block (see step 6 in "Preinsertion procedure").

Consider dilating the cervix to facilitate removal. You may find exerting downward traction on the cervix with a tenaculum helpful, as well.

If necessary, remove the device using alligator forceps, uterine packing forceps, a Novak curet, or a hook.

If the IUD thread is not visible, you can try removing the device in the office using uterine dressing forceps, a hooked uterine curet, or contact hysteroscopy. If necessary, the device can be removed in the hospital using hysteroscopy, dilation and curettage, or suction aspiration.

Suggested Readings

Hatcher RA, Guest FJ, Steward FH, et al: *Contraceptive Technology, 1984-1985,* ed 12. New York, Irving Publishers, 1984, pp. 81-89.

Pritchard JA, MacDonald PC: *Williams Obstetrics,* ed 16. New York, Appleton-Century-Crofts, 1980, pp. 1021-1028.

Romney SL, Gray MJ, Little B, et al: *Gynecology and Obstetrics: The Health Care of Women,* ed 2. New York, McGraw-Hill Book Co, 1981, pp. 831-835.

9

Newborn Circumcision with the Gomco Clamp

Paul S. Williamson, M.D.

While The American Academy of Pediatrics has declared that there are no absolute medical indications for circumcision of the newborn male*, controversy and argument about the advantages and disadvantages of the procedure abound. The majority of American newborn boys continue to be circumcised with "cleanliness" given as the most common reason parents desire the procedure. Traditional reasons given, such as the prevention of cervical or penile cancer, association with sexually transmitted diseases, and psychological reasons are not supported by data. Recent reports of an association between urinary tract infections and the uncircumcised male infant** are the strongest medical indication for newborn circumcision. Opponents of circumcision feel the foreskin is nature's protective covering, and that daily hygiene after the skin is retractable at 2 to 3 years of age is a perfectly acceptable alternative. Third party insurers are discontinuing payment for routine newborn circumcision (*AMA News,* May 9, 1986). Currently the decision to circumcise or not is made by the parents based on what they feel is best for their son.

There are, however, definite contraindications to performing newborn circumcision as follows:

Circumcision should not be performed on an infant who is less than 24 hours old, as it is essential that the newborn have this time to stabilize to the external environment. In a premature baby, the procedure should be deferred until such time as he is ready to leave the hospital. Any evidence of illness or suspicion that the infant is harboring an active infection is a contraindication to the procedure.

---

*Thompson HC, et al: Report of the AdHoc Task Force on Circumcision. *Pediatrics* 1975;56:610.

**Ginsburg CM, McCrackin GH: Urinary tract infection in young infants. *Pediatrics* 1982;69:409.

Lastly, circumcision should not be performed on an infant with a congenital anomaly such as hypospadias (in which foreskin is needed for reconstructing the urethra), incomplete foreskin, shortened penile shaft skin, or a family history of hemophilia.

The Gomco clamp method of circumcision is preferred over the Plastibell or Sheldon methods,[1] because the Gomco technique carries less risk of complications during surgery and fewer subsequent complications. With the Gomco technique, more of the membranous prepuce—the critical area for cancer risk—is excised. The Gomco technique occasions less risk of injury to the glans penis than the guillotine technique of the Sheldon clamp that often leaves "dog-ears" or "corner flaps" at the lateral edges of the preputial incision. With the Plastibell method, hemorrhagic problems may arise if there is loosening of the ligature holding prepuce to the bell; retention of the plastic ring may also cause complications.

Materials

- Infant restraint board with adjustable hook and loop tape (Velcro) straps
- Light source
- Warming light
- Sterile gloves
- Sterile towel drapes
- 4″ × 4″ gauze sponges
- 1 mL 1% lidocaine HCI (Xylocaine) *without* epinephrine and 1-mL syringe with 27-gauge × 1.2 cm needle
- Antiseptic skin prep material such as povidone-iodine solution (Betadine)
- Three mosquito clamps
- Suture scissors
- Blunt malleable probe
- Scalpel with blade
- 1″ × 9″ petrolatum-impregnated gauze dressing
- 1.1 and 1.3 Gomco circumcision clamps.

PROCEDURE

1. The infant should not be fed for 2-3 hours before surgery. Have in position a diaper-padded restraint board on a waist-high table, a light, all the sterile instrument packs, and a warming light.
2. Before donning sterile gloves, place the infant supine on the restraint board and close the straps over his extremities.
3. Do a 1-minute povidone-iodine surgical scrub of the genital area, concentrating on the penile shaft; wipe off excess with a 4″ × 4″ gauze sponge. Drape the infant with sterile towels.

4. Inject 1% lidocaine *without* epinephrine (0.2-0.4 mL, depending on the weight of the infant) on each side of the penile shaft over the dorsal penile nerves to block them locally. The anesthetic technique, as developed for infants by Kirya and Werthmann, involves stabilizing the penile shaft in one hand, then piercing the skin of the penile shaft at a 25-degree angle at the 10 o'clock and 2 o'clock positions, 1 cm distal from the pubic bone, inserting the needle no more than 0.25-0.5 cm.† Take care to enter the subcutaneous space, avoiding surface veins (Figure 9-1). Wait about 3 minutes for the anesthetic to take effect.

5. Identify the lumen of the prepuce; clamp the dorsal edge of skin with a mosquito hemostat and lift it. If the infant cries, release the clamp and wait a little longer; rarely, you may have to wait 6-8 minutes for the anesthetic to take effect.

6. Insert a second clamp (closed) through the preputial space to the dorsal base of the glans at the corona and open the clamp to dissect the prepuce laterally (Figure 9-2). Use a blunt malleable probe to complete dissection of the prepuce from the glans while continuing to elevate the prepuce with the first mosquito clamp.

Figure 9-1: Penile dorsal nerve block. Stabilize the penile shaft with one hand, then inject 1% lidocaine *without epinephrine* to the depth of 0.25-0.5 cm at 10 o'clock and 2 o'clock, 1 cm distal from the pubic bone.

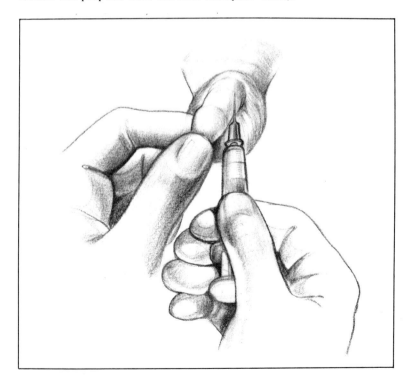

†Kirya C, Werthmann MW Jr: Neonatal circumcision and penile dorsal nerve block—A painless procedure. *J Pediatr* 1978;92:998-1000.

Figure 9-2: Lift the dorsal edge of the prepuce with a mosquito hemostat. Insert a closed hemostat through the preputial space to the dorsal base of the glans at the corona. Open the clamp to laterally dissect the prepuce. *Note:* If application of initial clamp to lift the prepuce elicits pain response, remove the clamp and wait 6-8 minutes for anesthetic to take effect.

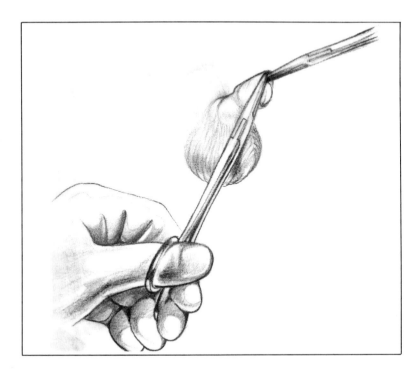

9-3: To maintain hemostasis as you divide the prepuce, place a clamp at the dorsal midline 1 mm from the distal edge of the corona and hold it shut for 5 seconds to crush the dorsal prepuce.

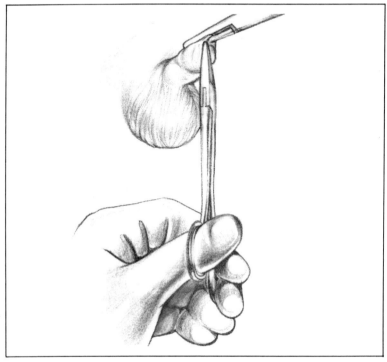

7. Carefully slide an opened clamp over the dorsal midline of the prepuce to 1 mm from the distal edge of the corona, keeping the point beneath the prepuce elevated to avoid trauma. Close the clamp to crush the dorsal prepuce (Figure 9-3), and keep it closed for 5 seconds. The crush will maintain hemostasis after you divide the prepuce down the middle of the crush.

8. Still holding the edge of the prepuce with a clamp adjacent to the crush line, insert the opened scissors along the crush line with the blunt side beneath the prepuce elevated to avoid trauma. Divide the prepuce down the center of the crush with the scissors to just above the coronal sulcus (Figure 9-4).

9. With a clamp at either edge of the slit in the prepuce, peel back the corners (Figure 9-5). Take care to include both the skin and mucosal layers in the tissue you clamp and peel back; if you don't, the surface of the glans will not be completely exposed. If the initial blunt probing did not fully dissect the glans-prepuce plane, use a 4″ × 4″ gauze sponge to peel back the remainder of the membranous portion until you see the coronal sulcus and the glans exposed in its entirety. You'll know you've achieved the correct plane and depth of dissection if you see a slight amount of smegma exposed in the coronal sulcus. After full dissection, bring the prepuce back up over the glans.

Figure 9-4: To divide the prepuce, insert open scissors along the crush line with the blunt side down to avoid trauma. Slit the prepuce down the crush line to a point just above the coronal sulcus.

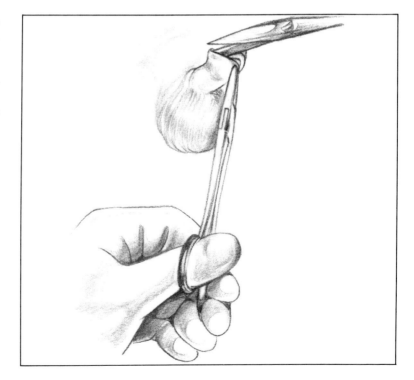

Figure 9-5: Clamp both edges of prepuce and peel back. *Note:* Be sure to peel skin *and* mucosal layer to fully expose glans. Full dissection is achieved when the coronal sulcus is clearly visible. After full dissection, bring the prepuce back up over the glans.

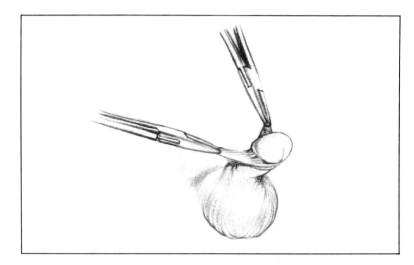

Figure 9-6: Third hemostat cross-clamps the prepuce up around the Gomco bell.

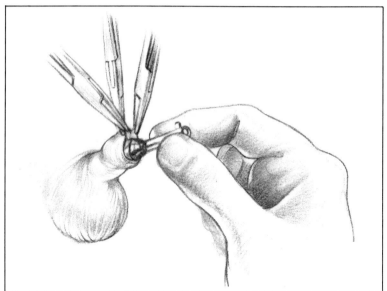

10. Select a 1.1 or 1.3 Gomco bell according to the size of the infant's penis, and insert it into the plane just dissected; it should easily reach as far as the coronal sulcus. Bring the two edges of the dorsal slit up around the shaft of the bell and cross clamp this incision with the third clamp (Figure 9-6). Remove corner clamps.

11. Place the open ring of the Gomco circumcision clamp plate over the shaft of the bell. Use a mosquito clamp to reach through the ring opening and parallel clamp the dorsal slit so you can remove the cross-clamp without losing either edge of the prepuce (Figure 9-7).

Figure 9-7: With the two side clamps removed, place the open ring of the circumcision clamp plate over the shaft of the bell. Place a mosquito clamp through the ring and parallel clamp the dorsal slit so you can remove the cross-clamp without losing the edge closure.

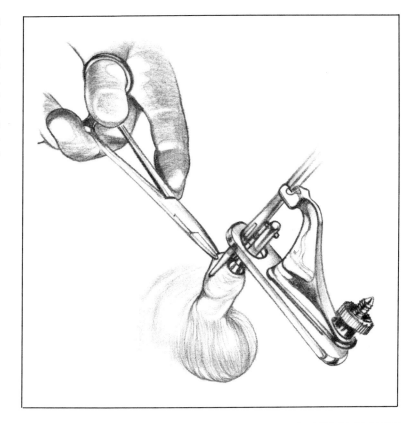

Figure 9-8: Loosen the thumbscrew until the crossbar of the bell shaft falls into the grooves of the clamp arm.

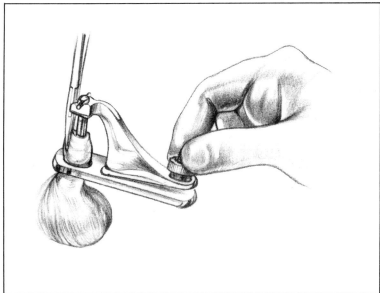

12. Fully loosen the thumbscrew knob of the Gomco clamp to allow the crossbar of the bell shaft to fall into the grooves of the clamp arm (Figure 9-8).

13. Hold the plate of the Gomco clamp horizontally and stretch about 0.75-1.0 cm of the prepuce onto the bell. *Important:* If you stretch it too tightly, too much skin will be removed; if too loosely, too little skin will be removed. This means pulling about as much skin through the ring as you leave below it. Take some time to adjust the skin so the clamp will make a symmetric crush around the prepuce.

14. When you are sure of the placement of the skin over the bell, tighten the thumbscrew of the Gomco clamp to produce a symmetric ring crush through the foreskin at the corona level. Leave the clamp in place 5 minutes for good hemostasis.

15. With the Gomco clamp still in place, trim the prepuce with a cold scalpel blade at the upper plate edge against the bell (Figure 9-9).

16. Loosen the thumbscrew, remove the clamp, and carefully loosen the bell from the incised edge of the penile skin. Wrap a petrolatum-impregnated gauze dressing around the raw edge of the incision to keep diapers from sticking to the area.

Follow-up

Keep the circumcised infant under observation for 24 hours for signs of bleeding or infection. Have the diapers changed promptly as needed and the incisional margins cleaned with warm water and mild soap at each diaper change. A light petrolatum coating should be applied around the incisional margin at each diaper change for about a week or until the incision is healed. Instruct parents to report promptly fever, swelling, skin redness around the incision, and any bleeding that is more than a slight spotting (see "Complications").

Complications

Circumcision is not a "minor procedure." Meticulous technique must be observed to avoid complications:

- Slight hemorrhage at the incision is the most common problem and can be controlled by direct pressure, by topical epinephrine on a cotton-tip applicator, or by a silver nitrate stick. *Caution:* Never use electrocautery because total sloughing necrosis of the penis has occurred with this technique. If a vessel is open, and these minor adjustments don't control bleeding, ligate the vessel at the margin of the incision. Most bleeding can be prevented by leaving the Gomco clamp on for a full 5 minutes before trimming the prepuce. Some minor spotting is to be expected after the procedure, and spotting may be observed in the diaper for the first day.

Figure 9-9: Trim prepuce at the upper plate edge with a cold scalpel blade.

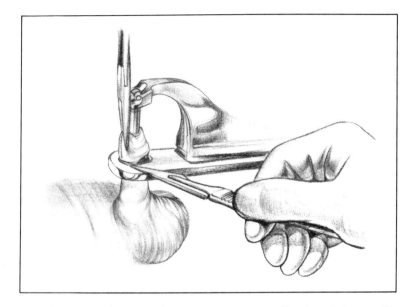

- Infection is the second most common complication. It is usually minor and local—and nearly always controlled by topical antibiotic ointment applied to cover the raw incision. Antibiotic ointment may be used in place of petrolatum for one week. In rare cases, major infectious complications can occur, such as Fournier's syndrome (a gangrenous infection of the penis, scrotum, and inguinal area), septicemia, or necrotizing fasciitis of the abdomen. Use of systemic antibiotics at the first sign of infection beyond the incision is mandatory for the prevention of these rare but serious occurrences.

- Surgical trauma can occur—usually as a result of careless dissection of the glans-prepuce plane or overdenudation of the penile shaft. Inadequate removal of the prepuce produces later adhesions and also can give the appearance of noncircumcision. Urethral fistulas have been produced by kinking the urethra into the Gomco clamp or freehand sewing of the incisional margin too deeply into the urethra. Bivalving of the glans and scrotal lacerations have also been reported.

Suggested Readings

Gee WF, Ansell JS: Neonatal circumcision: A ten-year overview: With comparison of the Gomco clamp and the Plastibell device. *Pediatrics* 1976;58 (6):824.

Kirya C, Werthmann MW: Neonatal circumcision and penile dorsal nerve block—A painless procedure. *J Pediatr* 1978;92 (6):998.

DIAGNOSTIC PROCEDURES

10

Tympanometry

Charles E. Driscoll, MD

Tympanometry provides an objective measurement of tympanic membrane mobility, affirms the presence of an intact membrane, and helps confirm the integrity of the ossicular chain, with results that are reproducible from test to test. The technique is sensitive to subtle changes produced by middle ear disease. Little training is required to perform satisfactory examinations with a modern tympanometer. The recommended devices are fully automatic and require little maintenance or calibration.

Tympanometry is the measurement of tympanic membrane mobility during variation of the air pressure in the sealed ear canal. Mobility is plotted graphically, with distance traveled by the membrane on the Y axis and pressure change on the X axis. Pressure is gradually decreased from a reference level of $+200$ mmH$_2$O, through 0, to at least -200 mmH$_2$O. You can also measure the volume of air required to fill the ear canal. This aids in diagnosis of tympanic membrane perforation when insufflated volume exceeds normal range. Mobility of the tympanic membrane and integrity of the ossicular chain may also be measured when you test the stapedial reflex by presenting a pure tone through the earphone probe unit.

This technique does not replace traditional pure tone audiometry, but it adds useful information on several conditions that alter the architecture or volume of the middle ear. It is especially helpful in detecting or following the progress of a middle ear condition such as effusion, cholesteatoma with possible perforation, or a retracted tympanic membrane with adhesions. The procedure is also indicated:

- To detect negative middle ear pressure.
- To detect tympanic membrane perforation.
- To detect ossicular chain disruptions.
- To check ventilation tubes for patency.
- To screen children who may need audiometry.

Tympanometry has no absolute contraindications. Otitis externa with purulent exudate that can cross-infect patients through contaminated equipment is a relative contraindication.

Materials

- Otoscope with ear specula of various sizes
- Cerumen spoon

- Automatic tympanometer composed of an ear probe unit for delivery of air and a pure tone pulse to the middle ear, and a recording unit with self-contained manometer and a strip chart recorder to provide hard copy of test results
- Soft rubber ear pieces of various sizes for the ear probe unit

PROCEDURE

1. Emphasize the need for the patient to sit quietly and to look straight ahead while you perform the test, without talking, swallowing, moving the jaw, or moving away from the ear probe (thereby breaking the hermetic seal). For accurate diagnosis in a patient unable to cooperate, such as a young child, you will need repeated measurements taken during quiet periods.
2. After inspecting the external ear, grasp the helix between your thumb and forefinger and move it in several directions to evaluate pain.
3. Using an otoscope, examine the ear canal to be sure it is free of cerumen or exudate (as in otitis externa). If cerumen occludes the canal, remove it with a cerumen spoon or by irrigation until you can see a portion of the tympanic membrane. Do not use irrigation if perforation is expected.
4. Inspect the tympanic membrane surface for architecture, perforation, and visible positive or negative signs of middle ear disease.
5. Turn on the automatic recording device so that it will be triggered when you apply the probe to the ear. You may also trigger it manually, if you prefer.
6. Select a soft rubber tip for the ear probe. The tip that fits properly occludes the opening of the external ear, producing a hermetic seal against the soft tissues of the ear, without being able to advance past the opening into the ear canal (Figure 10-1).
7. Grasp the helix of the ear firmly as before. Pull up and outward in older children and in adults, down and outward in young children, to straighten the ear canal while the probe is sealed (Figure 10-2). Remind the patient of the need to remain motionless. When the probe is properly positioned, the automatic recording device will be triggered.
8. Leave the ear probe sealed to the external ear canal until the tympanometer signals the conclusion of the test (3-8 seconds). The signal is a light or tone on most units. Concentrate on positioning the ear probe in the ear while the test is in progress; do not move and look at the tracing until the test is completed.
9. Repeat the procedure in the opposite ear. If you obtain any tracings of doubtful validity, repeat the test.

Figure 10-1: The rubber tip of the ear probe is the correct size if it creates a hermetic seal against the soft tissues of the ear, completely occluding the opening without advancing into the ear canal.

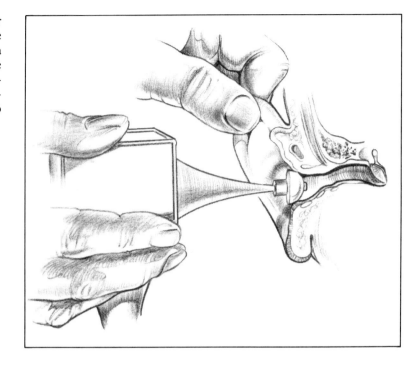

INTERPRETATION. Tympanogram tracings made by the method described (called the American method), usually fall into three types:

1. Type A is normal (Figure 10-3), with a peak of eardrum compliance at or near an air pressure of 0 mmH$_2$O, indicating that air pressure in the middle ear is in equilibrium with that of the atmosphere.

2. Type B (Figure 10-4) shows little change in compliance as the air pressure changes, suggesting the presence of fluid in the middle ear.

3. Type C (Figure 10-5) shows greatest compliance when air pressure in the ear canal is below atmospheric pressure, indicating low (negative) middle ear pressure.

You'll occasionally obtain maximum compliance at a pressure of +10 to +50 mmH$_2$O. This suggests either that the patient may be developing acute otitis media or that the patient applied positive pressure through the eustachian tubes during the test.

The volume needed to insufflate the ear canal and move the tympanic membrane is generally recorded on the tracing. Normal volume for children is 0.6-1.0 mL and for adults is 0.8-2.5 mL. If you need to insufflate an abnormally high volume of air to move the tympanic membrane, increase your suspicion of a perforation.

Figure 10-2: In an older child or adult, the arrow indicates the direction to pull the helix, which is up and outward.

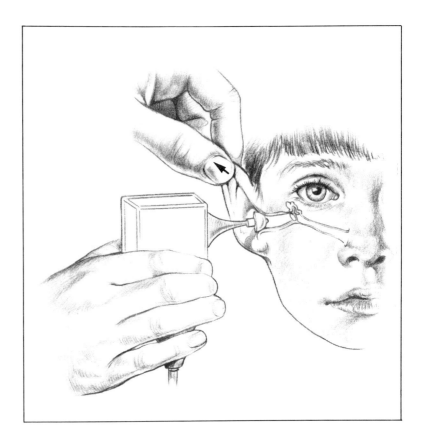

Figure 10-3: Type A tracings of the American method. Air pressure in the middle ear is in equilibrium with the atmospheric pressure.

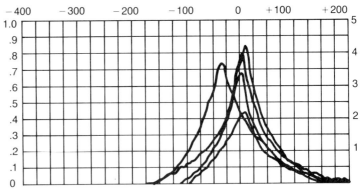

A normal variant can occur with hypermobile tympanic membranes. In that setting, the peak is near zero, but it is so high it seems to "go off the chart" (Figure 10-6). You can chart the peak by changing the air pressure applied to the tympanic membrane to bring the peak down to traceable range: Turn the switch to alter the amount of air

Figure 10-4: Type B tracings. Suggests presence of fluid in the middle ear.

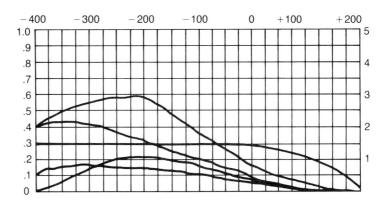

Figure 10-5: Type C tracings. Evidence of negative middle ear pressure.

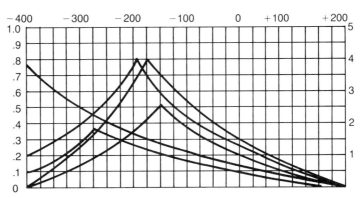

Figure 10-6: Illustrates hypermobile tympanic membrane. The peak is near zero and can be charted by adjusting the air pressure applied to the membrane to 5 mL, thereby accommodating the bigger swing, bringing the peak down to traceable range.

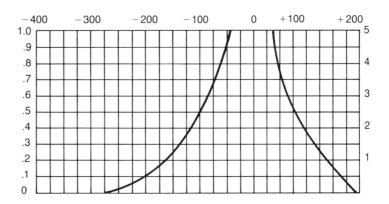

displacement from 1 mL, the usual "normal," to make 5 mL the "normal" level, thereby accommodating a bigger swing.

Stapedial reflex testing involves presenting a pure tone to the tympanic membrane to elicit movement that registers on the tympanogram. Failure to obtain motion of the tympanic membrane on pure tone stimulus in a patient with reduced hearing may indicate disruption of the ossicular chain.

Suggested Readings

Harford ER: Tympanometry, in Jerger J, Northern JL (eds): *Clinical Impedance Audiometry,* ed 2. American Electromedics Corp, Acton, Mass, 1980, pp. 40-64.

Stool SE: Medical relevancy of immittance measurements. *Ear Hear* 1984;5:309-13.

11

Punch Biopsy of the Skin

Richard E. Munns, MD

Punch biopsy is the best way to obtain small, full-thickness skin specimens. It is much easier and more effective than the traditional scalpel method, which requires the subsequent placement of sutures. Bleeding and scarring at the punch biopsy site are minimal, suture closure is seldom necessary, and secondary infection is essentially nonexistent.

You can use the punch biopsy technique whenever you need a small, full-thickness skin specimen from a lesion for microscopic examination.

Materials

For skin preparation:

- Antibacterial soap and water or alcohol swabs
- Gloves
- 3 mL of 1% lidocaine HCI (Xylocaine)
- 3-mL syringe
- 25-gauge, ⅝-in needle

For punch biopsy:

- Biopsy punches in 3-, 4-, 5-, and 6-mm sizes
- Skin hook
- Fine-pointed tissue forceps
- Iris scissors
- Specimen container
- Sterile gauze
- Adhesive strip
- 6.25% aluminum chloride in anhydrous ethyl alcohol 96% (v/v)-Xerac AC
- Cotton-tipped applicator
- Needle holder with small curved needle
- Suture material such as 4-0 monofilament
  Note: These suture materials are seldom necessary

PROCEDURE

1. Cleanse the biopsy site with antibacterial soap and water or an alcohol swab. Select the precise site carefully to encompass some of the lesion and some of the surrounding normal skin.

2. Using a 3-mL syringe with a 25-gauge, ⅝-in needle, infiltrate about 3 mL of 1% lidocaine into the subcutaneous tissue around the site. This serves to elevate the skin for biopsy as well as to provide anesthesia. The elevation protects deep tissue from injury in the unlikely case that you apply too much pressure when the punch enters the subcutaneous fat layer. Caution in applying pressure is especially important in elderly patients because of their relatively thin layer of subcutaneous fat.

Figure 11-1: Place punch perpendicular to the skin and advance it with moderate pressure while rotating it back and forth between thumb and forefinger.

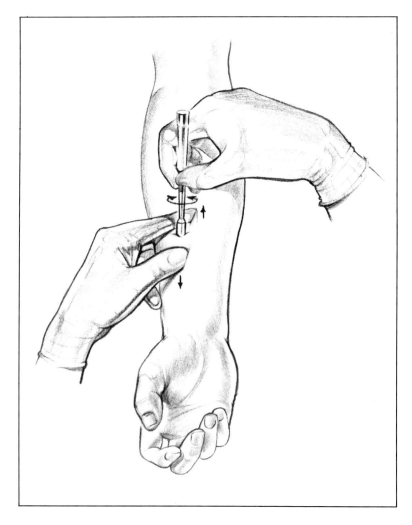

Figure 11-2: Lift specimen with tissue forceps and clip pedicle with iris scissors to free.

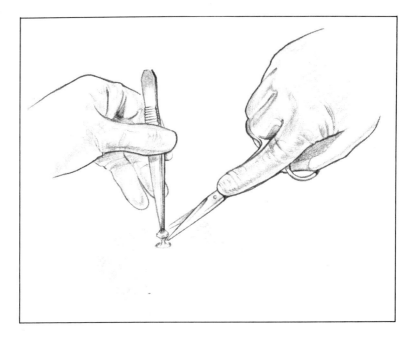

3. Select the smallest size punch that will pick up an adequate specimen—usually a 3- or 4-mm punch. Be sure to check and confirm that the punch is sharp. With one hand, slightly stretch the skin by digital pressure at right angles to the skin lines before you introduce the punch with the other hand. Keep it stretched as you advance the punch; this helps produce a moderately elliptic skin defect rather than a circular one and promotes quick healing.

4. Apply the punch perpendicular to the skin, advancing it with moderate pressure while rotating it back and forth between thumb and forefinger (Figure 11-1).

5. When you feel a marked decrease in resistance as the punch penetrates the dermis and enters the subcutaneous fatty layer, stop advancing the punch.

6. Remove the punch. Occasionally the specimen lifts out with the punch; if so, remove it with a small probe or skin hook. Usually the specimen remains in place. Lift the specimen up with tissue forceps and cut the pedicle with iris scissors (Figure 11-2). Be sure the specimen contains a bit of subcutaneous fatty tissue. Place the specimen in a container for transportation to your laboratory according to the laboratory protocol.

7. Apply light pressure to the wound with sterile gauze; this nearly always stops any bleeding. An adhesive strip is usually an adequate dressing. If you've used a larger punch, you might need to cauterize with aluminum chloride solution 6.25% on a cotton-tipped applicator, or suture, but even a 6-mm punch seldom creates the need for either of these.

Complications are very uncommon with punch biopsy. If bleeding is not controlled by pressure, a well-placed suture will solve the problem. Using only sharp punches will permit the specimen to be cut with minimum pressure, thus avoiding injury to deep tissue when the dermis is penetrated. Return visits should be scheduled as with a skin laceration so that adequate healing of the biopsy site can be documented.

Suggested Readings

Driscoll CE, Bope ER, Smith CW, et al: *Handbook of Family Practice.* Chicago, Year Book Medical Publishers Inc, 1986.

Epstein E: *Skin Surgery,* ed 4. Springfield, Illinois, Charles C. Thomas, 1977.

Fitzpatrick TB, Polano MK, Suurmond D: *Color Atlas and Synopsis of Clinical Dermatology.* New York, McGraw-Hill Book Co, 1983.

Schultz BC, McKinney P: *Office Practice of Skin Surgery.* Philadelphia, WB Saunders Co, 1985.

12

Thoracentesis for Fluid Removal

Leslie E. Weber, MD

When a patient presents with a pulmonary effusion of unknown origin, it is essential that it be classified as a "complicated" (or infectious) effusion, which requires drainage, or an uncomplicated effusion that resolves spontaneously. When fluid is present on X-ray, it should be sampled for laboratory study to obtain cell count and differential cytology, perform a Gram's stain and cultures to determine presence and type of bacteria, and analyze for protein, specific gravity, LDH, sugar, and amylase; it can also provide relief from dyspnea and respiratory distress caused by the accumulation of fluid in the pleural space.

Thoracentesis is simple to perform, and can be accomplished unaided. It should not be performed in patients with severe coagulopathy, and is best postponed or deferred in patients who have a small effusion that is not increasing in size, in patients who are physically agitated and cannot hold still, and in patients who are responding positively to drug therapy.

Materials

- Antiseptic skin prep such as povidone-iodine (Betadine)
- Sponges
- Sterile drape or sterile towels
- Sterile gloves
- 10 mL of local anesthetic such as 1% lidocaine HCl (Xylocaine)
- 5-mL Luer-Lok syringe
- 25-gauge, ⅝-in needle
- 22-gauge, 2-in needle

For thoracentesis:

- 50-mL Luer-Lok syringe
- Three-way stopcock with rubber tubing attached to stopcock sidearm
- 22-gauge, 2-in needle
- 18-gauge, 2-in needle

- 15-gauge, 2-in needle
- Two curved clamps
- Specimen bowl
- Three specimen tubes with stoppers
- Scalpel handle and No. 11 stab blade
- Sterile sponge dressings
- Pressure pads
- Adhesive strips

Optional for thoracentesis:

- Vacuum bottle

PROCEDURE

1. Get an upright chest X-ray no more than a day before the procedure is scheduled to determine the extent and location of pleural effusion.

Caution: Although thoracentesis is not especially difficult, it does require a high degree of patient cooperation; you can accidentally puncture a lung if the patient is agitated. Delay the procedure in a patient who is coughing or has hiccups.

2. For the procedure, have the patient sit leaning forward. One convenient arrangement is to have the patient on the edge of the bed leaning on a pillow placed on a bedside stand (Figure 12-1). He or she should be resting as comfortably as possible with arms elevated.

3. Impress upon the patient the importance of remaining as still as possible to avoid puncturing the lung, and tell him to expect some discomfort when you puncture the pleura. Also warn him against coughing and ask him to tell you if he feels a cough coming on.

4. Select a site for thoracentesis at a point well below the level of the fluid as indicated by chest film. In the posterior approach, the site is often the seventh or eighth interspace on the posterior axillary line. A slightly higher site may be used, but do not use a site lower than the ninth interspace to be sure of intercepting the pleura.

5. With the patient properly positioned, don gloves and prepare the skin with antiseptic solution, covering an area about 20 cm in diameter around the selected site.

6. You can use a drape with a hole 10 cm in diameter cut in it, taping the upper margins to the patient's skin. This has a tendency to fall off, however. As an alternative, simply attach a sterile towel across the back below the site of needle entry.

7. Anesthetize the skin with a local anesthetic such as 1% lidocaine solution, using a 5-mL Luer-Lok syringe and a 25-gauge $\times$ ⅝-inch needle to raise a wheal. Then inject about 1-3 mL down through the muscles of the chest wall. Select a track directed just above the upper

Figure 12-1: Patient in correct position for thoracentesis. He or she should be as comfortable as possible, with arms raised on a pillow.

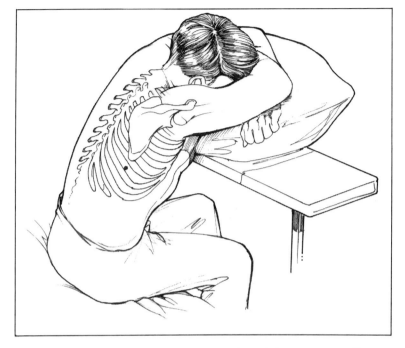

margin of the rib below the interspace selected, because a needle too close to the inferior rib margin above the intercostal space might compromise vascular strutures in the area (Figure 12-2). You will want to aspirate periodically as the needle goes in to confirm that you are not encountering blood vessels.

8. Switch to the 22-gauge × 2-inch needle and anesthetize the deeper structures with 3-5 mL of lidocaine. When you reach the pleura, the patient almost always feels pain that alerts you to needle-tip location. You won't always feel the traditional "popping" sensation on puncturing the pleura.

9. Carefully attempt to aspirate by using negative syringe pressure. If the aspirate is not pleural fluid, reposition the needle and reaspirate. When you get pleural fluid return, mark the needle's depth with a curved clamp and then withdraw the needle (Figure 12-3).

10. Attach the appropriate thoracentesis needle to the 50-mL syringe (22- or 18-gauge for sampling, 15-gauge for removing large quantities of fluid); mark the proper depth by clamping the needle at the same depth as on the anesthetizing needle (Figure 12-4). Insert the needle.

11. *To sample pleural fluid,* withdraw enough fluid to fill the specimen tubes. *To remove a large amount of fluid,* aspirate 50 mL and then turn the stopcock to permit emptying of the syringe through the rubber tubing into the specimen bowl. Repeat as necessary.

Figure 12-2: To inject
anesthetic, select a point of
insertion directly above the
upper margin of the rib
that lies directly below the
interspace you wish to enter. Aspirate periodically as
you advance the needle to
confirm that you are not
entering blood vessels.

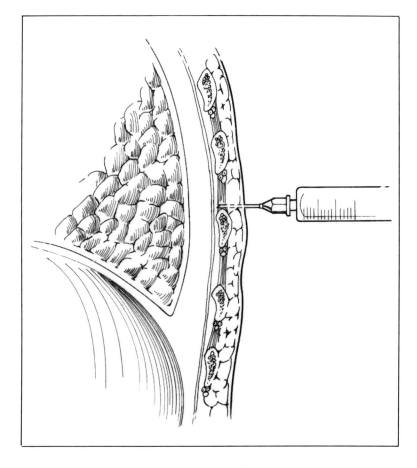

A vacuum bottle is occasionally useful if you're sure you will be
aspirating a large amount of fluid: Connect the vacuum bottle to the
15-gauge needle with rubber tubing, first having clamped off the
tubing. With the needle in the pleural space, open the tubing clamp,
allowing the vacuum to aspirate the fluid. This method benefits the
patient by permitting rapid aspiration.

12. When sufficient fluid has been aspirated, withdraw the needle
and apply finger pressure over the puncture site to prevent air from
entering. Hold the pressure for a few moments to close the site, then
apply a pressure pad with adhesive strips.

When the procedure is complete and the patient is resting,
instruct the nursing staff to observe the patient closely, and check
vital signs often for the next hour or so. Patients who have had large
amounts of fluid removed may develop pulmonary edema.

Watch for shortness of breath, which can indicate the development of pneumothorax. In the event that this does occur, the amount

Figure 12-3: When you think you have entered the pleural space, attempt to aspirate fluid. Reposition the needle if the aspirate is not pleural fluid. Upon pleural fluid return, mark the depth of the needle with a curved clamp and withdraw.

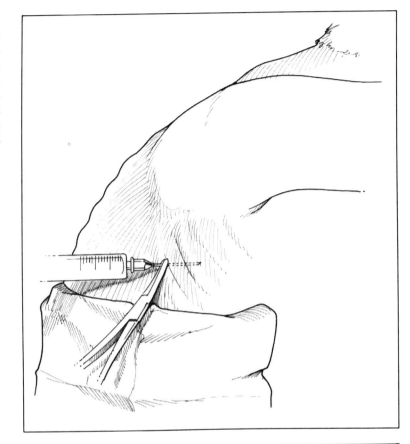

Figure 12-4: Mark the thoracentesis needle with a clamp in the same position as the clamp on the anesthetizing needle.

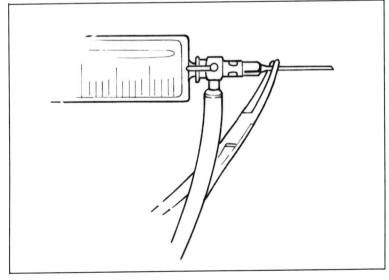

of air lost is usually small, even when a lung is inadvertently punctured.

Rarely, bleeding may occur. You can avoid this complication by selecting the puncture site carefully and directing the needle over the superior margin of the rib.

Suggested Readings

Orland MJ, Saltman RJ: *Manual of Medical Therapeutics,* ed 25. Boston, Little Brown & Co, 1986, pp. 173-174.

Pories WJ, Thomas FT: *Office Surgery for Family Physicians.* Boston, Butterworth Publishers, 1985, pp. 149-152.

Roberts PW: *Useful Procedures in Medical Practice.* Philadelphia, Lea & Febiger, 1986, pp. 449-455.

Wright CV, Mitts DL: Pleural effusions and empyema thoracis, in Rakel RE (ed): *Conn's Current Therapy.* Philadelphia, WB Saunders Co, 1986, pp. 127-128.

13

Paracentesis and Peritoneal Lavage

Leslie E. Weber, MD

Abdominal paracentesis is simple, safe, and easy to perform. It provides useful diagnostic information as well as therapeutic results. You can increase the accuracy of information obtained by including peritoneal lavage, which has largely replaced the four-quadrant abdominal tap.

In an emergency situation, paracentesis provides the information necessary to evaluate the need for laparotomy in a trauma patient, particularly when trauma was known to have been caused by a blunt blow to the abdomen. Trauma victims can also be assessed for other abdominal calamities, such as a possible splenic rupture.

In patients with ascites, paracentesis can help in the determination of the cause of the condition, and relieve their discomfort by removing fluid. *Note:* Avoid frequent therapeutic paracentesis, however, because fluid generally tends to reaccumulate rapidly.

Diagnostically, paracentesis aids in assessing the conditions of pancreatitis or peritonitis. In cases of peritonititis or acute pancreatitis, the concommitant use of peritoneal lavage may provide some relief. As the lavage, use a specifically balanced electrolyte solution containing 15 g/L of glucose, 500 USP units of heparin, 1 g kanamycin sulfate (Kantrex, Klebcil), and 100,000 USP units of bacitracin in normal saline, sufficient to make 1000 mL of lavage fluid.

In patients with a bleeding disorder or coagulopathy, paracentesis should be avoided. In emergency situations, however, patients with a mild to moderate bleeding tendency can be tapped using great caution. An absolute contraindication is cellulitis of the anterior abdominal wall.

Relative contraindications to paracentesis include patients with scars from a previous laparotomy or abdominal surgery that may have caused adhesion of an underlying bowel loop, an enlarged liver or spleen that extends into the lower quadrants, or a large, distended urinary bladder.

Materials

- Sterile gloves
- Povidone-iodine (Betadine) antiseptic solution
- Sterile drape (optional)
- 5- or 10-mL syringe
- 2-in, 21-gauge needle
- 2% lidocaine HCI (Xylocaine) with/without epinephrine, 2-3 mL
- 50-mL disposable syringe
- Short-bevel, 2-in, 14-gauge needle with stylus
- Sterile 16-gauge polyethylene intraluminal catheter, identical to that used for subclavian puncture
- 1,000 mL normal saline solution (500 mL for patients 50 kg [110 lb] and under)
- Specimen tubes
- Gauze pads

PROCEDURE

1. Empty the patient's bladder, by catheterization if necessary, and place him or her supine, with the head of the examining table or bed slightly elevated. Prep the skin with povidone-iodine solution. Drape the patient if you choose.

2. At a site in the midline about 3 cm (1¼ in) below the umbilicus, use the 2-in, 21-gauge needle and the 5- or 10-mL syringe to infiltrate the skin with 1-2 mL of 2% lidocaine. Advance the needle to the peritoneum and inject an additional 1 mL of lidocaine.

3. With the stylus in place, insert the 2-in, 14-gauge needle perpendicular to the skin. Advance it up to the hub. If you're concerned about an undue amount of pressure within the abdomen, using a Z-track insertion technique can lessen the likelihood of leakage once the procedure is completed. To do this, advance the needle a layer at a time, sliding the tissue as you go. Often, you will sense a "pop" as you penetrate the peritoneum. If ascites is present entry is confirmed by aspiration of ascitic fluid (Figure 13-1).

4. Remove the stylus, attach the 50-mL syringe, and aspirate. If you withdraw frank blood, consider the finding positive for significant intra-abdominal injury and stop the procedure. The patient will need immediate laparotomy. If ascitic fluid is present, you can remove it. But do so cautiously: The removal of more than 1,000 mL of fluid may precipitate hypotension.

5. If you have no return, proceed with lavage. Disconnect the syringe, insert the catheter through the needle (Figure 13-2), and remove the needle (Figure 13-3).

6. Connect the catheter to the bottle of saline solution. Elevate the

Figure 13-1: With stylus in place, needle is inserted perpendicular to the skin and advanced to the hub. Often there will be a "popping" sensation as you penetrate the peritoneum. If ascites is present, there will be fluid return.

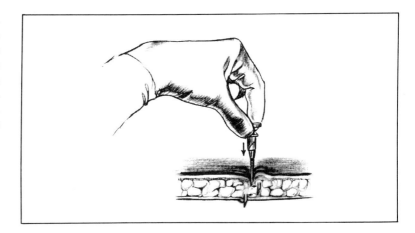

Figure 13-2: To proceed with lavage, disconnect the syringe and pass catheter through the needle.

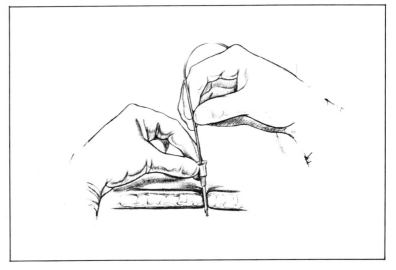

bottle and allow the solution to run rapidly, wide open, into the peritoneal cavity (Figure 13-4).

7. When the bottle is empty, place it on the floor and allow it to refill with solution. You may rock the patient slightly from side to side to facilitate the flow (Figure 13-5).

8. While the fluid is draining, disconnect the tubing momentarily and allow some fluid to run onto a white gauze square to see more clearly whether it is blood tinged. This technique allows you to detect as little as 0.25 mL of blood; the presence of a light pink tint makes the test positive.

9. Consider obtaining specimens of the returned fluid for analysis, especially in nonemergency situations. In most abdominal trauma

Figure 13-3: With catheter in place, remove the needle.

Figure 13-4: Connect catheter to bottle of saline and elevate bottle. Allow solution to run rapidly into peritoneal cavity.

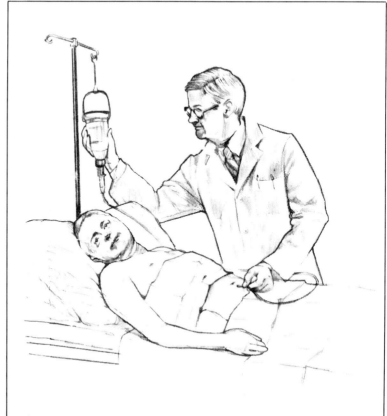

Figure 13-5: Place the empty bottle on the floor to allow the fluid to drain out. Gently rocking the patient from side to side facilitates flow.

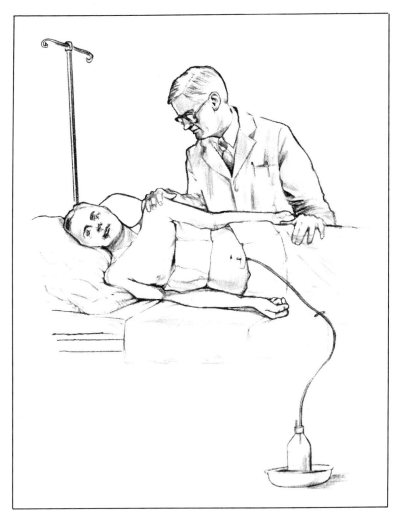

patients, visual examination of the returned fluid is sufficient for initial therapeutic decisions. If you suspect pancreatic trauma, you may choose to analyze the amylase level.

10. Remove the catheter and cover the skin wound with an adhesive bandage. Virtually all such wounds are self-healing and require no pressure.

11. Observe the patient for hypotension, fever, chills, and abdominal distention or tenderness.

Lab results

If the patient has sustained *blunt trauma* and the extent of damage is uncertain, an erythrocyte count greater than $100,000/mm^3$ or leukocyte count greater than $500/mm^3$ in the fluid indicates significant injury and the need for immediate laparotomy. With lower counts, you may treat and follow up conservatively.

If you suspect *pancreatitis,* order a peritoneal fluid amylase level for comparison with the serum amylase level. Peritoneal values several times higher than serum levels provide strong evidence for pancreatitis. Unlike serum levels, which often fall quickly after the onset of acute pancreatitis, peritoneal fluid amylase levels tend to remain elevated for several days. This distinction is particularly helpful when serum levels are only slightly elevated.

If you suspect *peritonitis,* obtain a Gram's stain and culture of the fluid.

If *ascites* is present, examine the fluid for albumin. Determine the gradient between serum and ascitic fluid by subtracting the ascitic fluid albumin level from the serum level. About 90% of patients with chronic liver disease have gradients of 1 g/dL or more. With a lesser value, portal hypertension is unlikely: The fluid probably arises from an exudative peritoneal lesion.

A cell block can be performed on a specimen of ascitic fluid concentrated by centrifugation. This specimen should consist of 100 mL or more and can be useful to determine the presence of a malignancy.

Also obtain a leukocyte count and differential, Wright's stain, Gram's stain, and culture. In some cases, you may also want amylase values and a determination for carcinoembryonic antigen.

Complications

Peritonitis related to the procedure has not been reported. Although other complications are rare, these are the ones you may find.

Bowel perforation, especially if the bowel is fixed by adhesion from a previous laparotomy. The perforation almost always heals itself when you withdraw the needle. Leakage is infrequent.

Bleeding from the puncture site that can be controlled by applying pressure.

Bleeding from laceration of an epigastric vessel, which is not likely if you introduce the needle as described: in the midline, below the umbilicus.

Suggested Readings

Bayless TM (ed): *Current Therapy in Gastroenterology and Liver Disease, 1984-1985.* St Louis, CV Mosby Co, 1984, pp. 476-477.

Hill GJ II: *Outpatient Surgery,* ed 2. Philadelphia, WB Saunders Co, 1980, pp. 105-107.

Ismail A, El Kafafy S, El Kafor AA: The role of peritoneal lavage in diagnosis of abdominal emergencies. *Br J Clin Pract* 1984;38:125-9.

Olsen WR, Hildreth DH: Abdominal paracentesis and peritoneal lavage in blunt abdominal trauma. *J Trauma* 1971;11:824-9.

Flexible Fiberoptic Sigmoidoscopy

Charles E. Driscoll, MD

Primary care physicians are using flexible fiberoptic sigmoidoscopy increasingly as the usual sites of colorectal cancer—the most common internal malignancy—shift. Not long ago, some 50% of bowel cancers were detectable by digital rectal examination. Today, only 10% are detectable this way, since common sites of colon cancer have shifted from the left toward the right side of the colon over the past two decades. Theoretically, rigid sigmoidoscopy can detect up to 50% of colon cancers—those that occur in the distal 25 cm. Yet rigid sigmoidoscopy generally reaches only 15-17 cm, which decreases the theoretical yield.

As colorectal cancer develops at more proximal levels, we must rely more on other detection methods such as occult blood testing, radiologic study using the barium enema, and flexible fiberoptic sigmoidoscopy. The latter can extend the examination field to 65 cm and permit detection of 75% of large bowel cancers.

Note: The technique can be learned easily but does require one-on-one training. Properly done, the procedure has an extremely low complication rate. Improperly done in a patient with a very friable bowel, however, flexible sigmoidoscopy may be more likely to dispose toward perforation. Flexible sigmoidoscopes come in lengths of 35, 60, 61, and 65 cm at an average price of $2,900, including light source and biopsy forceps. The longer (60-65 cm) scopes are preferred despite claims of easier technique with the 35-cm models. Manipulating the scope during the first 35 cm of insertion is the most difficult part of the procedure; extending your view to 60-65 cm should produce no additional difficulty or complications and generally increases the yield.

The American Cancer Society recommends that every asymptomatic person have sigmoidoscopy at age 50, again one year later, and then every 3-5 years, assuming results for the first two examinations were negative. In addition, flexible or rigid sigmoidoscopy is indicated in patients who have:

- Dark, tarry stools or bright red blood passed per rectum.
- Gastrointestinal pain or cramping.
- Change in bowel habits such as reduced stool caliber, differences in frequency, constipation, or diarrhea.
- Unexplained weight loss or anemia.
- Positive fecal occult blood test.
- A colorectal lesion discovered on X-ray.
- Suspected foreign body.

In addition, routine periodic sigmoidoscopic examination is recommended for patients with a:

- Personal history of colorectal lesions such as cancer, polyps, or inflammatory bowel disease.
- Family history of polyps or colorectal cancer.

Flexible sigmoidoscopy is contraindicated in patients with:

- Acute fulminating bowel disease. *Note:* While full insertion is contraindicated, the scope may be inserted safely as much as 15 cm.
- Acute diverticulitis with fever.
- Suspected perforation of the bowel.
- Paralytic ileus.
- Peritonitis.
- Severe cardiovascular disease or recent MI.
- Ischemic bowel disease.
- Patients with large aortic or iliac aneurysms.
- Patients with multiple abdominal surgeries and radiation therapy.
- Suspected complete intestinal obstruction.
- Toxic megacolon.
- Prosthetic heart valves—unless the patient has received prophylactic antibiotics one hour before examination.

(Rigid sigmoidoscopy is sometimes permissible despite these conditions depending on the depth and ease of insertion; digital examination is almost never contraindicated.)

Materials

- Adjustable examining table; ideally proctologic
- Water-soluble lubricant, such as K-Y Jelly or Surgilube
- Gloves
- Occult blood testing cards

- Anoscope
- Flexible fiberoptic sigmoidoscope with light source[1]
- Suction machine
- Air and water sources; best when incorporated in the light source
- Biopsy forceps and brush
- Camera attachment or teaching head (optional)

Preparation

Inadequate bowel prep is the most common cause of unsuccessful visualization of the colon. To ensure adequate preparation:

- Have the patient take two sodium phosphate-type enemas (Fleet), one at two hours before the procedure, the other at one hour before, repeating enemas until evacuated fluid is clear.
- For patients who are inactive or have chronic constipation, order a clear liquid diet for 24 hours before the procedure, a bisacodyl suppository (Dulcolax, Fleet Bisacodyl, Theralax, etc.) for the day before the procedure, and 10 oz of citrate of magnesia in the late afternoon of the day before.

Figure 14-1: Insert is detail of scope head. Use the left hand to manipulate controls of sigmoidoscope, and the right hand to advance and withdraw the scope shaft.

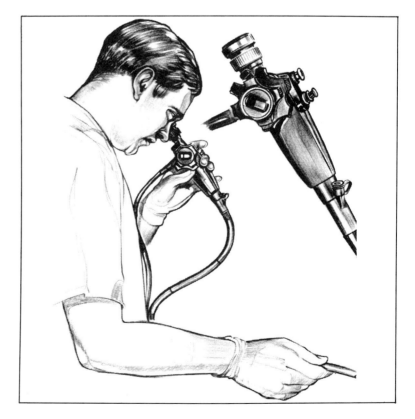

PROCEDURE

1. Patient cooperation is mandatory. Have the patient on the examining table in a left lateral decubitis, Sims', or knee-chest position, or supine with the right leg flexed, whichever you prefer and the patient finds comfortable. In any but the knee-chest position, the patient's buttocks should be at the edge of the table nearer you.

2. With the patient positioned, insert a well-lubricated glove finger into the rectum for digital examination, which helps relax the anal sphincter. Check for adequate bowel prep and determine the exact direction of the rectum. Test any material on your glove for occult blood.

3. Perform anoscopy to visualize the distal 8 cm, an area difficult to inspect with the flexible sigmoidoscope.

4. Generously lubricate the anal opening and adjacent buttocks; also lubricate the distal 5-10 cm of the sigmoidoscope, taking care to avoid the lens.

5. Hold the control head of the sigmoidoscope in your left hand so the controls for suction, air, water, and tip deflection are at your fingertips. Use your right hand to advance and withdraw the shaft of the sigmoidoscope (Figure 14-1).

6. With the shaft in straight extension, insert the scope under direct visualization, always keeping the lumen in view. Insufflate minimal amounts of air to distend the bowel and allow visualization. Warn the patient not to strain against the instrument and instruct him or her to report any significant discomfort during the procedure. (Pain is not customary with flexible sigmoidoscopy and may indicate too much pressure against the colon wall or too much stretching of the bowel on its peritoneal attachments. Aspirate air if the patient complains of cramping. If the patient at any point has extreme discomfort or intolerance, discontinue the insertion procedure.)

7. Stop just inside the rectum. Move the tip of the scope up and down until you completely visualize the posterior wall. If the lens becomes clouded or obscured by mucus or stool, squirt water over the lens to clear it, or use suction to clear thin mucus. In most scopes, the tip can be flexed 180 degrees, so you can look back to see the anal verge and entry of the scope through the anus. Reorient the scope and continue advancing it under direct visualization until you reach the rectosigmoid junction, where you must be prepared to negotiate a 90-degree angle.

As you continue the procedure, use *dithering* and *torquing* to advance the scope. Dithering is smooth and gentle insertion of the instrument shaft 5-6 cm alternating with slow partial withdrawal—a "jiggling" motion that pleats the colon along the shaft and permits

Figure 14-2: Arrows indicate direction of scope motion to advance. Note slight withdrawal with simultaneous downward rotation.

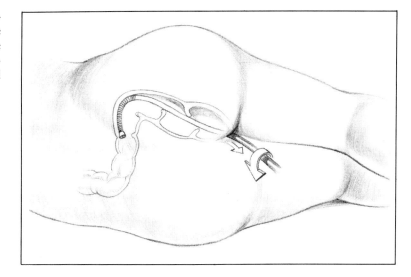

Figure 14-3: Immediately change direction by gently advancing scope while reversing rotation direction.

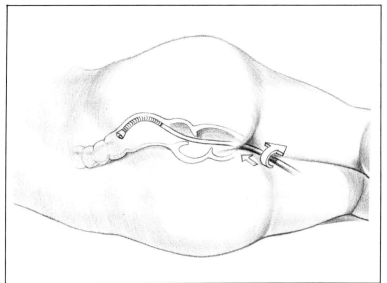

easier advancement. Torquing combines a clockwise or counterclockwise twist of the shaft with forward or backward motion. This technique helps shorten turns of the colon and permits easier passage between the sigmoid and descending colon.

8. Negotiate the rectosigmoid fold by dithering and torquing or by hooking the fold with the tip of the scope and gently pulling. This straightens the rectosigmoid angle somewhat and facilitates entry into the sigmoid colon (Figures 14-2, 14-3, 14-4). Study colon walls for

Figure 14-4: Scope has reached sigmoid colon.

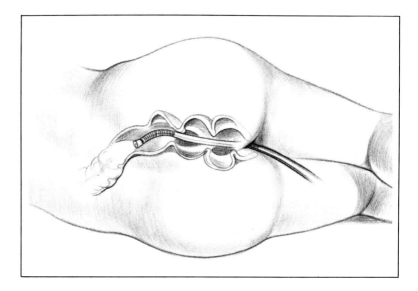

arcuate shadows and bubbles of flatus to help you find and follow the lumen. Withdraw the scope slightly and redirect it whenever you encounter any of the following:

- Resistance to movement of the scope. Make sure you can see the colonic mucosa sliding easily by the tip.
- "Redout" of your field of view. This indicates that you are pushing the tip of the scope against the bowel wall.
- Blanching of the colonic mucosa in your field of view. This indicates that you're putting the wall of the colon under too much pressure, which may lead to perforation.

Also check for blind pouches indicative of diverticulosis; they may be large, and you can enter them inadvertently with the scope if you confuse them with the lumen. This can lead to excessive pressure, distention, and possibly, perforation. Pouches usually have a slightly ovoid portal of entry and may contain stool.

9. There are landmarks and characteristics to help you as you advance the scope. You'll note the characteristic recticular pattern of blood vessels beneath the mucosa in the rectosigmoid area. Look for tubular folds in the sigmoid colon. Expect the descending colon to be pale pink in appearance due to its lack of prominent vascularity. While the rectosigmoid colon appears round to oval, the descending colon often appears slightly triangular.

10. Torque the scope clockwise to help you advance it into the sigmoid colon. Advance the scope through the sigmoid colon, which averages 35 cm in length, to the junction of the descending colon. If you are using a scope longer than 35 cm, advance the scope to full insertion in the descending colon, which is 20-30 cm long and relatively fixed to the left paracolic gutter.

11. Begin systematic examination of the colon as you gently withdraw the scope. When you encounter a fold, examine its hidden surface by gently hooking the edge of the fold with the flexible tip and allowing the colonic wall to straighten.

12. As you withdraw the scope and examine, do not attempt to evacuate blood clots, fecal particles, or foreign objects such as kernels or seeds. Only thin mucus and secretion can be aspirated through the narrow suction channel. During scope withdrawal, use the sigmoidoscopic biopsy forceps or brush to perform a biopsy of any lesions or suspicious areas. This can help avoid a second intubation: The technique is relatively simple but one-on-one training is highly recommended. *Do not use cautery* on any lesion unless a complete bowel prep has been done, because of the hazard of potentially explosive bowel gas that may be present. Just before removing the scope, aspirate all the air you introduced into the colon for visualization.

13. Carefully document in the patient's record all the findings of the exam, including the following:

- The indications for performing the exam
- Type of bowel prep
- Adequacy of bowel prep
- Findings of digital exam
- Findings of anoscopic exam
- Insertion technique and ease of insertion
- Findings of full visual mucosal inspection
- Depth of scope insertion
- Anatomic site of lesion
- Appearance of lesion
- Depth of lesion
- Sites of biopsy and/or photographs
- Patient's tolerance of the procedure

Instrument care. Clean the instrument promptly after each use before secretions dry out to reduce chances of infection. Wash the shaft, suction and biopsy channels, and biopsy instruments in a solution of surgical soap; rinse alternately with a 30% alcohol solution and clean tap water. Do not immerse the ocular head of the scope or the controlling knobs and levers; wipe these parts clean with disinfecting alcohol. To disinfect the shaft of the scope, immerse it in a cold sterilizing solution recommended by the manufacturer for 10 minutes, followed by thorough rinsing with tap water. Again, do not immerse the head. Gas sterilization is advisable following use in a patient with hepatitis or acquired immune deficiency syndrome.

Suggested Readings

American Cancer Society, "Guidelines for the Cancer-Related Checkup: Recommendations and Rationale", *Cancer* 1980;30(July-Aug.):194.

Hunt R, Waye J (Eds): *Colonoscopy: Techniques, Clinical Practice, and Colour Atlas.* London, Chapman and Hall Publishers, 1981.

Morgenstern L, Lee S: Spatial distribution of colonic carcinoma, *Archives of Surgery* 1978;113 (Oct.):1142.

Rodney WM, Felmar E: Flexible sigmoidoscopy: A "how-to" guide. *Your Patient and Cancer* 1984;4(2):57.

Shinya H: *Colonoscopy: Diagnosis and Treatment of Colonic Diseases.* New York, Igaku-Shoin Medical Publishers, 1982.

Lumbar Puncture in Adults

Elliott Schmerler, MD
Glenys O. Williams, MD

The lumbar puncture is an excellent diagnostic tool. It is as applicable in emergency situations as it is in routine workups.

Indications for performing a lumbar puncture include patients who present with symptoms of seizures, intractable vomiting, unexplained fever, headache, stiff neck, and positive Kernig's and Brudzinski's signs, raising the suspicion of meningitis. It will also help confirm suspicion of leukemia or a central nervous system malignancy.

In possible cases of subarachnoid bleeding, some physicians recommend postponing lumbar puncture until after seeing the results of a computed tomography (CT) scan, if such a test is available. This recommendation also applies to situations where the diagnostic workup is for dementia, syncope, asymmetric weakness, or hypoesthesia.

There are contraindications to lumbar puncture that must be noted. One is evidence of raised intracranial pressure, especially from a space-occupying lesion. Performing a lumbar puncture when this condition exists creates a risk of causing a possibly fatal cerebellar pressure cone, or a herniation of brain substance through the tentorial falx.

Patients with blood dyscrasias who are undergoing full anticoagulant therapy should not have a lumbar puncture. Nor should anyone with an infection of the skin in the area of a lumbar puncture, or a stiff and unyielding back.

Difficulties in performing a lumbar puncture arise in several situations. The obese patient presents a problem because landmarks needed to find a prescise puncture site are difficult to locate. The elderly patient, even a thin one, may have a long, bone-hard supraspinous ligament that is hard to penetrate. Lastly, patients with severe degenerative changes in the spin, and those who have trouble bending into the necessary position pose particular difficulties.

Materials

- Sterile gloves and towels
- Antiseptic solution containing iodine, such as povidone-iodine (Betadine)
- 70% alcohol solution
- Gauze pads, 2 × 2 in
- Spinal needle (22-25 gauge, 1-1½ in, with stylet)*
- 2-mL syringe
- Manometer with three-way stopcock
- 0.5-1.0 mL 1% lidocaine HCl (Xylocaine) and 2-mL syringe with 25-gauge needle
- Three sterile test tubes
- Adhesive strip

Preparation

1. Have the patient lie on one side. Occasionally a sitting position can be used if the patient cannot lie down, but this does not allow accurate measurement of CSF pressure. Also, the risk of herniation increases with the patient sitting; avoid this position when intracranial pressure is elevated.

2. See that the lumbar vertebrae are flexed on each other as far as possible, so that the inferior articular processes of the upper vertebrae ride up on the superior articular processes of the lower, the ligamenta flava are stretched, and the interlaminar spaces are increased, all of which expand the target area.

Flexion of the hips on the spine does not necessarily produce flexion of the lumbar vertebrae. Telling a patient, "Draw your knees up to your chin" is insufficient. A better instruction is, "Try to roll your head into your lap." Alternatively, you can put your fingertip on the lumbar area and say, "Push out this part of your back." If the patient is lying down, an assistant can firmly flex the neck and raise the knees to meet the head.

Caution: Be careful your assistant does not contaminate the sterile field with head or breath.

3. Identify the site for lumbar puncture by drawing an imaginary line between the highest points of the patient's two iliac crests. This line passes just below the fourth lumbar space (Figure 15-1).

4. Provided the level of puncture is below L-2, the exact location is unimportant: At this level the spinal cord becomes the cauda equina

---

*Several studies suggest that needles *without* stylets can lead to development of spinal epidermoid tumors, theoretically by displacing the core of the epidermis into the spinal cord.

Figure 15-1: With the patient in the correct position, try to imagine a line drawn between the highest points of the patient's iliac crests. This line passes just below the fourth lumbar space. As long as the puncture is directed below L-2, the exact location is unimportant.

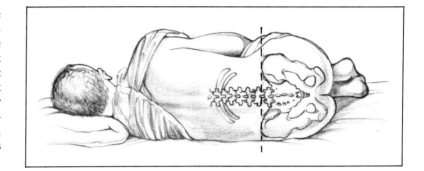

Figure 15-2: With the hub of the needle at eye level, advance it cautiously and slightly cephalad toward the umbilicus.

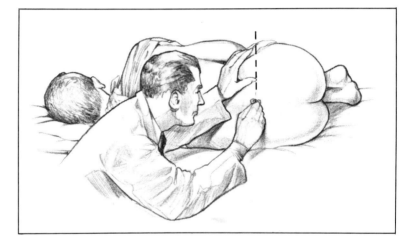

in adults. Distances between lumbar vertebrae may vary; choose the space where the gap is widest.

5. Observe strict antiseptic technique. Using gauze pads, scrub first with antiseptic, then with alcohol. Cleanse the puncture site first, then scrub the rest of the back in concentric circles around the intended puncture site.

6. Drape the back with sterile towels.

7. Using a 25-gauge needle and a 2-mL syringe, inject 0.5-1.0 mL 1% lidocaine SC at the site.

PROCEDURE

1. Line up your eye behind the hub of the needle, looking down the shaft. Keep the bevel facing cephalad. The median approach is recommended, although some physicans prefer a paramedian or lateral approach.

2. Direct the needle slightly cephalad, toward the umbilicus. Advance it cautiously, either in millimeter steps or continuously, in the median plane (Figure 15-2).

3. When you've advanced the needle 1.0-1.5 cm (⅜-⅝ in), you will feel a decrease in resistance as the needle penetrates the ligamentum flavum. The penetration sometimes gives the sensation that the needle is "popping" through the ligament.

4. Once the needle point enters the ligamentum flavum, remove the stylet, advance the needle a little further to puncture the dural arachnoid (dura and arachnoid are virtually homogeneous in the lumbar area). CSF should appear (Figure 15-3).

5. Check for free flow of CSF. If necessary, rotate, fractionally advance, or withdraw the needle. You may have to create negative pressure by attaching a 2-mL syringe and aspirating before CSF flows freely.

6. Once free-flowing CSF appears, attach a three-way stopcock and manometer to measure the CSF pressure (Figure 15-4). Then allow 0.5-1.0 mL CSF to drop into each of three sterile test tubes—the first for glucose and protein measurements; the second for Gram's stain, culture, and sensitivity; and the third for blood cell count and differential. (Other less common tests on CSF are fungal culture, culture and smear for acid-fast bodies, lactate dehydrogenase, VDRL, and cytology.)

Figure 15-3: The needle that returns CSF is in the dural arachnoid. You may have to create negative pressure by attaching a syringe in order to achieve a free flow of fluid.

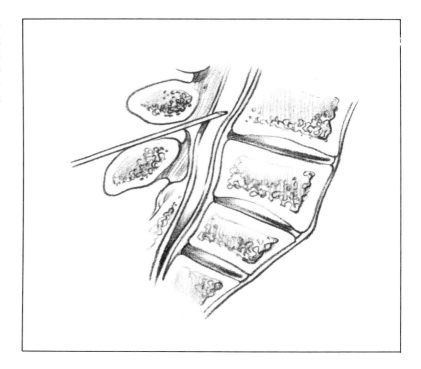

Figure 15-4: Attach a three-way stopcock and manometer to measure the CSF pressure.

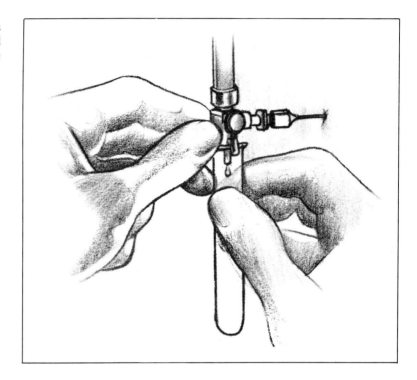

7. Measure the CSF pressure again.
8. Replace the stylet and withdraw the needle.
9. Dress the puncture site with an adhesive strip.

Complications

The complications that can occur following a lumbar puncture are listed below in order of frequency:

- Postpuncture headache occurs in one third of patients, who may be relieved by bedrest. It is necessary to keep all patients supine to prevent headaches and possible leakage of CSF from the puncture site.
- Blood-stained CSF from overadvancement of the needle with penetration of the venous plexus on the anterior aspect of the spinal canal. Such bleeding can cause irritation of spinal nerve roots with pain in the lower back and legs.
- Herniation of brain substance due to abnormally high intracranial pressure.
- Infection. A contaminated needle can introduce infection and cause bacterial meningitis.
- Epidermoid tumors, probably the result of epidermoid cores that are displaced into the spinal cord by spinal needles without stylets.

Suggested Readings

Carbaat PAT, VanCrevel H: Lumbar puncture headache: Controlled study on preventive effect of 24 hours' bed rest. *Lancet* 1981;2:1133.

Evans CH: *Spinal Anesthesia.* New York, Paul B. Hoeber Inc, 1929.

Lee JA, Atkinson RS: *Sir Robert Macintosh's Lumbar Puncture and Spinal Analgesia,* ed 4. Edinburgh, Churchill Livingstone Inc., 1978.

Van Allen MW: *Pictorial Manual of Neurologic Tests.* Chicago, Year Book Medical Publishers Inc, 1969.

Fine-Needle Aspiration of the Breast

Elizabeth Loeb, MD

Fine-needle aspiration of the breast is a quick and simple procedure of great efficacy. Although surgical biopsy has been the preferred and traditional method of breast tumor evaluation, currently the recommended method is to use examination of cytologic smears from the fine-needle aspiration in conjunction with mammography. This winning combination has reduced diagnostic errors to 1%. It is important to note, however, that it is unsafe to rely exclusively on mammogram results to confirm dysplastic changes, because false-negative reports can delay a diagnosis of cancer.

Because of its simple set-up, and ease in performance, the indications for fine-needle aspiration are numerous.

- Confirm cytologically that vague nodularities and thickenings are benign.
- Diagnose fibroadenoma in young women, allowing postponement of surgery to a more opportune time if desired.
- Confirm cytologically that a cyst is benign and to drain the cyst.
- Distinguish diffuse suppurative disease from neoplasm.
- Establish a positive diagnosis of cancer when considering pre-operative irradiation.
- Establish a diagnosis of operable cancer. This helps to convince a reluctant patient of the need for surgery and reduces anesthesia time by eliminating the need for frozen section.
- Analyze the estrogen receptor status of a carcinoma.
- Confirm the diagnosis of an inoperable cancer, such as inflammatory breast carcinoma, for possible irradiation or chemotherapy.

While there are no absolute contraindications to a fine-needle aspiration, there are a few limiting factors. Lesions that lie deep in a heavy breast are difficult to locate with a needle. And the results of an aspiration are only useful if they are accurately evaluated. Therefore, it is essential that your practice have access to a pathologist who is experienced in interpreting cytologic smears.

Materials

- Cameco syringe pistol or Aspir-Gun[1]
- 20-mL disposable syringe *without* Luer-Lok tip
- 22-gauge (0.6-1.0 mm external diameter) disposable needle, 3.8 or 8.8 cm long, with or without a mandrin
- 25-gauge needle
- 3 alcohol prep sponges
- Sterile gauze pads
- Glass microscope slides with frosted ends for labeling
- Spray fixative or a bottle of 95% methyl, ethyl, or isopropyl alcohol to hold slides for immediate fixation of wet smears
- 1% lidocaine HCI (Xylocaine)

PROCEDURE

To prepare for fine-needle aspiration, examine the patient's breast, supraclavicular region, and axilla including the posterior axillary folds. If the mass is difficult to palpate, soap the breast and palpate lightly, asking the patient where the mass is located. Examine any postmastectomy scars carefully for a local recurrence of carcinoma. If you find a tumor eroding the skin surface, use a scalpel to collect the specimen.

1. With the patient supine, attach the syringe to the syringe pistol. By applying light pressure, position the mass between index finger and thumb of your nondominant hand. With your other hand, prep the skin above the mass three times with alcohol prep sponges. If the patient is especially anxious, infiltrate the skin with 1% lidocaine.

2. Position the syringe pistol over the puncture site, insert the needle quickly through the skin, and advance it into the mass (Figure 16-1). The location and nature of the mass may influence your technique in this step:

- If you find skin dimpling, the skin is probably attached to the outer surface of the mass, and you can insert the needle directly through the dimple into the tumor.
- If you find vague, superficial nodules, inflammatory carcinoma, and suspected pagetoid skin, perform a superficial subepidermal aspiration using an angled 25-gauge needle.

Confirm that you have punctured the mass by moving the needle slightly from side to side and feeling the mass move between your fingers.

You may have trouble penetrating firm, dense, gritty scirrhous tumors. Grasp the scirrhous mass firmly, especially if it is deep, and use forceful movement with aspiration if necessary to extract tissue; this is often painful to the patient. Benign lesions, especially lipomas,

Figure 16-1: Position the mass between the index finger and thumb of the nondominant hand. Position the syringe directly over the mass and insert the needle quickly through the skin and into the mass.

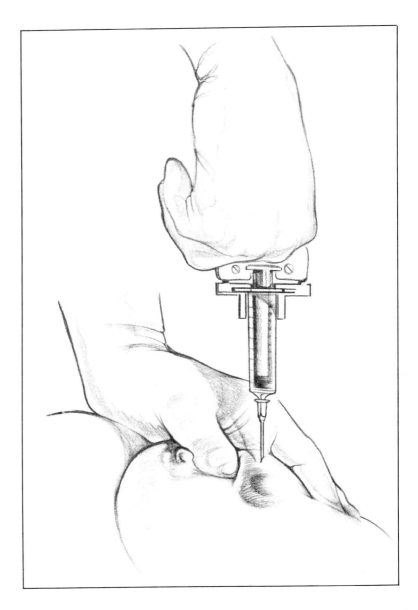

usually offer little or no resistance, depending on the extent of their fibrous stroma.

3. Apply full suction continuously while you move the needle back and forth within the tumor using short, jackhammer-like strokes in slightly different directions (Figure 16-2). Multiple punctures of small nodules give a higher yield of positive material.

4. Watch the needle hub. As soon as you see fluid, release the

Figure 16-2: Once the mass is entered, apply continuous suction while enacting a jackhammer-like stroke in slightly different directions. When fluid appears at the needle hub, release the syringe pistol to discontinue suction.

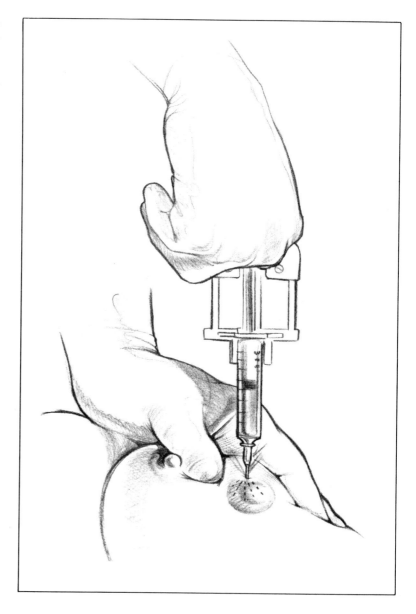

syringe pistol trigger to discontinue the suction and ensure that you'll obtain good quality cellular aspirates. Negative pressure on withdrawal can cause the specimen to leave the needle and enter the syringe. This ruins the cellular architecture and leads to poor microscopic exam. If you find no specimen in the syringe hub, make 10-12 passes into the tumor to assure good aspiration; some passes may miss a small tumor. if you detect a cyst at this stage, discard clear yellow fluid or fluid devoid of particulate matter and reaspirate any residual mass remaining after fluid removal with a fresh needle.

5. Remove the syringe and apply pressure to the puncture site with a sterile gauze pad. Blood rapidly appearing at the puncture site suggests a malignancy.

6. Disengage the syringe from the needle, fill the syringe with air, and reattach the needle. Expel the aspirate onto one or several slides. Fix the slide immediately and submit it with clinical data to the pathology laboratory. Centrifuge any turbid fluid obtained from a cyst, prepare a slide from the particulate matter, and submit that slide to pathology as well.

There are virtually no complications encountered with fine-needle aspiration. The occasional hematoma can usually be controlled by applying firm pressure to the site. Very rarely there may be an ensuing infection, and even more rarely, the development of pneumothorax caused by needle penetration of the chest wall. Tumor spread after fine-needle aspiration is yet to be documented.

Suggested Readings

Frable WJ: *Thin Needle Aspiration Biopsy. Major Problems in Pathology,* vol 14. Philadelphia, WB Saunders Co, 1983, pp. 7-73.

Kaminsky DB: Aspiration Biopsy for the Community Hospital. *Masson Monographs in Diagnostic Cytopathology,* vol 2. NY, Masson Publishing USA Inc, 1981, pp. 9-77.

Linsk JA, Franzen S (eds): *Clinical Aspiration Cytology.* Philadelphia, JB Lippincott Co, 1983, pp. 105-137.

Biopsy of the Uterine Cervix

R.J. Coble, MD

Although the decline in death rate from carcinoma of the cervix is not completely understood, part of it is due to patient and physician education in early detection and part is due to increased physician awareness of the need for step-by-step evaluation of the patient with an abnormal Pap smear.

When you encounter an abnormal Pap smear (class II or higher), repeat the smear right away to confirm the abnormal cytology and rule out laboratory error. If the abnormal result is confirmed, proceed to biopsy. While colposcopy with guided biopsy is a superior method, the procedure can be performed without colposcopy.

There are no absolute contraindications to the procedure, except pregnancy, when the lesion is located within the endocervix.

Materials

- Colposcope (optional)
- Large-tipped cotton batons and small-tipped cotton swabs
- 3-5% acetic acid solution
- Lugol's solution
- Kevorkian-Younge biopsy forceps or equivalent (for instance, Tischler or Eppendorfer instruments)
- Monsel's solution (ferric subsulfate)
- Vaginal speculum
- Specimen jars filled with 10% formalin

PROCEDURE

Under Colposcopy

1. Explain the procedure and obtain informed patient consent.
2. With the patient in the lithotomy position, insert the vaginal speculum as you would for a routine pelvic examination.
3. Clean the cervix and vaginal mucosa by wiping away the cervical mucus with a dry cotton baton. Paint the cervical area generously with 3-5% acetic acid solution to help identify abnormal blood vessels, mosaic mucosal patterns, punctate lesions, and white epithelium (Table 17-1).

121

TABLE 17-1

Some colposcopically significant cervical lesions		
Lesion	**Characteristics**	**Possible significance**
Atypical blood vessels	Well-demarcated areas of vessels markedly irregular in size, direction, shape, and arrangement	Invasive carcinoma
Mosaic mucosal patterns	Well-demarcated areas composed of segments of avascular pathologic epithelium outlined by capillaries	Dysplasia or carcinoma in situ
Punctate lesions	Well-demarcated areas of dilated, elongated hairpin capillaries, often slightly twisted and irregular	Dysplasia or carcinoma in situ
White epithelium	Well-demarcated areas of epithelium that appear white after application of acetic acid	Dysplasia or carcinoma in situ

4. Move the colposcope into place and focus on the cervical os and surrounding portio.

Note: Anesthesia is seldom necessary, but if you anticipate biopsy of a large area, administer local anesthesia by injecting 1-2 mL of 1% lidocaine HCl (Xylocaine) into the cervix sublesionally.

5. If you see gross lesions or areas with abnormal patterns, take punch biopsy specimens from these sites with the biopsy forceps. For each specimen, open the biopsy forceps fully and place the jaws over the entire lesion, if possible including some surrounding normal tissue. If the lesion is large, take one sample at an edge of the lesion to include some normal tissue and a second sample in the center of the lesion. Place each sample in a separate specimen jar labeled to identify the site. Bleeding during the procedure can usually be controlled easily with pressure or Monsel's solution; a hemostatic suture may occasionally be needed.

Note: Remember to send a good clinical history to the pathology laboratory with each specimen to aid in histologic interpretation.

6. With a cotton baton, apply Lugol's solution as a stain to help identify neoplastic epithelium; normal tissue appears deep reddish

Figure 17-1: Biopsy samples should be taken at 3, 6, 9, and 12 o'clock on the cervical circumference.

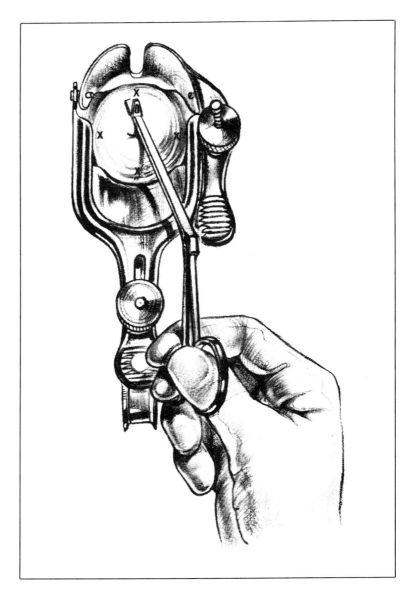

brown, while dysplastic tissue appears pale yellow. Take biopsy specimens from any areas of apparent dysplasia.

7. No special aftercare of biopsy sites is necessary.

Without Colposcopy

1. Follow steps 1-3 and 5-6 above, examining the cervix and patterns of staining as closely as possible with the unaided eye. Take biopsy specimens from any suspicious areas.

2. If no areas look suspicious even after staining with Lugol's solution, take random biopsy specimens at 3, 6, 9, and 12 o'clock on the cervical circumference (Figure 17-1).

3. No special aftercare of biopsy sites is necessary.

Vaginal bleeding more serious than spotting seldom occurs, but if it does the patient should return for examination.

Similarly, vaginal discharge or infection rarely occurs, but advise the patient to return if it does.

Follow-up care is dictated by the pathologist's report. If examination and biopsy without colposcopy fail to explain the abnormal Pap smear, refer the patient for colposcopically guided biopsy.

Suggested Readings

Duenhoelter JH: *Greenhill's Office Gynecology,* ed 10. Chicago, Year Book Medical Publishers Inc, 1983.

Jones HW, Jones GS: *Novak's Textbook of Gynecology,* ed 10. Baltimore, Williams & Wilkins Co, 1980.

Mishell DR, Brenner PF: *Management of Common Problems in Obstetrics and Gynecology.* Oradell, NJ, Medical Economics Books, 1983.

Endometrial Biopsy by Suction Curettage

Elizabeth A. Burns, MD

Endometrial biopsy by suction curettage is a procedure that is extremely well-suited for an outpatient setting. Set-up is simple, and patient tolerance is high, with little more necessary than premedication with a non-steroidal anti-inflammatory drug and local anesthesia by paracervical block.

Among its many indications, endometrial suction curettage provides 95% diagnostic accuracy in the detection of uterine cancer. It is also valuable as a step in the evaluation of infertility, and the workup for menstrual disorders, including dysfunctional uterine bleeding. Other patients who are candidates for this biopsy are those who present with postmenopausal bleeding, those in need of hormonal therapy (for pre-treatment assessment and post-treatment follow-up), and women with a history of pelvic irradiation (for detection of cell dysplasia).

Women in a high-risk category for endometrial cancer, i.e., those who are obese, have diabetes mellitus, hypertension, low parity, irregular menses, failure of ovulation, adenomatous hyperplasia, prolonged unopposed estrogen administration, an early menarche, or late menopause, can benefit from an endometrial biopsy.

The only absolute contraindications are evidence of active infection, and pregnancy.

Of relative contraindication are an inadequate pelvic exam, cervical stenosis, uterine flexion, coagulopathy, large leiomyoma, severe anemia, heart disease, and extreme patient anxiety.

Materials

- Sterile speculum
- Sterile gloves
- Povidone-iodine solution (Betadine)

- Bowl for solution
- Cotton balls or gauze sponges
- 22-gauge spinal needle
- 20-mL syringe
- 0.5% lidocaine HCl (Xylocaine)
- Laminaria or graduated dilators
- Sterile tenaculum
- 4-mm sterile endometrial suction curette with collecting apparatus and vacuum source (Milex Tis-U-Trap)
- Kevorkian-Younge endocervical curette
- Uterine sound (unless curette is designed to serve as a sound)
- Silver nitrate sticks
- Preservative (formaldehyde)

PROCEDURE

1. Explain the procedure to the patient and premedicate, if desired, about 30 minutes before beginning. Set up the suction curettage system (see Figure 18-1).

2. Perform a bimanual exam to determine the position of the uterus and check for signs of infection.

Figure 18-1: Endometrial suction curette with collection container.

Figure 18-2: Paracervical block of 10 mL 0.5% lidocaine at 9 o'clock and 3 o'clock, and 5 mL at 7 o'clock and 5 o'clock. After anesthetizing, tenaculum is applied to straighten the axis of the uterus.

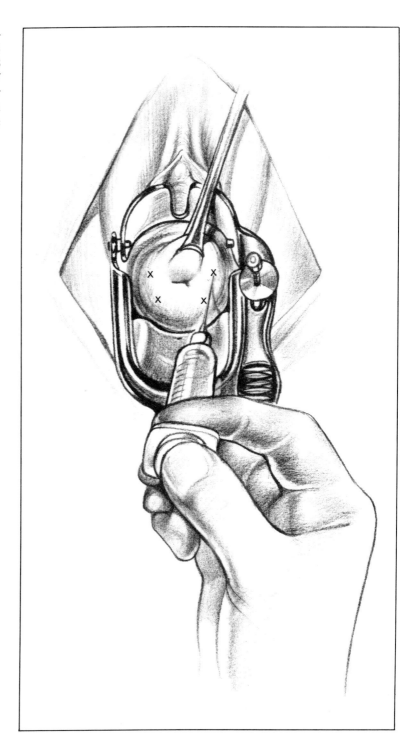

Figure 18-3: Insert the endometrial curette and occlude the suction release opening to allow pressure to build to 51-71 mg Hg. While withdrawing the curette, make sweeping motions to increase the surface area sampled.

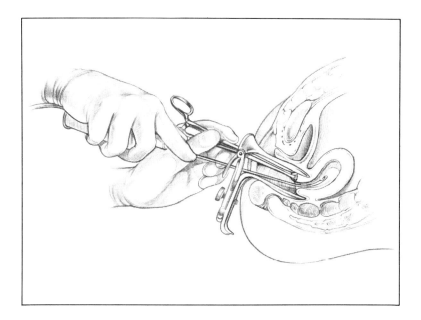

3. Insert the speculum to inspect the cervix. If you encounter stenosis, you may need laminaria or graduated dilators to complete the procedure. If you use laminaria, delay the procedure to give the cervical os time to dilate. If you use dilators, proceed with step 4, inserting the dilators at step 6.

4. Clean the patient's cervix and vagina with povidone-iodine.

5. If local anesthesia is desired, administer a paracervical block using the spinal needle (see Figure 18-2). Inject 10 mL of 0.5% lidocaine at 9 o'clock and at 3 o'clock to anesthetize the paracervical ligaments and 5 mL at 7 o'clock and at 5 o'clock to anesthetize the uterosacral ligaments.

6. With the tenaculum, grasp the anterior lip of the cervix and apply gentle traction to straighten the axis of the uterus. You may want to use dilators if the os is stenotic.

7. If endocervical curettage is indicated for postmenopausal bleeding, use a Kevorkian-Younge endocervical curette. Collect the sample on a filter paper or whatever collection vehicle your pathologist prefers and place it in preservative.

8. Sound the uterus. (Some endometrial curettes have centimeter markings and can be used as uterine sounds.)

9. For suction curettage of the endometrium, insert the endometrial curette (see Figure 18-3), occlude the suction release op ning at the proximal end to let suction build to 51-71 mg Hg pressure (this may take several seconds), and pull the curette out, making small sweeping motions to increase the surface area sampled.

For an infertility evaluation, sample at the 3-o'clock and 9-o'clock positions. For a diagnostic evaluation, curette at all hours of the clock and across the top of the fundus.

Note: To avoid severe cramping, *never apply suction* while positioning the curette in the uterus.

10. Aspirate some preservative into the system to collect any tissue remaining in the curette, disconnect the collecting chamber, and fill it with preservative. Send the sample to the lab for histologic diagnosis.

11. Use silver nitrate cautery if necessary to stop excessive bleeding from the tenaculum site. Have the patient remain recumbent for a few minutes to avert vasovagal syncope.

Pain and cramping are the most common post-procedure problems. Also watch for these possible complications: uterine perforation, vasovagal syncope, infection, and reaction to povidone-iodine or lidocaine.

Suggested Readings

Fuller AF: Role of the primary physician in the detection and treatment of gynecologic cancer. *Primary Care* 1981;8:111-29.

Hurt WG, Hall DJ: Outpatient endometrial sampling. *J Fam Pract* 1980;10:115-8.

Koss LG, Schreiber K, Oberlander SG, et al: Screening of asymptomatic women for endometrial cancer. *CA* 1981;31:300-17.

Richart RM, Pringle P: Choosing the right biopsy device. *Contemp OB/GYN* (special issue), October 1984, pp. 48-57.

THERAPEUTIC PROCEDURES

19

Removing a Skin Cyst

Gerald J. McGowan, MD

Most skin cysts do not require removal. However, when they become inflamed, infected, or otherwise unsightly and seriously bothersome to the patient, they are easily remedied. Excision is not difficult, scarring is minimal, and the postoperative course is usually uneventful. You can easily excise a sebaceous or epidermoid cyst—and other simple cutaneous tumors such as small lipomas, sclerosing hemangiomas, and pyogenic granulomas—in the office or similar ambulatory setting.

You may want to arrange surgical consultation if the patient has a cyst embedded in the outer table of the skull. Similarly, you may want to arrange consultation for a patient who has any large cutaneous tumor, or any tumor that is growing in a precarious location.

Materials

- Gloves
- Drape
- Povidone–iodine solution (Betadine)
- 10 mL 1% lidocaine HCl (Xylocaine) with 1:100,000 epinephrine
- 10-mL syringe with 25-gauge, 1-in needle
- Small Kelly clamp, straight or curved
- Small Metzenbaum scissors (optional)
- Small Allis clamp
- Sterile pads and dressing (according to cyst size)
- Small suture tray (scalpel, medium scissors, 3-0 plain catgut and 4-0 or 5-0 nylon suture)

PROCEDURE

1. If the cyst is inflamed or infected, consider incision and drainage or a course of antibiotics for 5 to 10 days, and hot packs, letting the inflammation subside before you attempt to perform excision.

2. Scrub the cyst and surrounding area with povidone-iodine solution. Using sterile technique, drape around the cyst. Inject 1% lidocaine with epinephrine around the cyst, not only to provide local

Figure 19-1: Make an elliptic incision over the cyst in the direction of the skin lines. Incise the ellipse through the dermis, separating both ends from the subcutaneous tissue.

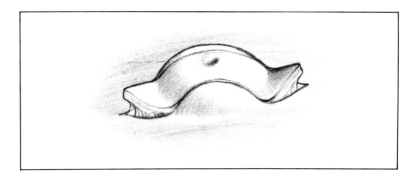

Figure 19-2: Spread the tissue at both ends of the ellipse with a Kelly clamp. Work slowly toward the center, carefully spreading tissue as you go.

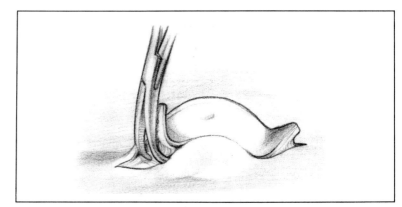

Figure 19-3: Use an Allis clamp to provide traction to the skin ellipse. When the underside is visible, remove the cyst with the skin intact.

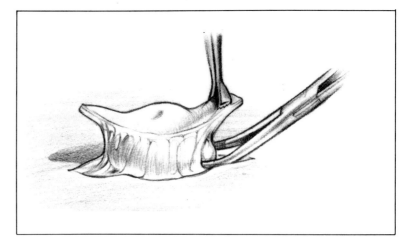

anesthesia but also to dissect the capsule of the cyst from surrounding tissue.

3. Make an elliptic incision over the cyst in the direction of skin lines. Maximum width of the ellipse should be about 3 mm (⅛ in). In length, the ellipse should extend beyond the edge of the cyst.

4. Incise the ellipse of skin through the dermis, separating both ends from the subcutaneous tissue as flaps (Figure 19-1).

5. Identify the cyst at both ends of the ellipse and carefully start to dissect it. With a small Kelly clamp or a small Metzenbaum scissors or both, spread the tissue at both ends of the ellipse (Figure 19-2). Work toward the center, spreading the tissue progressively, and cautiously separate the cyst from the surrounding tissue.

6. With careful blunt and sharp dissection, continue down and around the cyst, grasping the ellipse of skin with an Allis clamp if you need traction (Figure 19-3). When you identify the underside, remove the cyst with the ellipse intact.

7. Close the dead space with 3-0 plain catgut sutures in one or two layers. This also approximates the skin edges. If the ellipse is wide or the skin fails to come together well, undermine the dermis; you can then easily approximate the mobilized skin. For final closure, use interrupted 4-0 or 5-0 nylon sutures in order to minimize scarring.

8. Apply light pressure with a sterile dressing. The wound will be tender, but patients seldom require pain medication. Complications are rare. After suture removal in 4-7 days, depending on location, further visits are usually unnecessary.

Suggested Readings

Davis L: *Christopher's Textbook of Surgery,* ed 8. Philadelphia, WB Saunders Co, 1964, pp. 192-193.

Schultz BC, McKinney P: *Office Practice of Skin Surgery.* Philadelphia, WB Saunders Co, 1985.

Thorek P: *Surgical Diagnosis,* ed 2. Philadelphia, JB Lippincott Co, 1965, pp. 3, 107.

20

Incision and Drainage of Cutaneous Abscesses

Ralph H. Knudson, MD

Abscesses are the end result of infections, such as cellulitis, lymphadenitis, and wounds and lacerations that were contaminated. Incision and drainage is the best and virtually the only course of treatment.

In an abscess caused by bacterial infection, incision and drainage is indicated when liquefactive necrosis is present. This can be demonstrated by palpation of fluctuance, or, if the site of the abscess is difficult to palpate, by needle aspiration of pus.

Drainage not only provides relief from discomfort, it allows for diagnostic culturing and sensitivity testing of the abscess material. This can be helpful in determining a course of antibiotic therapy.

Using antibiotics to promote abscess healing after incision and drainage is questionable; many studies show no significant improvement. Thus, routine culturing of all abscesses incised and drained is not considered necessary in healthy patients. For the high-risk patient, the toxic patient, or the patient with a facial lesion that might be drained by the cavernous sinus, however, antibiotics *are* recommended. Select appropriate agents on the basis of a Gram's stain plus culture and sensitivity studies.

Abscess bacteriology shows mixed aerobic and anaerobic growth. *Staphylococcus aureus* is the predominant aerobic organism in cutaneous abscesses. Perineal abscesses tend to show more anaerobes and may grow *Neisseria gonorrhoeae* in vulvar gland areas. A penicillinase-resistant penicillin is generally a good choice for beginning antibiotic care.

No contraindications exist, although areas overlying nerves or vessels, deep lesions around the eyes, perianal abscesses, and deep palmar and plantar lesions should be surgically drained with careful follow-up and parenteral antibiotic treatment.

Materials

- Sterile gloves
- Sterile drapes
- Antiseptic such as isopropyl alcohol, hexachlorophene cleanser (pHisoHex), or povidone-iodine solution (Betadine)
- Razor
- 1% lidocaine HCl (Xylocaine)
- 5-mL syringe with 25-gauge needle
- 10-mL syringe with 22-gauge needle
- Blunt needle
- Ethyl chloride spray
- Scalpel with No. 11 blade
- Culture swab
- Sterile cotton-tipped swab
- Hydrogen peroxide
- ¼- or ½-in plain strip gauze
- Sterile scissors
- Forceps
- Hemostat tape
- 4 × 4-in gauze pads

PROCEDURE

1. Position the patient comfortably with good exposure of the site. Gently scrub the area overlying and surrounding the abscess for one minute. Vigorous scrubbing is unnecessary. Shave the site if needed for exposure. Drape the area.

2. Anesthetize the lesion:

- For a superficial lesion with obvious fluctuance, use ethyl chloride spray. The first contact of the spray on an abscess site is uncomfortable, so lead up to it by demonstrating the cooling effect on your own hand, then on the patient's hand, then on the lesion. Maintain a steady spray until a white "frost" appears, then proceed immediately to step 3.

- For a lesion that is too deep or large for a single brief incision, infiltrate the overlying dermis with 1% lidocaine. Injection is painful and adds to induration, so limit injection sites and the amount of lidocaine to the minimum necessary for anesthesia.

3. Locate fluctuance by two-finger gentle pressure or, if necessary,

use the 22-gauge needle for fine-needle aspiration of the site to demonstrate pus. Resort to fine-needle aspiration only if fluctuance is questionable, not when fluctuance is clearly not present.

Note: If you do not demonstrate fluctuance or purulence, *do not* proceed with incision, because it can open up tissue planes and spread infection. Instead, prescribe moist heat and elevation for 24 hours, treat any cellulitis with systemic antibiotics, and reexamine the patient. This helps reveal very early nonpalpable abscess sites and limit associated cellulitis.

4. When you achieve anesthesia, incise as follows:

With demonstrated fluctuance, make a single quick incision parallel to skin lines from edge to edge across the fluctuance (Figure 20-1). Expect spontaneous drainage of some pus, occasionally mixed with blood.

With pus demonstrated on needle aspiration, make a single stab incision following the needle path.

5. If no spontaneous flow occurs, try *light* pressure on the surrounding skin to recheck fluctuance and possibly extrude thicker purulence.

Note: Avoid this step if the site is on the face or mastoid area since it might infect the sinuses.

6. Collect a culture specimen if culture is indicated.

7. Gently probe the opened abscess with a sterile swab soaked in hydrogen peroxide to break up and clean out loculations (Figure 20-2). An abscess is seldom smoothly spherical. It is more likely to be irregular in shape, with fingerlike extensions that spread into tissue planes; it can be partially loculated by fibrous and necrotic debris.

8. After probing, lavage the abscess with saline or hydrogen peroxide, using the lidocaine syringe and a blunt needle.

9. When probing and lavage no longer yield pus, examine for

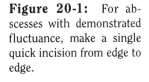
Figure 20-1: For abscesses with demonstrated fluctuance, make a single quick incision from edge to edge.

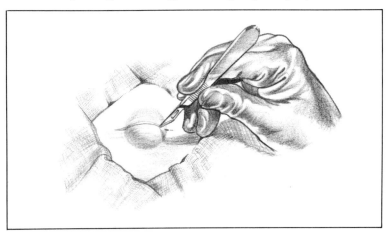

Figure 20-2: Following expression of pus, probe the cavity with a sterile cotton swab soaked in hydrogen peroxide.

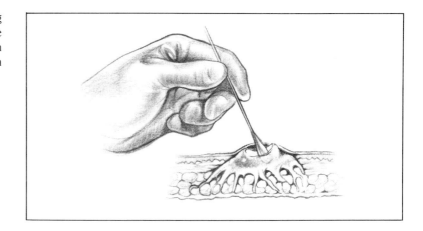

Figure 20-3: If the cavity is large, pack with ¼- or ½-inch sterile gauze strip. Then cover with sterile 4 × 4-in gauze pads.

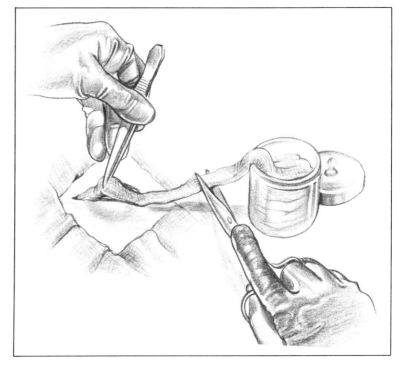

hemostasis. If the abscess is relatively large, packing will stop a slight oozing. In the rare case of persistent bleeding, you may resort to silver nitrate cautery or electrocautery.

Note: Do not use electrocautery in the presence of ethyl chloride, which is explosive.

10. Insert a sterile or medicated gauze wick or, if the abscess is relatively large, pack the abscess site with ¼- or ½-in plain strip gauze (Figure 20-3). Cover with sterile 4 × 4-in gauze pads, and inform the patient to expect some oozing of pus, exudate, and a little blood.

Follow-up

See the patient again in 1-2 days
- **Facial lesion.** Reevaluate in 24 hours. If erythema is resolving and drainage is minimal, no further packing is needed. If not, replace the wick or repack loosely and continue daily follow-up examinations and repacking until both erythema and drainage are minimal.
- **Other lesions.** Replace the wick or repack in 24-48 hours, then recheck every 1-3 days, depending on patient reliability, size of lesions, and resolution of erythema, drainage, and induration.

Instruct the patient to use warm peroxide-and-water soaks, 2-4 times per day for 5-7 days, followed by redressing. Caution the patient not to try to reinsert packing if it falls out. Healing time varies from 7 to 21 days depending on the dimensions, depth, and location of the abscess.

Complications

Complications are few and easily managed.
- Re-formation of the abscess, the most common complication, is usually due to inadequate incision, incomplete probing for loculations, inadequate lavage, or inadequate packing and soaking during aftercare. Correction usually entails reincision, using the old incision site, and aggressive drainage.
- Bleeding may occur if the abscess is in a highly vascular area or under unusual mechanical pressure or if granulation tissue is traumatized. This is nearly always corrected by packing, pressure, or cautery.
- Slow or poor healing may indicate inadequate drainage or lax aftercare.

Suggested Readings

Dodd RW, Seidenberg B: Abscess, incision and drainage, in Mayhew HE, Rodgers LA: *Basic Procedures in Family Practice.* New York, John Wiley & Sons, 1984, chap 1.

Llera JL, Levy RC: Treatment of cutaneous abscess: A double-blind clinical study. *Ann Emerg Med* 1985;14:15-9.

Meislin HW, Lerner SA, Graves MH, et al: Cutaneous abscesses—Anaerobic and aerobic bacteriology and outpatient management. *Ann Intern Med* 1977;87:145-9.

Munster AM: Infections, in Hill GJ II (ed): *Outpatient Surgery,* ed 2. Philadelphia, WB Saunders Co, 1980, pp. 134-159.

21

Cryotherapy for Skin Lesions

Lawrence W. Steinkraus, MD
Charles E. Driscoll, MD

Cryotherapy is an easy and effective procedure for destructive treatment of cutaneous lesions that achieves excellent cosmetic results and has minimal complications. Usually, very little scarring results from office cryotherapy, although hypopigmentation occurs occasionally, especially in blacks. Deeper and wider lesions such as malignancies carry some potential for permanent defects.

Different conditions require different depths of freeze, freeze-zone areas, and numbers of freeze-thaw cycles for best effect:

- Flat warts require very light freezing, often without blister formation.
- Superficial lesions in the elderly require shallow freezing because of natural thinning of the dermis. Extensive freezing, which can cause full-thickness destruction, may result in scarring and chronic ulceration.
- Periungual lesions require light, contained freezing to avoid excessive blister formation, subungual hemorrhages, and destruction of the nail bed.
- Large, thick lesions may require treatment spread over more than one session.

Even with a conservative approach, cryotherapy may not achieve total effect because of discomfort and possible scarring. This procedure is indicated for the:

- Destruction of benign cutaneous lesions including verrucae, condylomata, benign lentigines, seborrheic keratoses, hypertrophic sebaceous glands, the papules of molluscum contagiosum, epithelial nevi, and the lesions of xanthelasma.
- Destruction of precancerous skin lesions including actinic keratoses, leukoplakia, and cutaneous horns.
- Destruction of malignant lesions. If you suspect a tenacious type of skin cancer such as a basal cell carcinoma, obtain a biopsy before cryotherapy. That will allow cytopathologic identification and examination of the specimen's borders to help determine later on whether you have removed the entire lesion.

TABLE 21–1

Cryotherapy techniques compared							
Method	Rate of complications	Freeze depth	Cost	Ease of use	Accuracy/ adaptability	Specific indications	Comments
Cotton-ball wick	Low	1.5 mm	+	+ + +	+	Benign, relatively superficial lesions, such as seborrheic or actinic keratoses	Relatively messy; needs source and storage container for liquid nitrogen
Spray	Low-moderate	≤ 10 mm: roughly ¼ of freeze diameter	+ +	+	+ +	Larger or deeper lesions	Needs source and storage container for liquid nitrogen; risk of spraying adjacent structures; problems with clogging and freeze-up
Cryo-probe	Low-moderate	Roughly ½ of freeze diameter	+ + +	+ +	+ + +	Useful for nearly all types of mucosal and cutaneous lesions, such as hemorrhoids, cervical lesions, skin tags	Good for intraoral lesions; neat; requires bulky equipment; more working parts and more chance of breakdowns

Note: When treating malignant lesions with cryotherapy, take special care to ensure adequate freezing throughout the tumor as revealed by thermocouples inserted into the treated area.

The few absolute contraindications to cryotherapy are the presence of cryoglobulinemia, cryofibrinogenemia, or cold agglutination, or a patient with a cold-sensitivity disorder such as cold anaphylaxis. Note that it is important not to use cryotherapy to treat morphea or sclerosing basal cell carcinoma.

The relative contraindications to the procedure are the presence of:

- Autoimmune disorders. These necessitate special caution when employing cryosurgery.
- Raynaud's disease, when lesions are on an extremity or on the nose, penis, or ears.
- Lesions that occupy very thin epithelium immediately over subcutaneous structures that can be injured, such as the eyelid over the tarsal plate or thin skin over the nail bed in an infant or elderly patient.
- Sun-damaged skin, irradiated skin, and skin of patients who are on chronic corticosteroid therapy. Expect a more severe destructive action and use very conservative freezing methods.

Choices of technique.   Cryotherapy can be carried out with a cotton-tipped applicator dipped in liquid nitrogen, a liquid nitrogen spray apparatus, or a cryoprobe cooled by nitrous oxide. (For a survey of the advantages and disadvantages of these techniques, see Table 21-1.)

Materials

Cotton ball-wick method:

- Cotton-tipped wooden applicator sticks
- Cotton balls
- A 1-qt stainless steel-lined vacuum bottle (Thermos) with a venting hole in the lid. *Note:* Do not secure the lid tightly
- Source of liquid nitrogen in storage unit

Nitrogen spray method:

- Liquid nitrogen spray unit (Figure 21-1)
- Spray probe tips of various sizes
- Source of liquid nitrogen in storage unit

Cryoprobe method:

- Cryoprobe surgical gun with silver tips of various sizes (Figure 21-2)
- Tanks of nitrous oxide with pressure gauge and regulator

Preparation

To allay anxiety, explain the procedure and the anesthetic effects of cold. The patient sometimes feels an initial burning sensation, followed by some burning and throbbing sensations, but these usually are mild.

If the targeted area is particularly sensitive to cold—for instance, the genital and periungual areas—consider using local anesthesia:

Figure 21-1: Example of a liquid nitrogen spray unit.

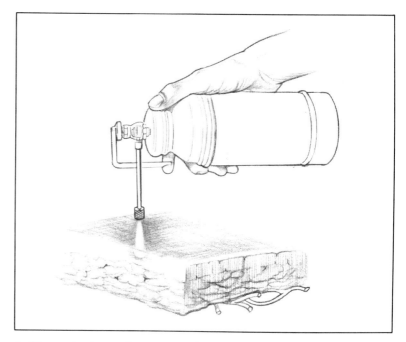

Infiltrate the immediate area with 2% lidocaine HCI (Xylocaine). Do *not* use anesthetics that contain epinephrine.

Pare down thick hyperkeratotic lesions as much as possible before cryosurgery to remove "insulation."

PROCEDURE

Cotton-ball wick (for small, shallow cutaneous lesions)

1. Place a supply of liquid nitrogen in a vacuum bottle and loosely secure the lid.

2. Reinforce the cotton-tipped applicator with extra cotton from a cotton ball, not too tightly wound, to carry the amount of refrigerant needed. Shape the tip to suit the targeted lesion, and be sure the cotton wad is not so bulky that it reduces your accuracy in limiting the freeze area.

3. Dip the applicator into the liquid nitrogen and apply it to the lesion. Because liquid nitrogen evaporates quickly, you probably will have to repeat the application several times to freeze the tissue adequately. Generally, you will have achieved adequate freezing when you create a freeze zone extending 2-4 mm into the normal tissue around the lesion, or when the frozen tissue takes approximately 30 seconds to thaw (for help in judging freeze depth, see Figures 21-3, 21-4, 21-5). Pressure on the lesion accelerates freezing but is not

Figure 21-2: Example of a cryoprobe gun with interchangeable silver tips.

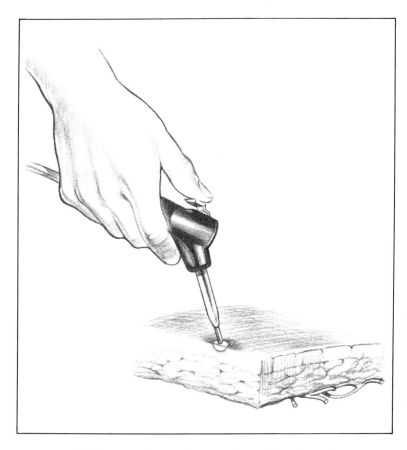

recommended because it may increase discomfort. In addition, complications are more likely with pressure applications, especially in elderly patients and over superficial nerves and bone.

Note: Two cycles of freezing and complete thaw usually are required, so you may want to freeze large lesions in portions. Thick lesions may require a third cycle.

Nitrogen spray (for most cutaneous lesions)

1. Fill the spray-unit container with liquid nitrogen and choose an appropriate tip—usually a fine, needle-type tip for better accuracy and increased concentration of refrigerant. You may choose wider tips and sprays for larger areas or for lighter freezing.

2. Spray the targeted area until you achieve a freeze zone that extends 2-4 mm into normal tissue or a 30-second thaw time. Normally, you'll want to hold the spray tip 8-10 cm from the skin. Reducing the distance causes deeper freezing. For optimal control of lateral spread, spray in short bursts rather than in one sustained spray.

Figure 21-3: Appropriate depth of freezing with the cotton applicator method.

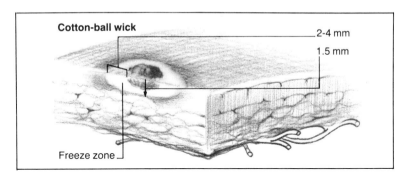

Figure 21-4: The depth of the freeze zone using the nitrogen spray procedure should be ¼ of the diameter of the lesion.

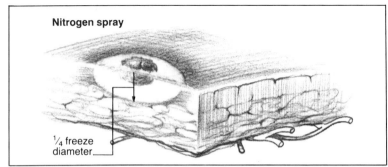

Figure 21-5: Depth of freeze zone using the cryoprobe gun.

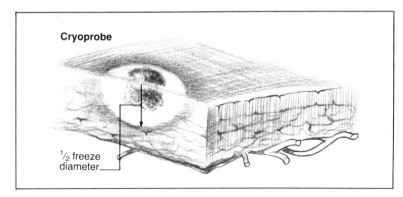

3. Repeat the freeze-thaw cycle once. (*Note:* Neoprene cones are used occasionally to limit the area treated, with petrolatum jelly smeared under the cone to prevent it from freezing to the skin. The depth of freeze is harder to judge with the cone in place, however, and overfreezing may result.)

Cryoprobe gun (for mucosal and cutaneous lesions)

1. Choose a tip large enough to cover the lesion, but not so large as to injure neighboring healthy tissue. Slightly rounded or flattened tips usually are more versatile; fine-point tips are less efficient in the conduction of cold to the lesion.

Remove the protective cover from the cryogun and screw on the cryoprobe tip, checking to see that you have a firm seal. *Note:* With devices that use 0-ring gaskets, the gaskets occasionally will fail when you turn on the pressure, causing a loud popping noise. Warn the patient of the possibility of this occurring so that he or she is not unduly startled.

2. Supply the silver-tipped cryoprobe gun with nitrous oxide via a regulator valve from a pressure-monitored tank.

3. Open the regulator valve and check the pressure indicator to verify that it is reading in the green (fully pressurized) range. This indicates that there is a sufficient amount of nitrous oxide in the tank.

Next, open the cryogun valve and test it by pulling the trigger to allow circulation of the refrigerant. You will hear a hiss and see frost on the cryoprobe tip. *Caution:* Do not touch the tip to test it.

4. Apply a small amount of lubricating jelly to the area to be treated using a cotton swab. The jelly conducts cold to the lesion and adheres the cryoprobe tip to the lesion during treatment which fosters better cold conduction and allows you to lift the lesion away from sensitive underlying structures such as superficial nerves and bony prominences.

Figure 21-6: As soon as the tip of the cryogun becomes frosted, and the lubricating jelly appears frozen, elevate the tip away from the lesion to avoid damaging underlying, healthy structures.

5. Stabilize the tip against the target area and pull the trigger to start the flow of refrigerant. As the tip cools, a firm frost forms and the jelly appears frozen. You now may elevate the tip slightly (1-2 mm) to avoid freezing nontarget underlying structures (Figure 21-6). The timing of this move comes with a little practice.

6. Continue the freeze until a freeze zone of 2-4 mm appears in surrounding normal skin. When you reach the desired depth and area of freeze, release the trigger, but do not remove the tip from the skin until the frost has disappeared—some five seconds.

7. Allow the area to thaw, then apply a second treatment.

Warn the patient that a blister usually forms within the first few hours, and that it may occasionally contain a small, insignificant hemorrhage (a "blood blister").

If you've treated a wart or other sessile lesion and the lesion lifts up to float on top of the sac in one or two days, you can remove it and the blister by cutting around the base of the blister with iris scissors. Alternatively, you can leave the blister intact and allow it to heal. Healing time is generally 2-3 weeks, with crust formation after the first 7-9 days. If you leave the blister intact, have the patient protect it with a dry dressing. Occasionally you'll have to drain a blister if it becomes infected or the patient has increasing discomfort. After drainage the patient can clean the area two or three times a day with hydrogen peroxide, apply a topical antibiotic if desired, and put on a clean dressing. Warn the patient to watch for signs of secondary infection, but such infections are rare.

Follow up in 3-4 weeks (4-10 days with larger lesions) and recheck to make sure healing is satisfactory and to decide whether further treatments are necessary.

Suggested Readings

Elton RF: The appropriate use of liquid nitrogen. *Primary Care* 1983; 10:459-78.

Elton RF: Complications of cutaneous cryosurgery. *J Am Acad Dermatol* 1983;8:513-9.

Hopkins P: Cryosurgery by the general practitioner. *Practitioner* 1983;227:1861-73.

Torre D: Cutaneous cryosurgery: Current state of the art. *J Dermatol Surg Oncol* 1985;11:292-3.

22

Aspiration and Injection of Joints

Steve Wilson, MD
Charles E. Driscoll, MD

The ability to aspirate and inject joints is extremely valuable in the primary care setting for diagnosis and treatment of various arthropathies. Aspiration also may be needed following trauma. The procedures are relatively safe and well tolerated, and no special equipment is required.

It is of therapeutic value in:

- Removing fluid or blood from painfully swollen joints following trauma
- Removing purulent or excessive inflammatory fluid from a joint
- Injecting steroids to suppress inflammation and pain, especially when nonsteroidal anti-inflammatory drugs have proved ineffective after a trial of at least two weeks
  and diagnostic value in:
- Obtaining joint fluid when any inflammatory joint disease is suspected, especially if there is swelling or no history of trauma
- Differentiating hemarthrosis from synovial effusion after acute trauma

Relative contraindications include skin infection near the needle entry site, or, for steroid injection only, previous injection of steroids into the joint—either one injection within the past month or a total of 2-3 previous injections.

Materials

- Antibacterial skin prep (povidone-iodine [Betadine] surgical scrub, chlorhexidine gluconate cleanser [Hibiclens], hexachlorophene [pHisoHex])
- Small sterile basin for skin prep solution
- Sterile 4″ × 4″ gauze sponges
- 70% alcohol solution
- Sterile gloves
- Skin drapes (optional)

- Mask (optional)
- 1% lidocaine HCl (Xylocaine) solution
- 2- to 3-mL sterile disposable syringe with 1-in, 30-gauge needle; 1½-in, 25-gauge needle (optional)
- Adhesive bandage
- *For aspiration:* 1½- or 2-in sterile needles, 18-, 20-, and 30-gauge; one or two 20- to 30-mL disposable syringes; collecting tubes (one sterile tube with heparin; one nonsterile tube with heparin or EDTA; one nonsterile tube with potassium oxalate; one nonsterile tube without preservative)
- *For injection:* two 1½-in, 25-gauge sterile needles*; steroid for injection (See Figures 22-1 – 22-7)

    Note: Maintaining sterile conditions throughout the procedure is of utmost importance.

Figure 22-1
Joint: Knee
Position of patient: Supine, knee fully extended
Approach: Anteromedial
Landmarks: Midpatella, medial aspect; medial femoral condyle
Needle insertion depth: 1.0-1.5 cm (⅜-⅝ in)
Technique: Locate joint space by moving medially from midpatella to point halfway between patella and underlying femoral condyle. Aim needle posteriorly (downward) and laterally to enter.

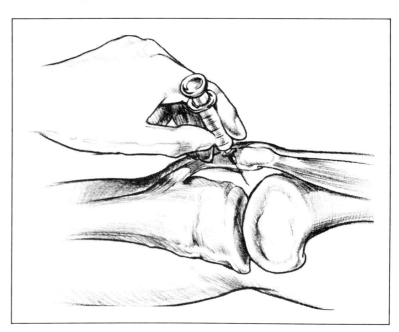

Preparation

1. Have the patient assume a position that is comfortable and provides good exposure to the joint. Determine landmarks (see illustrations) and mark the entry point by pressing with your fingernail or the tip of a ball-point pen with point retracted.

---

*Note: A second needle may be needed as a backup if the first needle clogs; or you may wish to enter the joint with one needle, leave it in place, detach the syringe, and use the other needle to draw up the drug.

Figure 22-2
Joint: Knee (when patient cannot extend knee)
Position of patient: Sitting, knee flexed 90 degrees over edge of examining table
Approach: Anteromedial or lateral
Landmarks: Infrapatellar tendon, tibial condyle, femoral condyle
Needle insertion depth: 3.5-4.5 cm (1⅜-1¾ in)
Technique: Locate triangle formed by tendon and condyles. Enter distal to apex of patella medially or laterally to tendon and aim needle slightly cephalad.

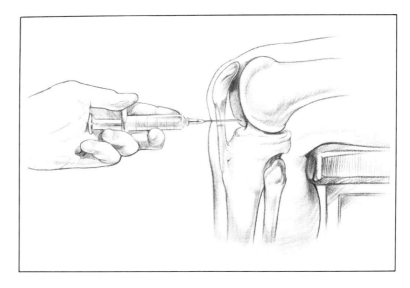

2. Thoroughly scrub the area with antibacterial skin prep for at least two minutes, then, using gauze sponges, clean with alcohol twice and allow to dry.

3. Wear sterile gloves if you need to palpate the joint further. For additional sterile protection, consider applying skin drapes and donning a mask.

4. For local anesthesia, inject 0.5-1.0 mL of 1% lidocaine through a 1-in, 30-gauge needle with 2- to 3-mL syringe. (You may want to use a 1½ in, 25-gauge needle to place anesthetic deeper in the tissues in larger joints and to explore the path of entry into the joint space before aspirating with a larger gauge needle.) If the patient is relaxed and you want to aspirate an easily accessible, large effusion, you may not need a local anesthetic.

PROCEDURE

Aspiration (with optional injection)

1. With a 1½- or 2-in, 18- or 20-gauge needle (30-gauge for finger joints) on a 30-mL syringe, gently enter the joint, directing the needle as indicated in the appropriate illustration. The patient may notice a sharp sensation as the needle pops through the slight resistance of the joint capsule. Withdraw and redirect the needle if you encounter bone or cartilage; be especially careful to avoid scraping the cartilage. Also, watch for blood entering the syringe in spurts, which indicates vascular trauma.

2. Remove as much fluid as possible, using gentle negative pressure

Figure 22-3
Joint: Ankle
Position of patient: Supine, foot in plantar flexion and slight inversion
Approach: Anteromedial
Landmarks: Medial malleolus, extensor hallucis tendon
Needle insertion depth: 3 cm (1¼ in)
Technique: Locate space between medial malleolus and extensor hallucis tendon. Enter lateral to the medial malleolus, medial to the tendon. Aim needle downward, laterally.

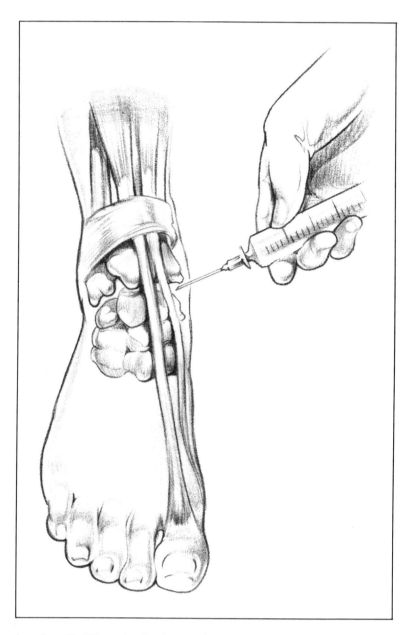

(see Step 5). When the fluid stops flowing, try rotating or repositioning the needle slightly and applying mild external pressure on the joint. This may help produce more. If you get a "dry tap," you still may be able to gain useful information. Even a small amount of fluid from the needle can be examined microscopically for the presence of crystals or organisms and, possibly, cultured.

Figure 22-4
Joint: Shoulder
Position of patient: Sitting, arm at side, shoulder rotated externally
Approach: Anterior
Landmarks: Tip of coracoid process, head of humerus
Needle insertion depth: 1.5-2.0 cm (⅝-¾ in)
Technique: Locate joint space medial to humerus. Enter inferior to tip of coracoid. Direct needle posteriorly and slightly superiorly and laterally.

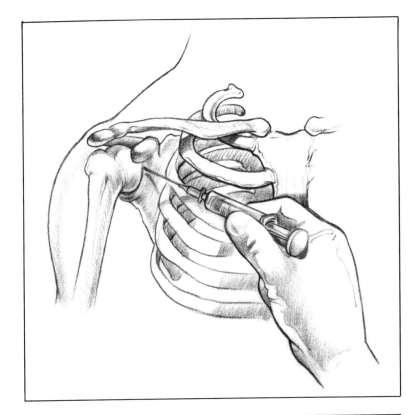

Figure 22-5
Joint: Finger
Position of patient: Hand pronated, traction on finger or finger in slight flexion
Approach: Dorsolateral or dorsomedial
Landmarks: Proximal and distal aspect of surrounding bones, extensor tendon
Needle insertion depth: 0.50-0.75 cm (³⁄₁₆-⁵⁄₁₆ in)
Technique: Locate articular capsule. Direct needle laterally or medially under extensor tendon.

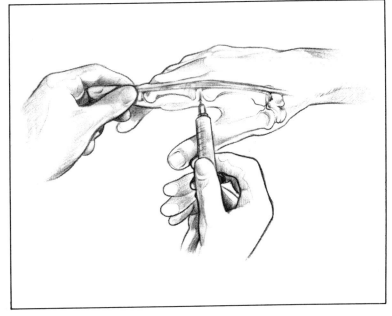

Figure 22-6
Joint: Elbow
Position of patient: Sitting, elbow flexed to 90 degrees, palm pronated on table
Approach: Posterolateral
Landmarks: Lateral epicondyle of humerus, olecranon process of ulna
Needle insertion depth: 1.5 cm (⅝ in)
Technique: Locate space between lateral epicondyle of humerus and olecranon process (1 cm [⅜ in] below epicondyle). Direct needle medially and slightly toward hand.

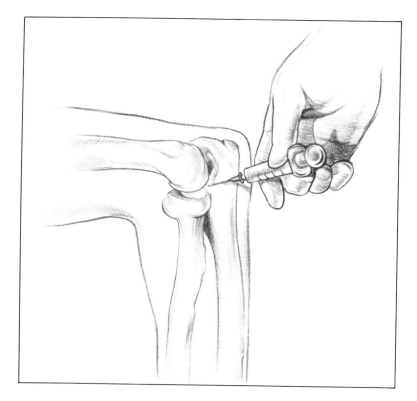

3. For injection, leave the needle in place and replace the syringe with a 2- to 3-mL syringe containing steroid medication; inject slowly. The amount of steroid injected is proportionate to the size of the joint and the size of the patient; use the following general dosage guide for prednisolone or equivalent: 2.5-15.0 mg for small joints of the hands and feet; 10-20 mg for wrist and elbow; 20-50 mg for knee, ankle, or shoulder.

4. Remove the needle, apply brief pressure to the site, then cover the site with a sterile adhesive strip bandage. If the joint was injected, gently move it through its range of motion to distribute the medication.

5. Collect fluid as follows:

- Add 2-5 mL of fluid to the sterile heparin tube for culture and send it to the laboratory immediately.
- Add 2-5 mL of fluid to the nonsterile heparin or EDTA tube for a complete blood cell count with differential and cytology; immediately shake the tube well to avoid clotting.
- Add 2-5 mL of fluid to the plain nonsterile tube for mucin clot and viscosity studies. Either this tube or the one containing nonsterile heparin or EDTA can be examined for crystals. Save one of them

Figure 22-7
Joint: Wrist
Position of patient: Sitting, palm pronated, wrist flexed 20-30 degrees over rolled towel with slight ulnar turn
Approach: Dorsal
Landmarks: Distal borders of radius and ulna, extensor pollicis longus tendon
Needle insertion depth: 1-2 cm (⅜-¾ in)
Technique: Enter distal to line between bony processes of radius and ulna and just lateral to the tendon. Enter perpendicular to skin and direct needle downward.

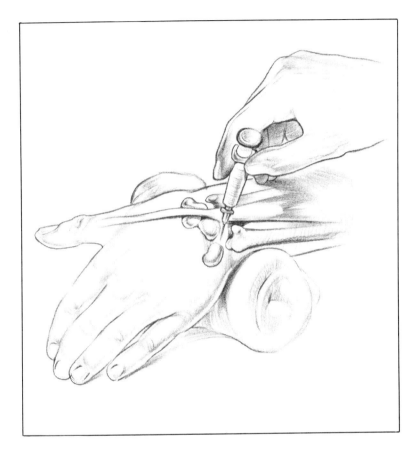

for this examination, making sure the examination takes place within a few days.

• Add 3-5 mL of fluid to the nonsterile potassium oxalate tube for glucose and other studies as indicated—rheumatoid factor, lupus erythematosus preparation, antinuclear antibody, complement level, and so on. If you are evaluating the complement level, immediately centrifuge the fluid sample and freeze it at −20°C (−4°F). To permit proper interpretation of the complement level, simultaneously draw a peripheral venous blood sample for evaluation; the same applies if you are doing glucose studies on the fluid sample.

6.   Evaluate the results of synovial fluid studies (see Table 22-1).

Patient instructions

Tell the patient who receives a steroid injection that he or she may have mildly increased pain in the joint for a few hours or, rarely,

TABLE 22–1

Synovial fluid analysis			
Presumptive diagnosis	**Appearance**	**Viscosity**	**Mucin clot formation**
NORMAL			
	Clear, straw-colored	High	Good
NONINFLAMMATORY (GROUP I)			
Trauma	Clear or turbid, red or xanthochromic	High	Good
Osteoarthritis	Clear, straw-colored	High	Fair to good
INFLAMMATORY (GROUP II)			
Systemic lupus erythematosus	Clear or turbid	High	Good
Rheumatoid arthritis	Turbid, greenish yellow	Low	Poor
Gout	Turbid, white	Low	Poor
Pseudogout	Clear or turbid	Low	Fair
Rheumatic fever	Slightly turbid	Low	Good
Reiter's disease	Turbid	Low	Fair
SEPTIC (GROUP III)			
Bacterial	Turbid, gray or yellow	Low	Poor
Tuberculosis	Turbid, gray or yellow	Low	Poor

Adapted with permission from Eknoyan G: *Medical Procedures Manual* Chicago Year Book Medical Pubs Inc, 1981, pp. 88-89.

WBC/mm$_3$	PMNs* (%)	Protein (gm/dL)	Glucose** (%)	Comments
30-150	<20	1-4	90	_____
750-20,000	<30	1.3-5.0	90	Many RBCs, few cartilage fragments
1,000-7,500	20-60	2.9-5.5	90	Many cartilage fragments
1,000-5,000	<20	1.5-4.0	90	Lupus erythematosus cells
5,000-100,000	60-95	3-6	80	Latex positive, ragocytes, low complement
1,000-70,000	50-95	2.8-5.0	90	Strongly negative birefringence, sodium urate crystals
500-80,000	30-95	_____	90	Weakly positive birefringence, many RBCs, calcium pyrophosphate crystals
300-100,000	60-90	1.5-5.0	90	_____
700-45,000	>60	2.5-6.0	—	PMNs in macrophages
5,000-5,000,000 (>75,000)	>90	2.8-6.8	20	Bacteria on Gram's stain, culture positive
2,500-100,000	50	4-6	50	Acid-fast seen on smear (20%); culture (80%) and biopsy (90%) positive

*Polymorphonuclear leukocytes.
**Expressed as a percent of serum glucose level.

for a few days. If you inject a weight-bearing joint, have the patient limit his activity to preinjection levels for a week to protect the joint and help prolong relief.

Ask the patient to report any signs or symptoms that suggest bleeding or infection in the joint. These complications are rare with the technique described here.

Suggested Readings

Currey-HL, Vernon-Roberts B: Examination of synovial fluid. *Clin Rheum Dis* 1976; 2:149-77

Eknoyan G: *Medical Procedures Manual.* Chicago, Year Book Medical Publishers Inc, 1981, pp. 77-94.

Fitzgerald RH Jr: Intrasynovial injection of steroids: Uses and abuses. *Mayo Clin Proc* 1976;51:655-9.

Germain BF: *Synovial Fluid Analysis in the Diagnosis of Diseases of the Joints.* New Orleans, Upjohn Company, 1976.

Miller JA Jr: Joint paracentesis from an anatomic point of view: I. Shoulder, elbow, wrist, and hand. *Surgery* 1956;40:993-1006.

Miller JA Jr: Joint paracentesis from an anatomic point of view: II. Hip, knee, ankle, and foot. *Surgery* 1957;41:999-1011.

Rodnan GP, Schumacher HR (eds): *Primer on the Rheumatic Diseases,* ed 8. Atlanta, Arthritis Foundation, 1983, pp. 197-199.

Steinbrocker O, Neustadt DH: *Aspiration and Injection Therapy in Arthritis and Musculoskeletal Disorders: A Handbook on Technique and Management.* Hagerstown, Md, Harper & Row Publishers, 1972.

23

Removing a Ring from a Swollen Finger

Charles D. Huss, MD

When you're faced with removing a ring from a swollen finger because of threatened neurovascular compromise, and lubrication is not enough, you can reach for a ring cutter, but this approach has the obvious disadvantage of severely damaging the ring. The wrapping method described here, which preserves the ring, is successful for all but the most grossly swollen fingers. The few failures usually occur in patients who have not removed the ring for years and have bony changes in the finger, such as arthritic malformations. Usually the proximal interphalangeal joint has the largest diameter and is the site of most resistance, but you can adapt the method to soft tissue swelling at any level of the digit.

Materials

- 2-3m (2-3 yd) of string—size 4 silk suture, for instance, preferably on a spool
- Adhesive tape
- 1.5 mL 1% lidocaine HCI (Xylocaine) *without* epinephrine (optional)
- 5-mL syringe and small gauge needle (25-, 27-, or 30-gauge) for digital nerve block (optional)

Digital nerve block. Although the procedure can usually be done without local anesthesia, some patients may require it to alleviate discomfort from the wrapping. Properly done, the digital block affords excellent anesthesia without appreciably increasing swelling distal to the ring. To administer the block:

1. On each side of the affected finger, identify the area of the neurovascular bundle of the volar aspect of the bone of the proximal phalanx.

2. Approach the midweb space at the base of the finger, just volar to the lateral edge of the bone on each side. Advance the needle

161

proximally and volarly at about a 45-degree angle to the palmar and longitudinal planes (Figure 23-1).

3. Infiltrate the area on each side with 0.50-0.75 mL of 1% lidocaine *without* epinephrine. Wait a minute or two until bilateral anesthesia of the digit develops before proceeding.

PROCEDURE

1. Move the ring to its loosest position on the proximal phalanx, frequently near the proximal end. Thread one end of the string

Figure 23-1: To administer a digital nerve block, locate the neurovascular bundle on the volar aspect of the bone of the ring finger. Advance the needle proximally and volarly at a 45-degree angle to the palmar and longitudinal planes, just lateral to the edge of the bone.

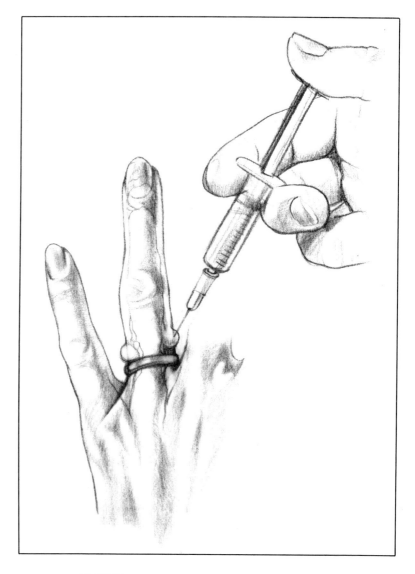

underneath the ring proximally and pull several inches of string through. Tape the proximal end to the hand. You may want to have the patient or an assistant retract adjacent fingers into flexion at the metacarpophalangeal joints for better exposure of the affected finger.

2. Beginning immediately adjacent to the distal edge of the ring, wrap the string circumferentially around the finger. (Wrapping is considerably easier if you unwind the string from a spool rather than battle coils of loose string.) Continue wrapping the string in a smooth single layer, moving distally (Figure 23-2). Use moderate tension to compress the soft tissues.

3. Continue single-layer wrapping until it is distal to the area of greatest swelling. Then tape the distal end of the string to the finger, distal to the last wind.

4. Untape the proximal end of the string and pull distally. Maintain tension along the long axis of the finger, moving the ring distally as you unwind the string (Figure 23-3). If you encounter resistance, try lubricating the wrapping of string ahead of the ring.

5. Continue unwinding the string, moving the ring past the area of the greatest diameter; the ring will then slide off easily.

Figure 23-2: Taking the thread directly off the spool, wrap the finger distally starting at the distal edge of the ring to make a smooth single layer.

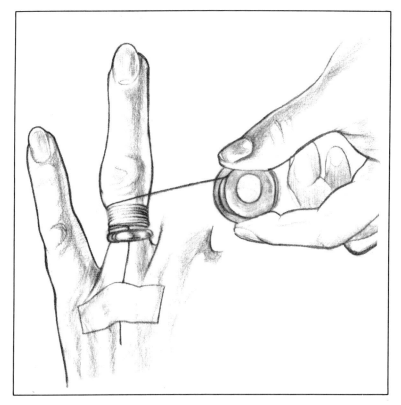

Figure 23-3: When you reach the area of greatest swelling, tape the distal end of the thread to the finger and untape the proximal end. Begin to pull on the proximal end while maintaining tension along the long axis of the finger. As you unwind the thread, keep the ring sliding distally. If the ring is not moving along easily, try coating the layer of thread with some lubricating jelly.

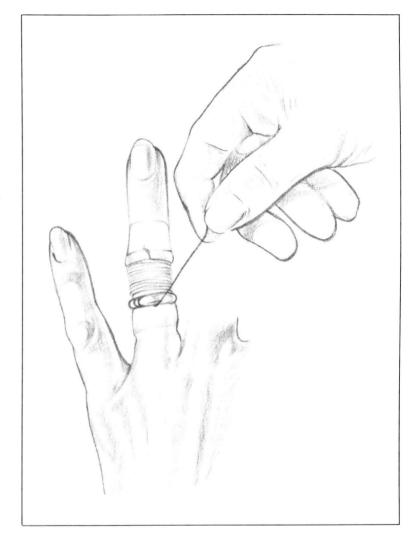

Suggested Readings

Flatt AE: *The Care of Minor Hand Injuries,* ed 4. St. Louis, CV Mosby Co, 1979.

Roberts JR, Hedges JR: *Clinical Procedures in Emergency Medicine.* Philadelphia, WB Saunders Co, 1985.

Schwartz G: *Principles and Practice of Emergency Medicine.* Philadelphia, WB Saunders Co, 1978.

24

Controlling Posterior Epistaxis

Leroy R. Schlesselman, MD
R. Ivan Iriarte, MD

Ninety percent of nosebleeds are anterior. These usually involve Kiesselbach's plexus of the nasal septum. The other 10% are posterior and arise from the sphenopalatine or ethmoidal vessels that supply the upper recesses of the nasal chamber (Figure 24-1).

In patients under age 40, bleeds are usually anterior and venous, most of them resulting from trauma. In patients age 40 and older, bleeds are often posterior, arterial, and associated with systemic disease, although the precise etiology is frequently not clear. Possible causes include degenerative processes of the blood vessels, neoplasms of the nose and paranasal sinuses, infections, hypertension, and bleeding diathesis. Many cases, however, must be classified as idiopathic spontaneous epistaxis.

Anterior epistaxis usually responds to pressure, application of 4% cocaine, or cauterization with silver nitrate. Patients with posterior epistaxis, however, often require sedation, posterior nasal packing, and hospitalization.*

A conventional gauze nasal pack is difficult to insert and remove, is poorly tolerated by most patients, and has a high rate of complications. Several types of intranasal balloons minimize these disadvantages, but a Foley catheter serves the same purpose and is available in most primary care settings.

---

*High posterior bleeds are rarely controlled by packing; they usually require ligation. Some authorities recommend treating a *severe* posterior bleed with arterial ligation initially.

165

In addition, the catheter procedure allows for quicker insertion than the conventional packing method. It is also less painful to insert and remove, is less uncomfortable while in place, is less likely to cause a nasal infection, and is less odoriferous.

The only absolute contraindication to the procedure is an obstruction of the oral airway.

Materials

- 4% topical cocaine solution
- Cotton swabs
- Foley catheter, No. 12 or No. 13 French, with 30-mL balloon
- 20-mL syringe
- Absorbable gelatin sponge (Gelfoam) (optional)
- Petrolatum gauze for nose packing
- Antibiotic ointment
- Umbilical clamp
- Piece of foam rubber or other padding
- Nasal speculum
- Bayonet forceps

PROCEDURE

1. Anesthetize the nasal fossa with topical cocaine solution.
2. Remove and discard the tip of the Foley catheter distal to the balloon. Lubricate the catheter with antibiotic ointment. Introduce the catheter into the bleeding nasal fossa past the choana.
3. With a syringe, introduce 5 mL of air or saline into the balloon and apply gentle traction to bring the balloon into contact with the choana. Then fill the balloon with an additional 10-15 mL of air or saline (Figure 24-2).
4. Continue to apply constant moderate traction to the catheter, or have an assistant do so. Using bayonet forceps, fill the posterior and medial portions of the nasal cavity with absorbable gelatin sponge smeared with antibiotic ointment, then pack the anterior part of the nasal fossa with antibiotic-coated petrolatum gauze in a conventional ribbon-layer manner (Figure 24-3). If the gelatin sponge is unavailable, pack the entire cavity with petrolatum gauze.
5. After completing the anterior packing, fix the Foley catheter in position with an umbilical clamp, using a piece of foam or other padding between the clamp and the nose. Fasten the remaining length of catheter around the ear with tape (Figure 24-4). Plan to keep the patient under observation for 24 hours. To prevent pressure necrosis of the skin under the clamp, have the position of the clamp adjusted every few hours.
6. On cessation of bleeding, deflate the balloon gradually and leave the catheter in place for 4-6 hours in case of rebleed.

Figure 24-1: Vessels involved in posterior epistaxis.

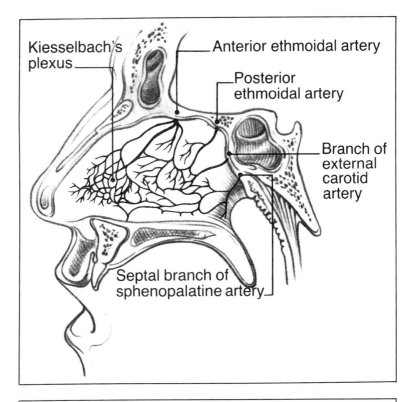

Figure 24-2: Lubricate a Foley catheter with antibiotic ointment and insert it into the bleeding nasal fossa, past the choana. With a syringe, inflate the balloon.

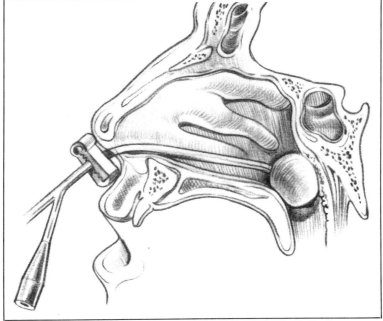

Figure 24-3: Pack the anterior portion of the nasal fossa with antibiotic-coated petrolatum gauze (if available), using bayonet forceps.

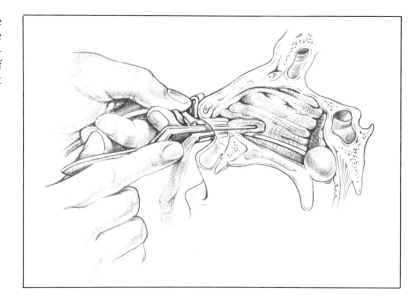

Figure 24-4: Fix the catheter in position by applying an umbilical clamp, which should be padded by a piece of foam or gauze. Hook the free end of the catheter around the ear.

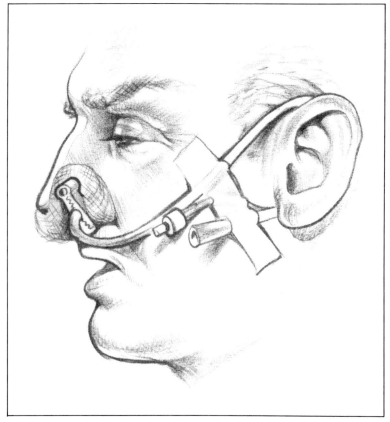

7. If no rebleed occurs, remove the catheter, leaving the anterior pack in place if possible; remove the pack in 24 hours if bleeding does not recur.

Note: If this method fails to control bleeding, arterial ligation may be indicated: Consult an otolaryngologist.

Complications

The following complications are possible and should be watched for:
- Acute sinusitis from blocked drainage
- Hemotympanum, middle ear effusion, or acute otitis media from blocked eustachian tube
- Hypoxia
- Balloon leakage (if air is used to inflate)
- Rupture of balloon and aspiration of saline (if liquid is used to inflate)
- Necrosis of mucous membranes from balloon pressure (rare)
- Pressure necrosis of skin under the umbilical clamp

Suggested Readings

Bierman SF: To air is humane. *N Engl J Med* 1983;309:243.

De La Haye, Davies H: Managing epistaxis. *Practitioner* 1983; 227:1011-4.

Kirchner JA: Current concepts in otolaryngology: Epistaxis. *N Engl J Med* 1982;307:1126-8.

Nassif AC: How I do it—head and neck and plastic surgery. A new procedure in nasal packing to stop bleeding. *Laryngoscope* 1983;93:1222-4.

Wang L, Vogel DH: Posterior epistaxis: Comparison of treatment. *Otolaryngol Head Neck Surg* 1981;89:1001-6

25

Removing Impacted Cerumen from the Ear

Elizabeth A. Burns, MD
Bev L. True, PharmD

Earwax impacted in the external meatus hinders the thorough examination of the auditory canal, particularly in children. In as many as 30% of all children who present with signs and symptoms of acute otitis media (AOM), cerumen removal was required before the physician could make an accurate diagnosis. It is incorrect to assume that the heat generated by the middle ear infection will melt or loosen the earwax. Cerumenosis and AOM can and do coexist.

The contraindications and safety points to keep in mind mostly concern small children. Do not irrigate or syringe the auditory canal in young children or infants if it is not absolutely necessary. Perforations are more likely to occur in this age group.

Other contraindications to irrigation include the presence of tympanostomy tubes, a perforated tympanic membrane, a previous membrane perforation that has healed poorly, or recent surgery of the middle ear.

Note: If you have already begun the cleaning procedure with a syringe and you find a perforation that you did not know was present, administer a systemic antibiotic prophylactically.

Keep in mind that the procedure usually causes reddening of the tympanic membrane, which may obscure a diagnosis of AOM. If you strongly suspect AOM at the start, remove earwax without irrigating, or check for membrane motility after removing the irrigation fluid from the canal. Tympanometry can be performed in equivocal cases (see Chapter 10).

TABLE 25–1

Agents commonly used to soften earwax

Ceruminolytics may aid removal if earwax is hard and dry although they are not necessary in all cases of impaction.
- Most ceruminolytics take 3-4 days to be effective. They are virtually useless if administered just before irrigation.
- When you prescribe a ceruminolytic, advise the patient or parent to instill the solution into the ear canal at bedtime, plug the canal with cotton, and remove the cotton in the morning. If a twice-daily regimen is required, any remaining solution should be drained by gravity before the next dose.

Brand name	Ingredients
Auro Ear Drops (OTC)	6.5% Carbamide peroxide
Cerumenex Drops (Rx)*	10% Triethanolamine polypeptide oleate-condensate, 0.5% chlorobutanol, propylene glycol
Colace liquid (OTC)**,***	Docusate sodium
Debrox Drops (OTC) Murine Ear Drops (OTC)	6.5% Carbamide peroxide glycerin
Various	Baby oil (OTC) Mineral oil (OTC) Virgin olive oil (OTC)

*This product achieves effectiveness in 15-30 minutes.
**Earwax removal is not an FDA-recognized indication for this product.
***Use liquid, not syrup, forms of docusate products.

Avoid using a curette to remove earwax when you can't be sure that the patient's head will remain immobile. Even with good head control, the procedure incurs some risk for eardrum and auditory canal trauma. Be aware that pulling out hardened earwax can cause bleeding.

Materials

- Blunt ear curette (Buck) size 0 or wire curette (commonly called cerumen spoons)
- No. 5 and No. 7 French suction tips
- Pomeroy ear syringe or suitable substitute
- Oral hygiene appliance (Water Pik)
- Bulb syringe (can be used by the patient at home)
- Towels or plastic apron

- Ear basin
- A container of tap water at body temperature (optional additives: several tablespoons of hydrogen peroxide or 1 tsp baking soda/pint water)
- Wax softening agents (optional; see Table 25-1)
- Monsel's solution

PROCEDURE

1.   If irrigation is contraindicated, proceed to step 5. Otherwise plan to use either an ear syringe or a Water Pik to flush impacted cerumen from the external meatus.

Figure 25-1:   With the patient sitting, have them hold an ear basin under the ear to catch draining fluid. Aim body-temperature water toward the wall of the canal that is not obscured by earwax. This allows pressure to build behind the plug, which helps push it out.

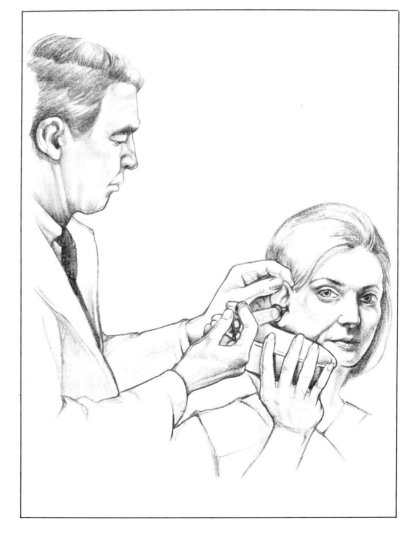

2. Be sure the water used for irrigation is at body temperature to avoid triggering the vestibular reflex and producing vertigo, nausea, and vomiting.

3. For best results, have the patient assume a sitting position and direct the liquid toward the wall of the canal not obscured by the earwax plug (usually superiorly) to build up pressure behind the plug and push it out (Figure 25-1). To reduce the risk of trauma, take care to use the lowest possible pressure. Use an ear basin to collect the irrigating fluid.

4. If the wax plug dislodges, dry the canal with 70% alcohol to prevent maceration and subsequent otitis externa. If the plug does not dislodge, continue with step 5.

5. Use a blunt or wire curette to remove cerumen. If the patient is a young child, have an assistant restrain him or her firmly (Figure 25-2).

6. Insert the curette alongside and just past the plug and spoon or roll out the wax plug (Figure 25-3). Exercise extreme caution to avoid nicking or irritating the ear canal.

7. If bleeding occurs, swab the area with Monsel's solution and administer a combination antibiotic such as hydrocortisone, neomycin sulfate and polymyxin B sulfate (AK-Sporin H.C. Otic, Cortisporin Otic) or hydrocortisone and polymyxin B sulfate (Otobiotic Otic) prophylactically to avoid an external ear infection.

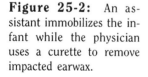

Figure 25-2: An assistant immobilizes the infant while the physician uses a curette to remove impacted earwax.

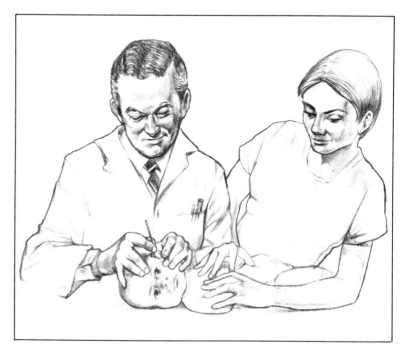

Figure 25-3: Gently slide curette past the cerumen plug and spoon or roll the plug out. Try not to nick the ear canal.

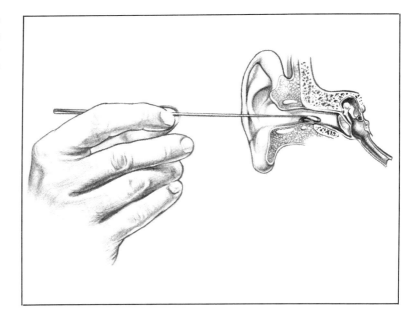

The key to a successful procedure outcome and proper follow-up care is patient education.

Urge your patients not to use cotton-tipped swabs to remove earwax, as these devices can push the wax deeper into the auditory canal, thereby increasing the chance of impaction. Always point out the extreme hazards of putting anything into the ear, such as bobby pins, or paper clips, or any other common objects people use to get at earwax. These objects easily traumatize the lining of the ear canal, and therefore increase the risk of otitis externa.

Let the patient know that over-the-counter wax-softening products do not remove earwax, as they may be advertised to do. These products do, however, soften the wax enough to facilitate removal by a professional. Sometimes it is helpful to instruct a patient a few days before an appointment for earwax removal to instill one of these products in the ears. Baby oil or mineral oil are also effective, and have a long shelf life.

Before your patient leaves the office, demonstrate the careful and proper use of the bulb syringe as adjunct home therapy for the patient who has a continuing earwax problem, and is capable and willing to perform the irrigation procedure him- or herself.

Suggested Readings

Bailey BJ: Removal of cerumen. *JAMA* 1984;251:1681.

Carne S: Ear syringing. *Br Med J* 1980;280:374-6.

Schwartz RH, Rodriguez WJ, McAveney W, et al: Cerumen removal: How necessary is it to diagnose acute otitis media? *Am J Dis Child* 1983;137:1064-5.

26

Rubber Band Ligation of Hemorrhoids

Timothy Appenheimer, MD

Although ligation of hemorrhoids predates Hippocrates, only in the past three decades have methods and technologies emerged that make it a practical and effective office treatment of internal hemorrhoids.

Recent studies suggest that hemorrhoids result from downward displacement of small masses of somewhat erectile tissue called anal cushions. These cushions represent congregations of the hemorrhoidal venous plexus. Usually three anal cushions are located just above the pectinate line; they are thought to facilitate complete anal closure. Straining at stool engorges these vascular cushions, and repeated straining may cause downward displacement, producing internal hemorrhoids. The downward displacement may be accompanied by discomfort and bright red bleeding from ruptured engorged capillaries. When an internal hemorrhoid is pushed outside the anal canal, it is said to be prolapsed.

Application of constricting elastic bands to mucosa overlying or just proximal to the internal hemorrhoid results in fibrosis that fixes the anal cushion in position and may decrease its vascularity. This relieves discomfort and bleeding while preserving the function of the anal cushion.

While hemorrhoids can cause discomfort and a great deal of anxiety, the mere presence of internal hemorrhoids, without signs or symptoms, does not justify intervention.

Ligation can be considered when there is prolapse of internal hemorrhoids, persistent bleeding, rectal itching or fecal soiling.

The procedure should not be performed if there is an active local infection, a history of inflammatory bowel disease, a clotting disorder, chronic liver disease (in which case portal vein pressure may be increased), or the presence of an anal fissure or other rectal pathology.

Caution: Ligation is *not* the appropriate treatment for external hemorrhoids (those originating below the pectinate line). Sensitive dermal nerve endings in external hemorrhoid tissues make this procedure extremely painful.

Materials

- Anoscope (a fenestrated model of the Hinkel-James type is preferred)
- Water-soluble lubricant such as K-Y Lubricating Jelly or Surgilube
- Hemorrhoidal ligator (McGivney) with appropriate rubber bands (This is a modification of earlier instruments designed by Blaisdell and Barron.)

- Forceps (Allis, McGivney, or alligator)
- Hemostat
- Surgical scissors
- Adjustable proctologic table (optional)

PROCEDURE

Always have a barium enema study done and perform or order flexible sigmoidoscopy before you make a firm decision to ligate so you can rule out a lesion higher in the rectum. Such a lesion could be obstructing venous return, causing hemorrhoids to become symptomatic. Surgery in that setting would probably be the treatment of choice, obviating the need for ligation. The technique assumes adequate digital examination before ligation. Bowel preparation is

Figure 26-1: Attach cone to ligator ring and slide two rubber bands over the cone onto the ring. *Note:* Loading two rubber bands at a time provides a back-up should one of the bands break.

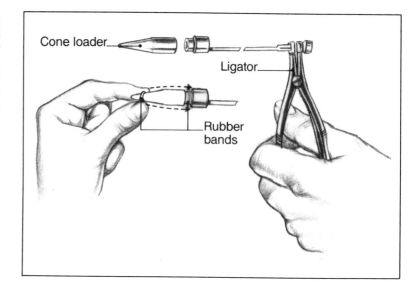

seldom necessary, but the bowel should be emptied voluntarily or by phospho-soda enema (Fleet) prior to the procedure to avoid the need for defecation in the first 24 hours following ligation.

1. Load one or, preferably, two rubber bands onto the ligator by attaching the cone to the ligator ring and sliding the bands over the cone until they are seated on the ligator ring (Figure 26-1). Remove the cone. Two bands are suggested so that one band would remain in place if the other should rupture.

2. Place the patient in the jackknife position on a proctologic table or in the knee-chest position on a standard examining table.

3. Apply lubricant to the fenestrated anoscope and insert the scope. Remove the obturator and slowly withdraw the anoscope to identify enlarged hemorrhoidal cushions. Normally, you'll find hemorrhoids in fields of redundant rectal mucosa. Identify the most prominent hemorrhoid.

4. Remove the anoscope, replace the obturator, and reinsert the anoscope with the fenestration in the direction of the most prominent hemorrhoid.

5. Again slowly withdraw until redundant hemorrhoidal mucosa protrudes into the anoscope. Have the patient perform Valsalva's maneuver to make the protrusion more pronounced.

6. With an assistant holding the anoscope in position, place the loaded ligator ring over the bulging mucosa. Insert forceps through

Figure 26-2: Have an assistant hold the anoscope in position. Insert forceps through the ligator ring and grasp the mucosal bulge.

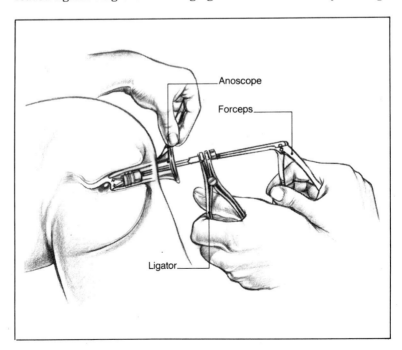

Figure 26-3: Squeeze the ligator handle to release a rubber band onto the base of the mucosal mass.

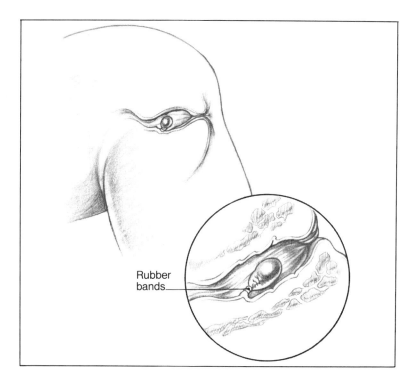

Rubber bands

the ring and gently grasp the leading portion of mucosa (Figure 26-2). If the patient feels marked pain at this point, the tissue is probably below the pectinate line. Discontinue the procedure.

7. If the patient feels little or no pain, pull the mucosal protrusion through the ligator ring.

8. Carefully push the ligator ring against the rectal wall and relax traction on the hemorrhoid to protect the rectal mucosa against the sudden shearing force exerted at the base of the hemorrhoid when you release the bands.

9. Squeeze the ligator handle to release the rubber bands onto the base of the mucosal mass (Figure 26-3) and remove forceps, ligator, and anoscope.

When rubber band ligation is done properly, most patients experience very little rectal discomfort. Pain immediately following the procedure indicates poor placement of the rubber band and prompts removal, using a hemostat and surgical scissors as needed.

If the patient has pain that begins after he or she leaves your office, recommend a nonprescription analgesic. Instruct the patient to phone again if this fails to provide relief. Persistent pain can indicate infection, sphincter spasm, or perianal hematoma, and always warrants reexamination.

Be sure to alert the patient to the scant bleeding and/or mucus discharge he will probably experience 4-8 days after the ligation is performed. Assure him that this is the normal process of events, as the necrotic tissue separates from the rectal wall.

Patient education is key in the prevention of further hemorrhoidal development. Advise the patient that hemorrhoids are likely to recur if he or she continues to be constipated. Emphasize the importance of adequate dietary fiber intake, and, if necessary, supplement the diet with psyllium-containing bulking agents such as Metamucil or Syllact.

Most patients remain ambulatory after the procedure and are able to return to work the same day. It is not unusual for a patient to require two or more rubber band ligation procedures for complete relief of symptoms. After you treat the most prominent hemorrhoid at the first visit, others may later become more symptomatic. It is wise to schedule a follow-up examination at 2-3 weeks to determine whether additional ligations will be necessary.

While some experienced operators routinely band two separate hemorrhoid sites 180 degrees apart during a single ligation session, you will probably have better results and certainly better patient tolerance if you restrict yourself to treating one hemorrhoid at a time. If symptoms persist, three or four repeat procedures at four-week intervals may be needed.

Patient satisfaction after ligation is about 88-92%, only slightly less than after surgical hemorrhoidectomy.

Suggested Readings

Alexander-Williams J, Crapp AR: Conservative management of haemorrhoids. Part I: Injection, freezing and ligation. *Clin Gastroenterol* 1975;4:595-618.

Thompson WH: The nature of haemorrhoids. *Br J Surg* 1975;62:542-52.

27

Treatment of Ingrown Toenail

Timothy Appenheimer, MD

Ingrown toenails usually occur on the tibial side of the great toe, and are accompanied by pain and erythema.

Management approaches suggested for ingrown toenails run the gamut from conservative nonsurgical procedures to bone removal. Recurrence is a significant problem in many commonly used treatments. The following guidelines yield good results:

For *initial lesions* of less than two months' duration with minimal infection and granuloma, consider using cotton wick insertion.

For *recurrent lesions,* lesions of more than two months' duration, and lesions with significant infection and granuloma formation, consider partial avulsion of the nail plate with phenolization. *Note:* According to several studies, simple avulsion of a strip of nail or the entire nail plate *without* phenolization often produces recurrence rates of 60-80%.

Either procedure can be done easily in the office and provides a satisfactory cosmetic result with an acceptable recurrence rate.

These procedures have no absolute contraindications. Relative contraindications are:

- Diabetes mellitus.
- Peripheral vascular disease.
- Bleeding abnormalities.
- Pregnancy—The use of phenol is contraindicated during pregnancy because of the possibility of systemic absorption. It has not been established whether the use of injectable lidocaine HCl (Xylocaine) is safe during pregnancy.

Materials

For digital block:

- 4-5 mL 1% lidocaine HCl *without* epinephrine
- 5-mL syringe and 25-gauge, ⅞-in needle

For cotton wick insertion:

- Povidone-iodine (Betadine) or other antiseptic skin cleanser

- Sterile or clean cotton ball
- Blunt splinter forceps
- Surgical scissors
- Tincture of iodine
- Silver nitrate sticks

For partial nail plate avulsion with phenolization:

- Large rubber band or small Penrose drain for use as tourniquet
- 6-in hemostat
- Sterile surgical scissors
- Small straight (mosquito) hemostat
- Sterile cotton swabs
- Silver nitrate sticks
- Phenol (80% or 88%)
- Alcohol swabs
- Alcohol
- Antibiotic ointment
- Nonadherent dressing
- Bandage roll (Tubegauz)

PROCEDURE

For digital nerve block, cotton wick insertion, or partial nail avulsion with phenolization, have the patient supine, with knees and hips flexed to position the foot flat on the examining table.

Digital nerve block

You can use digital nerve anesthesia for both treatment methods, although in early cases of ingrown toenail application of the cotton wick may not require anesthesia.

1. Using a 5-mL syringe and 25-gauge, ⅞-in needle, inject 0.5 mL of lidocaine beneath the skin overlying the proximal phalanx on the extensor surface of the affected side of the great toe (Figure 27-1).
2. Insert the needle to the hub in a plantar direction alongside the proximal phalanx but do not pierce the plantar skin surface. By placing a finger on the plantar surface, you'll be able to feel the approach of the needle and stop in time. As you slowly withdraw the needle, inject approximately 1-2 mL of lidocaine (see Figure 27-2).
3. When the needle tip approaches the skin surface, redirect it across the extensor surface of the toe. Then reinsert the needle and inject another 1 mL of lidocaine during withdrawal (see Figure 27-2).
4. Enter the toe dorsally on the opposite side and repeat step 2.
5. Allow at least five minutes for the nerve block to take effect.

Figure 27-1: Placing the digital nerve block. Inject 0.5 mL of lidocaine HCl beneath the skin overlying the proximal phalanx on the extensor surface of the affected side of the toe.

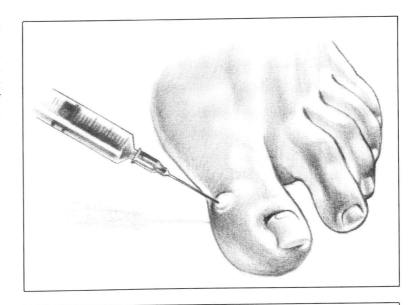

Figure 27-2: Place a finger on the plantar surface of the toe to enable you to detect the approach of the needle tip. As you feel it through the skin surface, stop advancing the needle. Withdraw the needle slowly while injecting more lidocaine. Redirect the needle in the direction of the arrows.

Cotton wick insertion

Consider this procedure clean rather than sterile.

1. Roll some cotton to a thickness of about 3 mm (⅛ in) and an initial length of at least 2.5 cm (1 in).

Figure 27-3: Push the wick into the distal portion of the lateral nail groove, separating the nail edge from the underlying tissue.

Figure 27-4: Place the small blade of the scissors in the track left by the hemostat and incise the nail to the base.

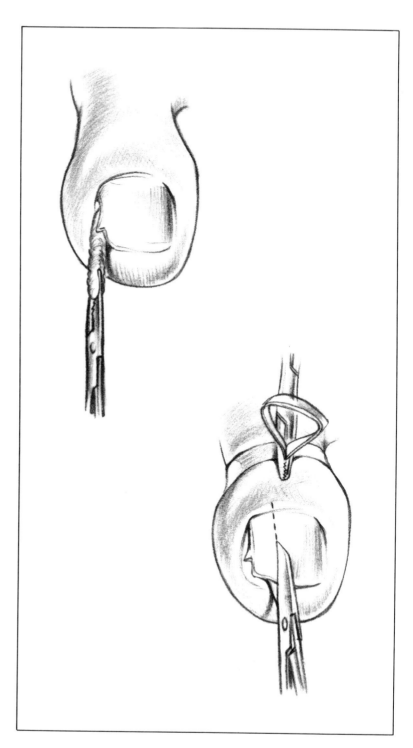

2. With splinter forceps, push the wick gently into the distal part of the lateral nail groove on the affected side, separating the nail edge from the underlying soft tissue (see Figure 27-3). When you can identify the offending corner or spike of nail, remove it with the scissors. Insert the wick far enough to separate the remaining distal nail from the underlying nail groove. About 1 cm (⅜ in) of the wick should remain free.

3. Apply tincture of iodine to the wick.

4. Cauterize any areas of granulation by firmly pressing a silver nitrate stick onto the tissue.

5. If you use silver nitrate, place an adhesive bandage over the granulation tissue. Instruct the patient to change it daily and to apply tincture of iodine to the wick every other day. Have him or her return weekly for replacement of the wick; at each visit, reevaluate the toe and apply further silver nitrate if indicated. Anticipate 4-6 treatments.

Partial nail plate avulsion with phenolization

1. Following nerve block, scrub the toe with antiseptic, rinse, and dry, drape the foot if desired.

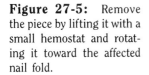

Figure 27-5: Remove the piece by lifting it with a small hemostat and rotating it toward the affected nail fold.

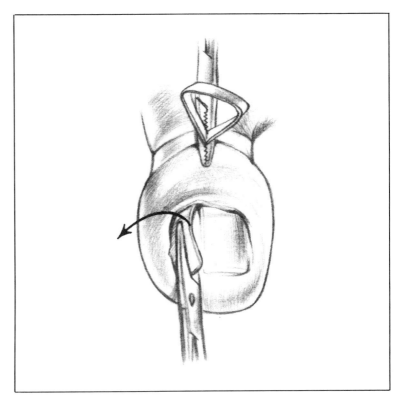

Figure 27-6: Notching the center of the nail with a "V" may reduce the odds of an ingrown nail recurring.

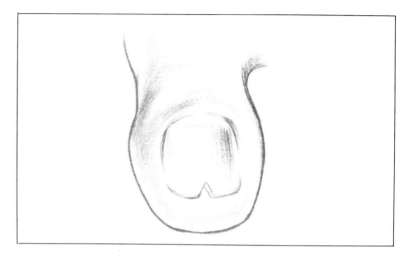

2. Place the tourniquet around the base of the toe, and secure it with the 6-in hemostat.

3. Near the affected edge of the nail, locate the point at which the nail plate begins to curve in the plantar direction. Open the small (mosquito) hemostat and fully insert a single blade between the nail plate and the nail bed at the point of curvature. Remove the hemostat.

4. Place the small blade of the surgical scissors in the track just opened by the small hemostat and incise the nail to the base (Figure 27-4).

5. Grasp the length of the nail portion to be removed with the small hemostat and remove it by gentle rotation toward the affected nail fold. Be sure this fragment includes the offending spike or corner of nail (Figure 27-5).

6. With cotton swabs, carefully dry the newly exposed nail bed, especially the proximal region beneath the cuticle at the germinal matrix of the nail. Phenol can effectively ablate the germinal matrix only if the matrix is completely dry.

7. Saturate a clean cotton swab with phenol, place the swab in contact with the germinal matrix beneath the cuticle, and rub. Resaturate the swab as needed to maintain contact for a couple of minutes.

8. Apply phenol to the remainder of the freshly exposed nail bed. Take care to avoid spilling the phenol, and use an alcohol swab to remove immediately any phenol that touches normal skin.

9. Cauterize any areas of granulation by firmly pressing a silver nitrate stick onto the tissue.

10. Remove the tourniquet and elevate the patient's foot for 15 minutes to aid hemostasis. Apply antibiotic ointment and place a nonadherent dressing to the wound. Cover with Tubegauz.

11. Have the patient return in two days so you can remove the dressing and reexamine the toe. At that visit, instruct him to cleanse the toe with soap and water and redress it daily using a less bulky dressing, and to return in five days for reassessment. The patient can continue to care for the toe at home until healing is complete, applying a dressing during waking hours only. He can wear a shoe when dressing size and comfort allow.

Advise the patient to wear shoes with an ample toe box. If the patient is a woman, advise her to avoid high-heeled shoes. When the nonablated nail regrows, the patient should take care to trim it straight across without rounding the corners. Notching the center of the distal border of the nail with a "V" (Figure 27-6) may reduce the odds of recurrence.

Suggested Readings

Cameron PF: Ingrowing toenails: An evaluation of two treatments. *Br Med J* 1981;283:821-2.

Fishman H: Practical therapy for ingrown toenails. *Cutis* 1983;32:159-60.

Rinaldi R, Sabia M, Gross J: The treatment and prevention of infection in phenol alcohol matricectomies. *J Am Podiatry Assoc* 1982;72:453-75.

EMERGENCY PROCEDURES

28

Repair of Simple Lacerations

Paul S. Williamson, MD

Most traumatic lacerations are minor. If the wound is superficial, with no vessel, tendon, joint, or nerve involvement, you can repair it as a simple laceration on an outpatient basis. A good assistant is invaluable in most laceration repairs.

This procedure is recommended for simple laceration up to full thickness (through the epidermis and dermis but not into subdermal structures). *Note:* Lacerations with linear, sharp, visible margins, such as those caused by sharp metal or glass, are generally easiest to repair. Stellate, beveled, or flap-shaped lacerations, sometimes contaminated with foreign material, are more difficult but still usually treated on an outpatient basis. Contaminated wounds needing extensive cleaning and debridement and crushed wound areas such as those resulting from wringer-type injuries often have extensive devitalized tissue and should be repaired only after demarcation with debridement.

The following are beyond the scope of this procedure:

- Lacerations that involve deep structures such as muscle, bone, fascia, nerves, parotid duct, or lacrimal apparatus; through-and-through lacerations of the eyelid, lip, or cheek; and lacerations requiring a large flap or graft. These should be dealt with in the operating room.
- Wounds more than 6-8 hours old (or up to 24 hours old if clean) and bite wounds. These should be allowed to heal secondarily and be revised as needed later, often after debridement.
- High-pressure injection injuries. These often appear minor but can be extensive under the surface. Primary closure is not indicated.
- Thermal injuries, including electrical and chemical wounds.
- Wounds with extensive edema, ecchymosis, and soft tissue injury. These may require open treatment with secondary closure to avoid compartment syndromes.
- Significant facial lacerations. Plastic surgery may be needed.

Materials

- Antibacterial skin prep, such as povidone-iodine (Betadine) or chlorhexidine gluconate (Hibiclens), in a 1-oz medicine cup
- About 12 sterile 4 × 4-in gauze sponges
- Sterile gloves
- Skin drapes
- 1% lidocaine HCl (Xylocaine) with and without epinephrine
- 5-mL, sterile, disposable syringe with a 1-in, 18-gauge needle to draw up the anesthetic and a 1½-in, 25- or 27-gauge needle to infiltrate the anesthetic
- 10-50 mL irrigation syringe with a blunt 18-gauge needle
- Warm saline
- Good operative light
- Needle holder
- Suture scissors
- Pick-up forceps with teeth (thumb)
- Pick-up forceps without teeth
- Skin hooks (optional)
- Two mosquito hemostats, one straight, one curved
- Scalpel blade with a No. 4 handle
- Small pair of curved scissors for undermining (optional)
- Suture in various sizes, usually 4.0 nylon monofilament (5.0 nylon monofilament for the face) or another nonabsorbable suture such as polypropylene (Prolene, Surgilene); synthetic absorbable suture such as polyglactic acid (Vicryl) or polyglycolic acid (Dexon) for subcuticular stitches

Preparation

In your record of the patient's pertinent medical history, include allergies (especially allergies to local anesthetics, topical antibiotics, tape and other materials used in the repair), any bleeding disorders, and tetanus immunization status. Record the time of the injury, location of the incident, and the patient's own description of what happened. On initial examination, record the location and size of the laceration, estimated depth, sensory changes, structures involved, and the amount of bleeding.

Remove any clothing that obstructs the wound; remove the patient's watch and any rings if near the wound.

Stop the bleeding with direct pressure, or use a blood pressure cuff as a temporary tourniquet if the bleeding is in an extremity. If pressure does not produce hemostasis, you may need to explore the wound for the bleeding source. Electrocautery is sometimes used to stop small bleeders.

Scrub the skin surrounding the wound with antibacterial skin prep or soak it for five minutes in a sterile pan of warm soap solution. Clean the wound itself with saline irrigation using the 10-50 mL syringe with 18-gauge blunt needle, expelling the saline fast enough to produce sufficient cleaning pressure. Debride necrotic, dirty, or ragged edges mechanically if necessary.

Note: Do *not* apply antiseptic within an open wound; it will impair the immune response and inhibit initial cellular repair. Do *not* shave the hair around the wound; this may increase the rate of infection. (Also, if the wound is above an eye, remember that eyebrows once shaved may not regrow normally.)

PROCEDURE

1. Examine the wound under sterile conditions for depth and involved structures. If called for, assess tendon function and ductal structures before repair. Record pinprick sensation distal to the wound before local anesthesia. Search for and remove any foreign bodies in the wound. Record your search for foreign bodies whether or not you find any. Use X-ray or xeroradiography if necessary to rule out foreign bodies such as glass or associated orthopedic fracture.

2. Administer local anesthesia, aspirating before injection to make sure the needle is not in a vein. Inject approximately 1 mL of 1% lidocaine for every 2 cm (¾ in) of laceration, to a maximum of 4 mg/kg for repair of multiple lacerations, or 28 mL for a 70-kg (154-lb) person. Infiltrate all dermal tissue within about 1 cm (⅜ in) of the wound edge. If the wound is clean, inject through the open wound surface; if contaminated, inject through the surrounding scrubbed skin surface. Inject slowly in the subdermal space to minimize pain, then allow five minutes for diffusion and anesthetic effect before suturing.

Note: Lidocaine with epinephrine will prevent some vasodilation and rebleeding caused by local infiltration, but epinephrine is con-traindicated in fingers, toes, penis, and earlobes.

3. Excise obviously necrotic tissue and any jagged wound edges, being conservative around vital tissues and in areas where the skin is tight. Where necessary, undermine the dermis to mobilize the skin edges and permit approximating them *without tension*. Square off oblique cuts to leave perpendicular skin edges for approximating (Figure 28-1). Try to preserve landmarks and leave square wound edges that can be approximated by appropriately matched layers. Eliminate dead space in subcutaneous adipose tissue by approximating it with a few absorbable synthetic sutures (Figure 28-2) to leave the smallest scar possible. Reestablish hemostasis with pressure or ab-sorbable-suture ligature of small veins. If the wound is now clean, linear, and no more than skin deep, proceed with suturing.

Figure 28-1: Dotted lines illustrate squaring-off of an oblique laceration perpendicular to the skin edges.

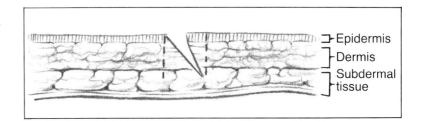

Figure 28-2: Eliminate dead space in subcutaneous adipose tissue by approximating it with a few absorbable sutures. Reestablish hemostasis with pressure.

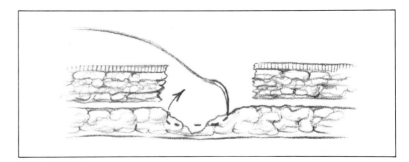

4. Choose the smallest monofilament suture that will hold the wound well—usually 2-0 or 3-0 on the back, 4-0 on the extremities, and 5-0 on the face. Plan the first suture to realign landmarks such as the vermilion border, skin wrinkles, or hair lines. For a V-shaped or flap laceration, place the first stitch at the vertex to realign tissue structures (Figure 28-3). For a T-shaped laceration, use the first stitch to approximate both flaps with the area where they were originally attached (Figure 28-4). Stabilize one edge of the wound with a skin hook or pick-up forceps lightly held to avoid crushing tissue.

5. Hold the suture needle perpendicular to the skin surface, as far

Figure 28-3: Plan the first suture to realign landmarks. For a V-shaped or flap laceration, place the first stitch at the vertex.

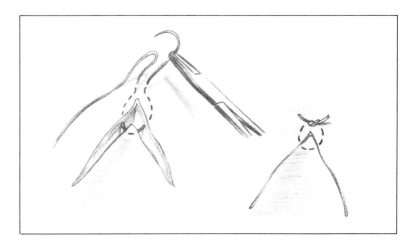

Figure 28-4: For a T-shaped laceration, use the first stitch to approximate both flaps with the area they were originally attached to.

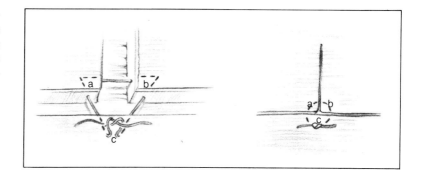

Figure 28-5: Hold the suture needle perpendicular to the skin surface, as far from the wound edge as the skin is thick, and twist the needle through the layers. Do not push the needle.

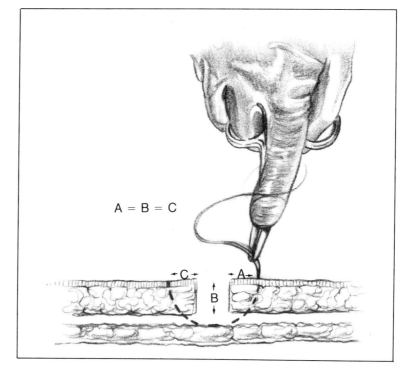

from the wound edge as the skin is thick (Figure 28-5), and rotate your wrist to twist, not push, the needle through the skin. Hemostasis at this point is essential, since a clot interposed between skin edges will delay healing and encourage infection. Use electrocoagulation if necessary, with the proper precautions.

6. If the gap between the wound edges is small, continue moving the needle up through the opposing skin edge, exiting about one skin thickness from the wound edge.

7. With some 2 cm of suture remaining on the side of the wound where the suture needle entered, instrument-tie the suture with just enough tension to approximate but not strangulate the skin edges. Try to leave wound edges slightly everted.

8. Place subsequent sutures as far apart as possible (0.5-1.0 cm [³⁄₁₆-³⁄₈ in]) while allowing no gaping at the wound edges. Handle "dog-ears" by removing a small triangular area of skin at the end of the laceration with the dog-ear and close with a vertex flap stitch.

9. Dress the wound with sterile gauze and tape.

Instruct the patient to leave the initial dressing in place for 24 hours and, if it bleeds through, to pack it over the top with more gauze and tape, then see you immediately for reexamination. Analgesics such as aspirin or acetaminophen may be needed for discomfort as the local anesthetic wears off.

Have the patient change the dressing daily and wash the wound with hydrogen peroxide, then coat the wound with an antibiotic ointment for the first three days. Starting with day 4, the wound may be washed with soap and water, but eschar should be kept covered with gauze until the sutures are removed. The wound infection rate for "clean wounds" is approximately 5%.

If the initial wound was contaminated with bacteria, reexamine it in 24-48 hours. Instruct the patient with a contaminated wound to return the same day if he or she develops fever, if the wound becomes red or swollen, or if it drains pus.

Have the patient return for suture removal in a specified number of days, generally 3 days for lacerations of the face, 5-7 days for the scalp, 7-10 days for the extremities and abdomen, and 10-14 days for the foot, hand, or back.

Note the condition of the wound at suture removal time. To remove a suture, elevate the knot with a hemostat, clip the suture on one side of the knot, and pull toward, rather than away from the healing wound line to avoid tearing the wound open. If indicated, redress the wound with a dry gauze bandage for one day. Some weaker wounds needing further support may be covered with adhesive strips for a few days.

Suggested Readings

Richless LK: Acute wound management. *Fam Prac Recert* 1985;7:39.

Stuzin JM, Engrav LH, Buehler PK: Emergency treatment of facial lacerations. *Postgrad Med* 1982;71:81.

29

Removing a Foreign Body From the Eye

Phillip G. Couchman, MD

Most particles that get into the eye from the environment produce no symptoms or only mildly annoying ones and are washed away by tears. Even when symptoms are severe or prolonged, some patients may be able to remove the particle safely and successfully, perhaps with your telephone instructions. Caution every call-in patient to avoid rubbing his or her eyelids. Then ask whether the eye has been traumatized by a rapidly moving object—a circumstance that indicates immediate examination and possibly referral to an ophthalmologist. If you can rule out dangerous trauma, suggest that the patient try remedies such as the following if he hasn't already done so:

- If the foreign body is visible in the lower conjunctival sac, the patient or a second person can try to remove it with the corner of a clean handkerchief or a paper tissue.
- If the patient feels the foreign body behind his upper lid, advise him to look down, then grasp the upper eyelid and lift it away from the globe. This often decreases pain and allows tears to wash away the irritant.
- If the patient is resourceful enough, encourage him to irrigate the eye once or twice with an eyecup or by simply flooding the eye, using a salt water solution (½ tsp salt dissolved in an 8-oz glass of warm water).

Tell the patient to call you promptly if these measures do not work. If home remedies don't help, or if telephone instructions are inappropriate to begin with, arrange an immediate appointment for evaluation and referral or removal of the foreign body, using the techniques described. When the patient arrives, see him promptly.

Materials

- Topical anesthetic such as 0.5% proparacaine HCl (Alcaine, Ophthaine, Ophthetic, etc.)
- Sterile fluorescein sodium strips (Fluor-I-Strip, Fluor-I-Strip-A.T., Ful-Glo)
- Sterile cotton-tipped applicators
- Sterile saline and eyedropper
- Sterile eye spud or 18-gauge needle
- Bright light source
- Magnifying glasses
- Snellen's chart

Optional equipment often useful:

- Sterile eye patches and 1-in paper tape
- Cycloplegic drops such as 2% cyclopentolate HCl (Cyclogyl Ophthalmic)
- Examination table
- Wood's light
- Ophthalmoscope (20-40 diopter lens)

Preparation

For easier examination, have the patient supine on the examination table.

Anesthetize the affected eye with 1-2 drops of the topical anesthetic. This is not mandatory, but a patient quickly relieved of much acute pain responds better to your questions and treatment. While you anesthetize the eye, review or take the history. Explain that the anesthetic will not block sensation completely but will prevent severe pain and will take effect within one minute. As soon as anesthesia is achieved, proceed with the examination.

Examination

Most eye injuries resulting from foreign bodies are superficial, in the cornea or conjunctiva. Unless emergency referral is indicated be sure to examine all areas even when you find a foreign body in one area; multiple particles may be present.

1. Expose the eyeball by opening the lids wide, using thumb and index finger. You may want to use a bright light and magnifying glass to examine the sclera and cornea.

Introduce fluorescein dye. Avoid the multiple-dose dropper bottles; fluorescein is a fertile culture medium for *Pseudomonas*. Use fluorescein strips instead.

Moisten a strip with saline or anesthetic solution and place it in the lower conjunctival sac for 3-5 seconds. The dye quickly disperses throughout the conjunctiva. Flush the eye with saline or anesthetic solution; denuded areas that have accepted the brilliant yellow stain will be easily identifiable. The dye may reveal mucus or tears around a foreign body in the conjunctival sac.

A Wood's light sometimes helps reveal a small foreign body in the cornea surrounded by a halo of stained tissue. It might also show a corneal scratch that the patient feels as a foreign body.

If you find a foreign body in the cornea, check the patient's visual acuity by Snellen's chart. If you locate the foreign body outside the visual axis or just superficially embedded in the visual axis, remove it before proceeding with the exam.

Caution: Refer the patient immediately to an ophthalmologist if the patient is uncooperative or if you find:

- A penetrating wound
- A foreign body inside the eyeball or deeply lodged in the sclera or cornea
- Blood in the anterior chamber of the eye
- Fixed, distorted, or dilated pupils

Unless you are highly experienced or remote from an ophthalmologist, also refer if you see a fleck of steel or iron surrounded by a rust ring in the patient's visual axis. Inadequate removal of the rust ring may result in low-grade inflammation and impaired vision. Removal of excessive corneal tissue along with the rust may produce a distorted cornea or excess scarring.

2. Evert the upper eyelid to permit examination of the upper conjunctiva. Have the patient gaze downward. Grasp the upper eyelashes between thumb and index finger and, with the tip of the other index finger or the side of the pad of a cotton-tipped applicator, press gently on the skin at the upper lateral border of the tarsal plate (Figure 29-1). Pull outward on the lashes and rotate the tarsal plate

Figure 29-1: Grasp the upper eyelashes with one hand, and with the other, press gently on the skin at the upper lateral border of the tarsal plate with a cotton-tipped applicator.

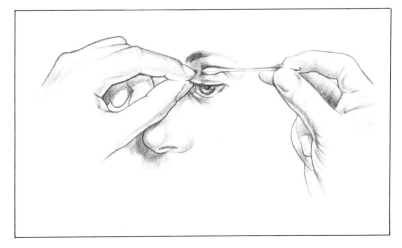

upward until it forms a right angle with the eyeball. A gentle tug upward should flip the plate into eversion, clearly exposing the conjunctival surface of the upper lid (Figure 29-2). Withdraw your finger or the applicator; the lid will remain everted until you have the patient look upward after examination. If you find a foreign body, remove it as described under "Procedure (Particle in conjunctiva)," and proceed with the exam.

3. Have the patient fix his gaze upward. Gently grasp the lower eyelashes between thumb and index finger and pull the lid away from the eyeball. Place the tip of your free index finger on the cheek over the inferior orbital margin and push the skin upward to help lift the lower lid further from the eyeball. If you see a foreign body, proceed to the procedure.

PROCEDURE

Particle in cornea

1. Have the patient fix his gaze on a distant object. Holding the eyelids apart with thumb and index finger, begin by wiping the cornea *once* with a moistened cotton swab. This occasionally dislodges the particle.

Figure 29-2: Pull outward on the lashes. A gentle tug out and up should flip the tarsal plate into eversion, exposing the conjunctival surface. The lid should stay everted on its own so you can remove the cotton-tipped applicator.

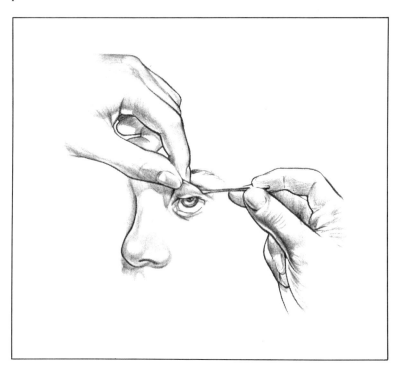

2. If this is unsuccessful, slip an eye spud or the point of an 18-gauge needle under the particle and lift it off the cornea. When using a needle, hold it bevel side up. You may have to make several attempts. Keep the instrument parallel to the surface of the cornea to avoid perforation (Figure 29-3).

If rust stain is present and you are confident of your ability to remove it safely, scoop it up bit by bit with the tip of the needle or spud. Magnifying glasses (8-10 power) are useful here; an ophthalmoscope (20-40 diopter lens) can help locate any residual fragments.

3. Once you have removed the foreign body, retest the patient's vision.

Particle in conjunctiva

Remove a foreign body from the conjunctiva by wiping with a moistened cotton swab. Rarely, you may need to use a spud or needle to lift a particle out.

After removing the foreign body, remind the patient that the anesthesia lasts about 15 minutes and that while paresthesias may occur while the effect is dissipating, he must avoid rubbing the eye. Except when corneal scratching is extensive, antibiotic drops, cycloplegic drops, and eye patches are seldom necessary. They are often counterproductive in that they interfere with the patient's activities. Healing usually occurs within 24 hours after removal of a foreign body.

If the corneal lesion is painful after treatment, have the patient

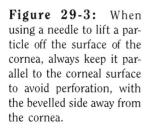

Figure 29-3: When using a needle to lift a particle off the surface of the cornea, always keep it parallel to the corneal surface to avoid perforation, with the bevelled side away from the cornea.

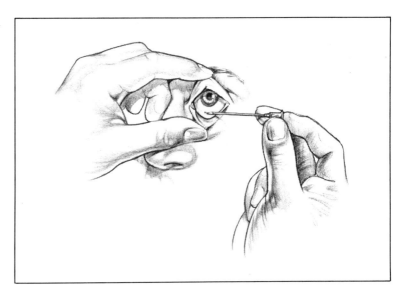

apply moist compresses as needed to provide relief. Have him stop application as soon as the discomfort abates to avoid iatrogenic disability.

If the cornea has been scratched, follow up with a fluorescein stain in 1-2 days. If healing is not complete, repeat every 1-2 days until the injured area will not accept the stain, closely watching for signs of infection and referring if necessary.

Note: At some point during your follow-up care of the patient, remind him to wear safety goggles when appropriate to help prevent foreign body entry into the eye.

Suggested Readings

Banks JLK: *Clinical Ophthalmology.* London, Churchill Livingstone Inc., 1982, pp. 45-54.

Miller D: *Ophthalmology: The Essentials.* New York, John Wiley & Sons, 1979, pp.219-268.

30

Compressive Ankle Splinting

Charles D. Huss, MD

several methods of treatment for ankle sprains are available, some using compressive dressings and others immobilization. This method incorporates the benefits of both approaches. Compression helps control swelling in the acute postinjury period, and plaster splinting provides immobilization, an important element for pain control. This procedure is applicable to all moderate-to-severe ankle sprains, and stable, closed fractures of the foot or ankle when a temporary measure is desired. In the early postfracture period, this technique provides immobilization without risk of neurovascular complications that can be associated with circumferential casts when extreme swelling occurs. This method is particularly useful when surgical treatment of a fracture will be delayed.

It is not, however, recommended for an unstable fracture, which may require casting, or a referral.

Materials

- 12 5 × 30-in plaster splints
- Rolls of 6 × ¾-in cotton sheeting
- Rolls of 6-in stretchable gauze (Kerlix or SOF Band)
- 6-in elastic bandages
- Plaster bucket with water (temperature according to individual preference)
- Crutches

PROCEDURE

1. Have the patient sit with legs hanging over the edge of the table or patient cart.
2. Roll the cotton sheeting circumferentially around the foot, ankle, and lower leg, starting at the toes and moving proximally. Be sure the sheeting lies flat and extends from the toes to about 5 cm (2 in) below the popliteal crease. The applied wrap should be 1-2 layers thick.
3. Roll the stretchable gauze circumferentially over the cotton sheeting, again moving proximally (Figure 30-1). Apply enough

Figure 30-1: With the patient seated and the affected leg hanging off the table, wrap cotton sheeting circumferentially around the leg from toes to below the popliteal crease. Roll stretchable gauze circumferentially over the sheeting with enough tension to smoothly compress the sheeting against the leg.

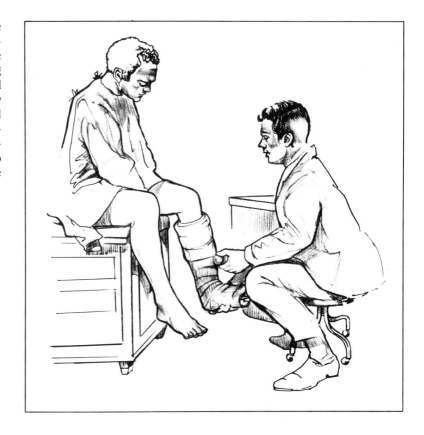

tension to mildly compress the underlying cotton wrap. Be sure you apply tension uniformly to avoid creating ridges in the compressive wrap.

4. For positioning, lay dry plaster splints (approximately 12 for an adult) over the gauze wrap from the posterior aspect of the lower leg to the plantar aspect of the foot and the tips of the toes. Tear the splints to length or trim them with shears or a knife.

5. Place the patient's ankle in a neutral position between plantar flexion and dorsiflexion, or with the sole of the foot at an angle of about 90 degrees to the lower leg. Maintain this ankle position with an assistant's help if necessary as you proceed.

6. Stack the 12 plaster splints and dip them into the plaster bucket until they are thoroughly wet, then remove them and strip off the excess water. The stripping also works moistened plaster into the gauze mesh wrappings of the splints. Apply the wet splints to the compressive wrap from the plantar surface of the toes up along the posterior aspect of the leg (Figure 30-2). Be sure the ankle remains in a neutral position during this application.

Figure 30-2: Apply wet splints to the compressive wrap from the plantar surface of the toes up along the posterior aspect of the leg.

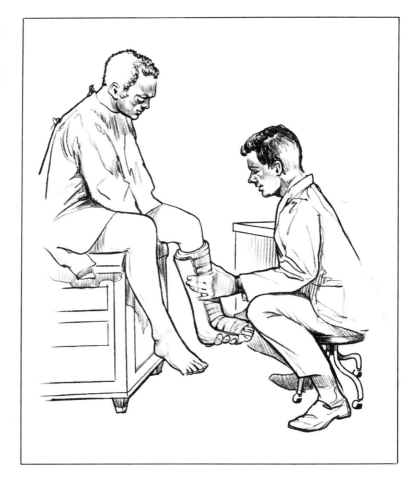

7. To finish the procedure, roll a 6-in elastic bandage circumferentially over the foot, ankle, and lower leg to cover the gauze and splints.
8. Stabilize the joint manually, or have your assistant do so, while the plaster begins to harden. Then have the patient elevate the leg on a pillow for final hardening, an overall period of 15 minutes. Be careful not to make ridges in the plaster.
9. After the plaster has hardened, fit the patient for crutches and demonstrate their use. Urge the patient to keep weight off the splinted region and to avoid exposing the splint to water. Schedule a follow-up visit in 3-5 days. See the patient earlier if the splint becomes soft.

At the second office visit, remove the splint by unwrapping the elastic bandage and cutting the gauze along the dorsum of the foot and anteriorly up the leg (Figure 30-3). Separate the cotton sheeting along the same line. If the patient is still unable to bear weight comfortably, you may reapply the same splint.

Figure 30-3: Remove the splint by cutting the gauze along the dorsum of the foot and anteriorly up the leg. Separate the underlying cotton sheeting along the same path.

Suggested Readings

Iverson LD, Clawson DK: *Manual of Acute Orthopaedic Therapeutics,* ed 2. Boston, Little Brown and Co, 1982, pp. 45-51.

Shaw DC, Heckman JD: Principles and techniques of splinting musculocutaneous injuries. *Emerg Med Clin N Am* 1984;2(2):391.

31

Immobilizing Clavicular Fractures

Charles E. Driscoll, MD

The incidence of clavicular fracture, one of the most frequent fractures in the general population, appears to be rising—largely due to burgeoning automobile and recreational sports-related accidents. Clavicular fracture in the neonate is a well-known complication of passage through the birth canal; and at the opposite end of life, heavy falls on an outstretched hand often cause this injury in the elderly.

Fractures of the middle third account for at least 80% of all clavicular fractures, followed by those of the lateral and then the medial thirds. In children, medial- and lateral-third fractures carry the risk of injury to the growth plate.

Clavicular injury produces a predictable type of fracture. Direct force on the middle third usually results in a transverse fracture at the junction of the outer and middle thirds (see Figure 31-1). A force on the top of the shoulder near the acromioclavicular juncture forces the clavicle down against the first rib, usually resulting in a spiral fracture of the middle third (see Figure 31-2). Indirect force—as from falling on the outstretched hand with the arm abducted and flexed—also usually produces a spiral fracture of the middle third by transmitting the force along the shaft of the humerus with the stenoclavicular joint as a counterpoint (see Figure 31-3). Palpate this joint in all clavicular fractures to rule out joint injury. A careful neurovascular examination of the afflicted arm is also important.

Fractures of the lateral third may be complicated by ligamentous injury to the coracoclavicular ligament or the articular surface. When the acromioclavicular and coracoclavicular ligaments remain intact (Type I fractures), displacement is minimal, and treatment is relatively easy by external means. With ligament injury, however, the distal fragment tends to remain anchored to the acromion while the proximal fragment rides up and backward. This creates marked,

Figure 31-1: Direct force on the middle third of the clavicle usually results in a transverse fracture at the junction of the outer and middle thirds.

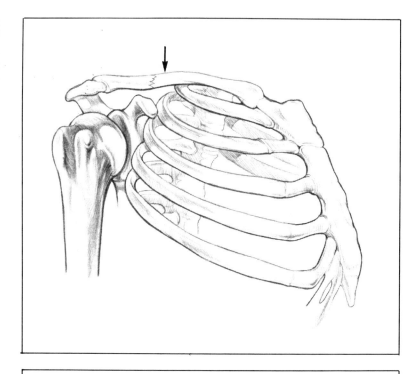

Figure 31-2: Spiral fracture of the middle third.

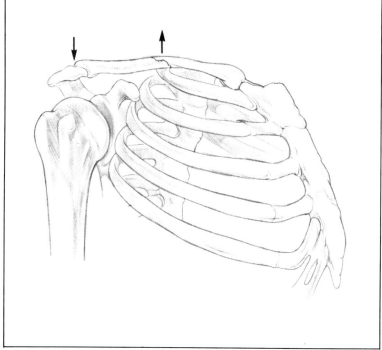

Figure 31-3: Spiral fracture of the middle third from indirect force, such as falling on outstretched hand.

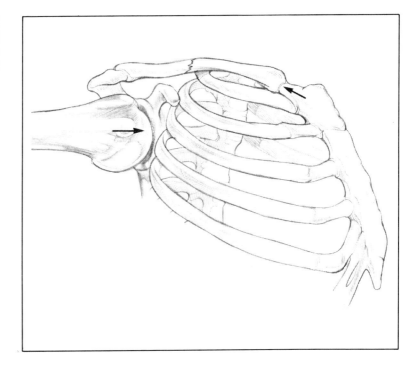

noticeable displacement, and this Type II fracture may require surgery.

The patient's age is the principal determinant of treatment and follow-up. Newborns require little more than pinning the sleeve of the baby's long-sleeved cotton undershirt to the trunk of the shirt as a sling for 2-3 weeks. Remodeling of the clavicle is excellent, and deformity rarely persists.

For simple, nondisplaced, subperiosteal fractures in children, use only a sling; it should be tied across the opposite shoulder to support the weight of the arm under the elbow. In moderately displaced fractures, use a padded figure-of-8 bandage or commercial clavicle strap to maintain alignment.

In adults and adolescents with little or no displacement, use the soft stockinette, figure-of-8 dressing; a sling may be needed for comfort. For more serious displacement, the fracture should be immobilized with a plaster dressing. In the elderly, a sling is almost always the safest treatment.

Indications for immobilization by external methods include fractures of the middle third of the clavicle with minimal or moderate displacement (less than 15 mm), and Type I lateral fractures (proximal to the acromioclavicular and coracoclavicular ligaments).

Contraindications to external immobilization include the following types of fractures.
- Fractures of the middle third, which usually compromise neurovascular structures.
- Type II or III lateral clavicular fractures involving the articular surface.
- Fractures with much dislocation of fragments.
- Fractures with shortening, usually indicated by gross deformity and wide separation of the ends of the fracture site.
- Fractures in patients with multiple chest injuries and an unstable shoulder girdle.
- Fractures with symptomatic, confirmed nonunion.

When external immobilization is contraindicated, the patient is a candidate for referral or surgical intervention.

Materials

- 100-mL syringe with 1.5-in, 21-gauge needle and 1% lidocaine HCl (Xylocaine HCl) for anesthesia
- Povidone-iodine (Betadine) swabs or alcohol pads
- 20-30 ft of 3-in stockinette
- Foam rubber or felt padding
- Cotton batting
- 4-in plaster, several rolls
- Large safety pins
- 3½-4 ft length of 1-in dowel or a discarded broom handle
- Triangular sling bandage
- As an alternative, commercially produced clavicle straps or canvas arm sling, though these are more expensive; for the treatment of Type I fractures, the Kenny-Howard sling may be preferable

PROCEDURE

Reduction technique

Conservative measures are usually quite adequate in treating clavicular fractures. Open reduction is rarely indicated, except as noted earlier, and may result in scarring or a higher incidence of nonunion. Most patients do not need manipulation or replacement of fracture fragments.

With displacement and overriding of fragments, however, reduction is necessary to restore the normal length of the clavicle. It should be done before immobilization, as follows:

1. Sterilize the skin with povidone-iodine or alcohol swabs, and inject 3-5 mL of 1% lidocaine HCl into the fracture hematoma.

Figure 31-4: Pull shoulders up, back, and out while applying counter-pressure against the back with knee.

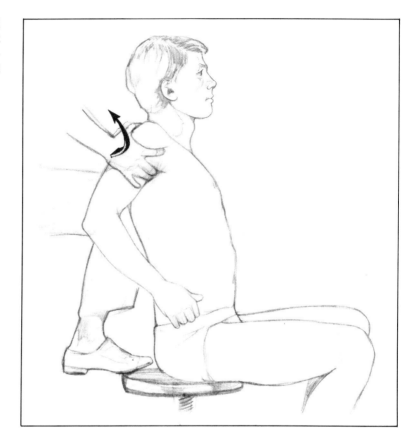

2. When the patient is satisfactorily anesthetized, seat him or her on a stool and put a hand on each shoulder from behind. Pull the shoulders upward, backward, and outward simultaneously while applying counterpressure in the midscapular area, usually by placing your knee in the middle of the patient's back (Figure 31-4). This maneuver usually realigns the fracture fragments. (A well-muscled adult may need plaster casting to maintain the reduction.)

3. Have the patient maintain this position by hooking both arms over a dowel or broom handle held horizontally across the back about level with the lower scapula borders (Figure 31-5) as you prepare the bandage for immobilizing the fracture.

Applying figure-of-8 immobilization

Use the stockinette bandage invaginated into itself in triple thickness; the single thickness has too much stretch to maintain good positioning.

Figure 31-5: Arms hooked over dowel maintains reduction during bandage preparation.

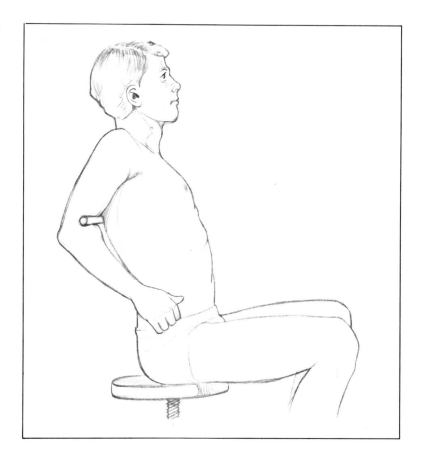

1. Approximate the length of stockinette for the bandage by placing the end at the middle of the patient's back and looping forward under the right axilla, over the top of the shoulder on the right, down to the middle of the back, looping under the axilla on the left and over the top of the left shoulder, returning to the middle of the back (Figure 31-6). Triple this measurement, and cut the stockinette.

2. To invaginate the stockinette into itself, mark off one third of the material, and hold it at that point with one hand. Reach through the entire length with the other hand, grasp the end, and pull that third back through itself, leaving about two thirds of the original length.

3. Visually divide this portion in half, mark that division with one hand, and reach the other hand through the doubled-up segment. Grasp the loose, single-thickness end, and pull it back through the double thickness to produce the desired triple thickness.

4. Position the patient, keeping the dowel or broom handle in place.

5. Envelope two large pieces (about 3 × 6 in) of felt or foam rubber in a single thickness of stockinette, and position them in the axillae for

Figure 31-6: Determining length of stockinette for immobilization.

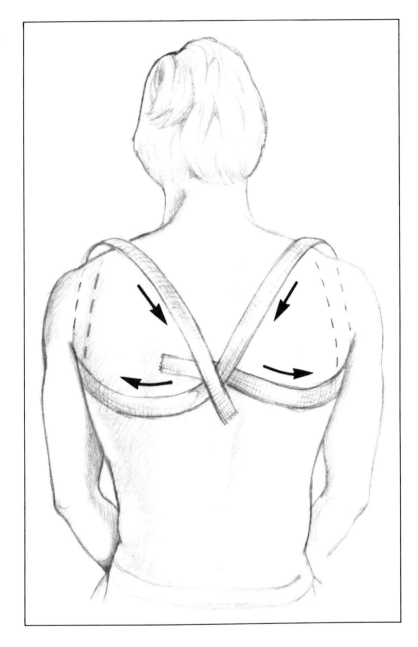

padding. Or you can make a slit at each end of the padding and thread the stockinette through to hold it in place (Figure 31-7).

6. Apply the figure-of-8 dressing in the same way you took the initial measurements, place the loose ends of the dressing in the middle of the patient's back, and pin them together with a large safety pin.

Figure 31-7: Foam rubber padding threaded over stockinette.

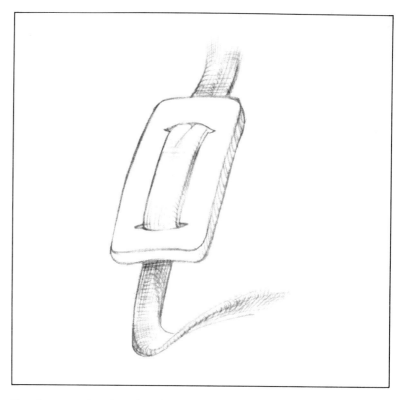

7. Remove the dowel or broom handle, and inspect the patient's shoulders for proper alignment. They should be held up, outward, and backward with proper length and alignment of the clavicle restored and maintained by the weight of the arms over the axillary pads.

Note: When there are overridiing fracture fragments and marked displacement, the stockinette dressing may not be enough. A plaster figure-of-8 dressing is necessary. Follow steps four through seven, with these adjustments:

- While maintaining the appropriate shoulder position, first pad the patient with five or more turns of cotton batting in a posterior figure-of-8 dressing.
- Hold the axilla pads in position while wrapping 10 to 12 turns of a 5-in plaster bandage in a posterior figure-of-8 dressing.
- When the plaster is firmly set, check immobilization by X-ray, and maintain this for 6-8 weeks until a callus forms and fragments are stable.

Note: To treat Type I fractures of the lateral third, you may prefer the Kenny-Howard sling. The shoulder strap applies downward pressure over the padding and holds the end of the clavicle down while the arm portion of the sling supports the forearm and maintains the acromion in an elevated position (see Figure 31-8). An across-the-chest halter pulls the shoulder and sling portions of the brace inward toward the contralateral axilla, which helps to hold the fracture in place. The sling must be worn for 4-6 weeks.

Figure 31-8: The Kenny-Howard sling provides downward pressure on clavicle and maintains the acromion in elevated position.

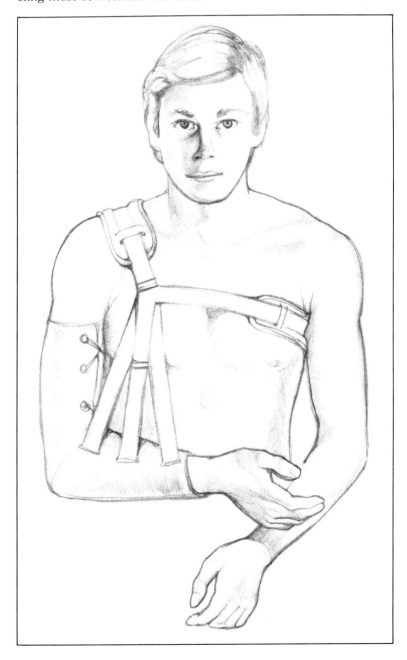

Follow-up

Healing takes 3-4 weeks in children and 4-6 weeks in adults.

In adolescents and adults with moderate displacement and a soft stockinette figure-of-8 dressing, follow-up should be completed in 6-8 weeks. After four weeks, stability usually allows switching to a simple sling for the remaining 2-3 weeks of healing.

In patients with a more serious displacement and a plaster figure-of-8 dressing, determine stability with an X-ray.

In elderly patients, particularly those with fragile skin and very little subcutaneous tissue for padding, a sling is safer and quite adequate for pain relief and immobilization during healing.

Suggested Readings

DePalma AF: *Surgery of the Shoulder,* ed 3. Philadelphia, JB Lippincott Co, 1983, pp. 348-362.

Eskola A, Vainionpaa S, Myllynen P, et al: Outcome of clavicular fracture in 89 patients. *Arch Orthop Trauma Surg* 1986;105:337-8.

Kessel L: *Clinical Disorders of the Shoulder,* New York, Churchill Livingstone Inc, 1982, pp. 109-124.

32

Managing Temporomandibular Joint Dislocation

Dan Heslinga, MD
Charles E. Driscoll, MD

Acute dislocation of the temporomandibular joint (TMJ) can usually be managed by primary care physicians with minimal effort and risk. The TMJ is a sliding joint controlled by the muscles of mastication. At rest, the mandibular condyle sits in the middle of the mandibular fossa of the temporal bone (Figure 32-1). With opening of the mouth, the mandibular condyle slides forward and downward along the articular eminence of the temporal bone.

Sometimes movement continues anterior to the articular eminence without causing difficulty. In many patients, however, this excessive forward motion results in dysfunction with muscle spasm and locks the condyle anterior to the articular eminence (Figure 32-2), probably through excessive and prolonged stretching of the capsular ligament and connective tissues of the TMJ. Dislocation can occur during yawning, certain dental procedures, endotracheal intubation, and other situations involving stretching.

The patient with acute TMJ dislocation is typically in excruciating pain, and efforts to close the mouth increase the pain. Usually, he or she is extremely apprehensive, with muscles of mastication in spasm and no control over saliva. The patient may have a history of other episodes of jaw dislocation.

Three management techniques are recommended in primary care. In order of preference, they are the extraoral, intraoral, and anesthetic approaches. The extraoral method is successful in most patients, keeps your fingers out of harm's way, and is simple enough that the patient can self-administer if he suffers recurrent dislocations. The intraoral method can be held in reserve, with the anesthetic method serving as a last resort.

While TMJ dislocation can usually be managed in the office or emergency department, if it is the result of significant jaw trauma, as

Figure 32-1: Illustration of temporomandibular joint at rest.

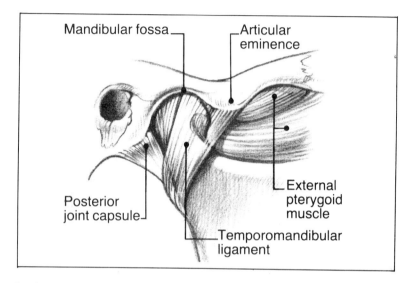

Figure 32-2: Illustration of the condyle locked anterior to the articular eminence.

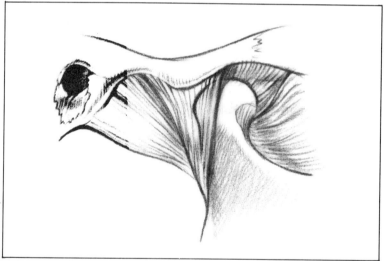

in a car accident, immediate referral to an oral or ENT surgeon is in order.

Materials

Extraoral and intraoral techniques require no equipment; the anesthetic technique requires the following:
- Sterile gloves
- Topical disinfectant
- Intraoral syringe with 25-gauge, 1⅞-in needle
- 2% lidocaine HCl (Xylocaine), 1.8-mL dental cartridge (Carpule)

PROCEDURE

Extraoral

1. At the outset, reassure the patient that simple measures will very likely bring prompt relief.

2. Stand behind the seated patient and place your fingers on the lateral and superior aspects of the mandibular condyles, easily palpated 2-3 cm (¾-1¼ in) anterior to the tragus of the ear.

3. With your fingers, apply a light downward force bilaterally over the condyles. As the condyles move, change the direction of the applied force so that it is directed more and more posteriorly (Figure 32-3). Continue the rotating movement, gently sliding the condyles in an inferior and posterior direction until you feel them return to the mandibular fossa.

Figure 32-3: Extraoral technique of managing dislocation. Fingers rest on the lateral and superior aspects of the manibular condyles. Apply light downward pressure bilaterally. As you feel the condyles move, change direction of force more posteriorly.

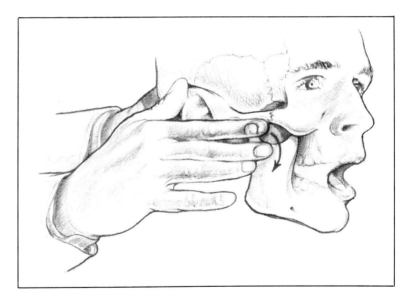

Intraoral

1. Stand in front of the seated patient and place your thumbs in his mouth on the lower molars, your fingers under his chin.

2. Exert downward pressure on the molars while pressing upward on the chin (Figure 32-4) until you feel the condyles return to the mandibular fossa.

Note: Some physicians also exert a posterior force to bring the condyle back over the articular eminence, but excessive pressure of this nature can damage the condyle or articular cartilage of the joint.

Figure 32-4: Intraoral technique. Exert downward pressure with thumbs on molars, while rest of hand presses up against chin.

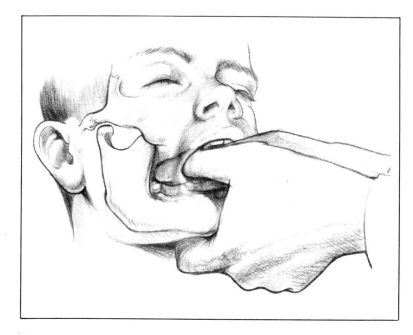

Figure 32-5: Insert needle into the subcutaneous tissue of the mandibular fossa and direct it medially and slightly anteriorly toward the condylar head, slowly injecting anesthetic as you advance the needle.

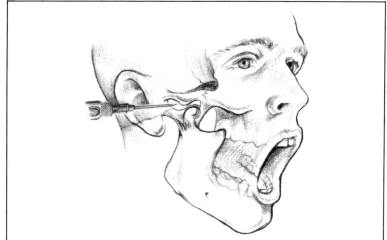

Anesthetic

1. Prepare either the right or left periauricular area of the face with topical disinfectant; even with bilateral dislocation you need inject only unilaterally.

2. With a gloved index finger, palpate the mandibular fossa. This is relatively easy to locate because the heads of the condylar processes are locked anterior to the eminences in the articular plane.

Figure 32-6: When you feel the needle touch the posterior slope of the eminence or the head of the condylar process, withdraw it slightly. Aspirate to check that you are not in a vein, then inject the remaining anesthetic.

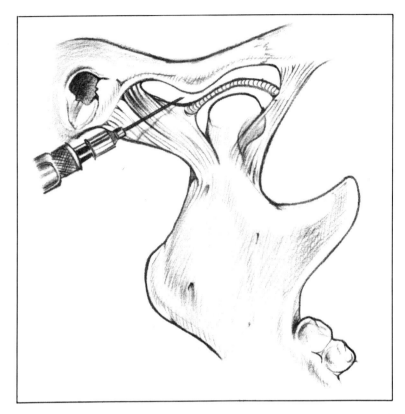

3. Load the 1.8-mL dental cartridge of lidocaine into the breech of the syringe. Insert the needle into the subcutaneous tissues of the mandibular fossa and direct it medially and slightly anteriorly toward the condylar head, injecting anesthetic solution slowly as you advance the needle (Figure 32-5).

4. When the needle touches the posterior slope of the eminence or the head of the condylar process, withdraw it slightly, aspirate to make sure the needle is not in a vein, and inject the remaining anesthetic solution into the tissue surrounding the mandibular fossa (Figure 32-6). Withdraw the needle. The injection should produce spontaneous reduction without manipulation.

Suggested Readings

Littler BO: The role of local anaesthesia in the reduction of longstanding dislocation of the temporomandibular joint. *Br J Oral Surg* 1980;18:81-5.

Vincent JW: Reduction of luxation of the temporomandibular joint—An extraoral approach. *J Prosthet Dent* 1980;44:445-6.

33

Cardiopulmonary Resuscitation in Adults

Gayle Nelson, RN
Charles E. Driscoll, MD

These instructions are based on the assumption that you are the only person present who is qualified to deliver CPR and that emergency medical facilities are not immediately available. If a qualified assistant is present, you can use this method with one person attending to ventilation and the other to chest compression. *Note:* In two-person CPR, the ratio of compressions to ventilations should be 5:1 rather than 15:2 as recommended below (see "Procedure," step 9,).

PROCEDURE

1. Establish unresponsiveness by noting the absence of breathing, the absence of a carotid pulse for at least 5-10 seconds, and the resultant deathlike pallor.

Note: If you find respiratory arrest without cardiac arrest, follow steps 2-5 and then ventilate once every five seconds.

2. Call for help immediately and have someone summon the nearest emergency medical service.

Note: Do not delay beginning CPR to telephone for help. If no one else is immediately available, administer no more than one minute of CPR before leaving the victim to call for help. Rapid application of advanced life support procedures (specifically defibrillation) seems to be critical to survival of out-of-hospital cardiac arrest.

3. Position the victim on a firm surface, moving him or her with care if you suspect a cervical spine injury.

4. Place one hand on the forehead and with the other hand, grasp the bony prominence of the chin and lift to open the airway (Figure 33-1). The airway is likely to be blocked by the tongue when the unconscious person is supine. Check again for breathlessness by watching chest movement and feeling for air movement (Figure 33-2).

Figure 33-1: Position the victim on a firm surface. Place one hand on the forehead and with the other hand, grasp the bony prominence of the chin and lift to open airway.

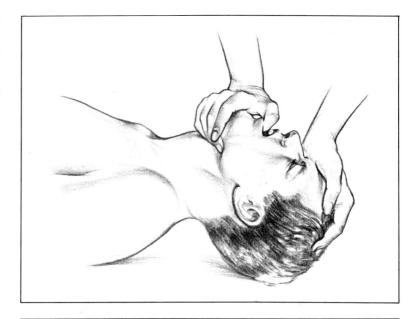

Figure 33-2: Check for absence of breathing by feeling for air movement. If you find no breath response, immediately begin mouth-to-mouth resuscitation.

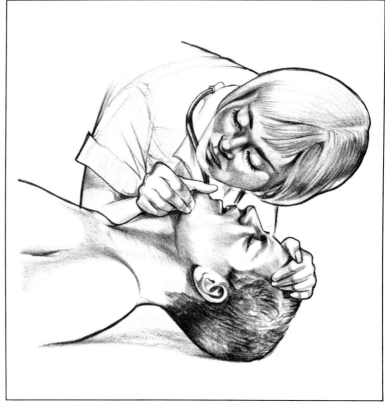

Note: Avoid this maneuver if you suspect cervical spine injury. Open the airway by placing the fingers at the angles of the jaw and anteriorly displacing the mandible, keeping the neck in a neutral position.

5. If you find no breath response, immediately begin mouth-to-mouth resuscitation. Pinch the victim's nostrils closed with the thumb and forefinger as your hand rests on his forehead and seal your mouth firmly over his (Figure 33-3). Blow air into his mouth and watch for responsive chest movement. Listen for escaping air during exhalation as a further sign of lung responsiveness. Transmit two slow, full breaths allowing full lung deflation (1½ seconds each). If you do not see or feel results from your ventilatory efforts, reposition the head and neck and reventilate or begin obstructed-airway procedures if foreign body obstruction is present.

Note: Use mouth-to-nose ventilation when you cannot open the patient's mouth, when the mouth has been traumatized, or when edentia prevents you from keeping a tight mouth-to-mouth seal. Hold the mouth closed as you quickly ventilate mouth to nose.

6. After initiating rescue breathing, begin external cardiac compression. Kneel or stand at the patient's side, locate the lower margin of the rib cage, and identify the xiphoid process.

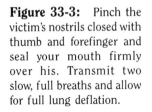

Figure 33-3: Pinch the victim's nostrils closed with thumb and forefinger and seal your mouth firmly over his. Transmit two slow, full breaths and allow for full lung deflation.

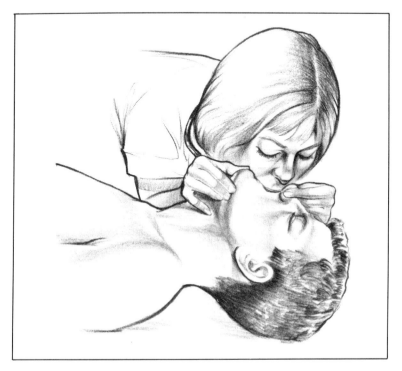

Figure 33-4: Place the heel of one hand on the long axis of the sternum approximately two-finger widths cephalad from the xiphisternal notch. Place the other hand on top of the first so fingers are parallel.

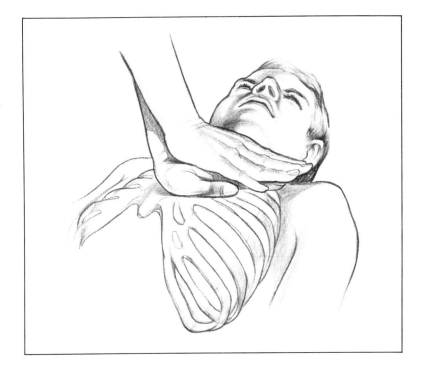

7. Place the heel of one hand—the one closer to the victim's head—on the long axis of the sternum about two-finger widths cephalad from the xiphisternal notch. Place your other hand on top of the first so the fingers are parallel (Figure 33-4). Make sure only the heel of the bottom hand touches the chest.

8. Straighten your elbows and position your shoulders directly over your hands for more efficient application of force. Depress the sternum and release the pressure completely without removing your hands. Aim for depressions of 4-5 cm (1½-2 in) in an adult of average size. Repeat rhythmically and smoothly for a total of 15 compression-release cycles, trying to deliver the compressions at a rate of 80-100/min, so that the series of 15 takes from 8-12 seconds.

9. After the series of 15 compressions, pause to deliver two full ventilations in 4-7 seconds allowing the patient to partially exhale between breaths. Together, the 15 compressions and two ventilations should take from 12-19 seconds. Repeat the cycle of 15 compressions and two ventilations at least four times initially before stopping to check for spontaneous pulse and respirations. Thereafter, pulse and respiration should be checked every 3-5 minutes.

Note: Do not interrupt CPR for more than a few seconds, except to institute endotracheal intubation or to transport the victim. In either case, allow no more than 30 seconds interruption.

10. Continue CPR until emergency personnel and equipment for advanced life support take over or you pronounce the patient dead. Cardiovascular unresponsiveness is generally a more reliable basis for terminating CPR than the ominous signs of cerebral death. Continue CPR for longer periods in special cases, such as in patients who are hypothermic; recovery has been achieved after long periods of unconsciousness in such patients.

Even with skillfully performed CPR, complications may occur, including rib fractures, pneumothorax, hemothorax, gastric distention, and lung contusions. Do not allow concern about possible complications to interfere with prompt administration of CPR.

Suggested Readings

Lampier TA: *Guidelines for Medical and Surgical Emergencies.* New York, Masson Publishing USA, 1983, pp. 234-245.

Mills J, Ho MT, Trunkey DD: *Current Emergency Diagnosis and Treatment.* California, Lange Medical Publications, 1983, pp. 1-22.

Safar P: *Cardiopulmonary Cerebral Resuscitation.* Philadelphia, WB Saunders Co, 1981.

Schwartz G, Safar P, Stone J, et al: The pathology of dying and reanimation, in *Principles and Practices of Emergency Medicine.* Philadelphia, WB Saunders Co, 1985.

Standards and guidelines for cardiopulmonary resuscitation (CPR) and emergency cardiac care (ECC). *JAMA* 1986;21(255):2915.

Wilkens E, Dineen J, Moncure A, et al: Cardiopulmonary resuscitation, in *MGH Textbook of Emergency Medicine.* Baltimore, Williams & Wilkins Co, 1983, pp. 25-39.

34

Emergency Cricothyroidotomy

Lawrence W. Steinkraus, MD
Gayle Nelson, RN

The cricothyroid is an excellent site for securing an emergency surgical airway. It is usually easy to identify in the adult, the trachea is most superficial at the cricothyroid, and serious bleeding can be minimized since major vessels are located elsewhere. By contrast, emergency tracheostomy is difficult, usually results in profuse bleeding, and may take too long to perform.

In children under age 12, needle cricothyroidotomy, also referred to as the jet insufflation method, is a good alternative to the surgical method. Use a catheter-over-needle cannula of at least 12-14 gauge, and a syringe. Insert the needle through the cricothyroid membrane, aiming caudally. When you can easily aspirate air into the syringe, advance the catheter into the trachea. This technique is similar to cannulating a vein.

Connect the catheter to an oxygen source with either a Y-connector or tubing in which a side hole has been cut. For intermittent ventilation, cover the open end of the Y-connector or the hole in the tubing periodically. This technique should not be used for more than an hour because exhalation is inadequate and excess carbon dioxide may accumulate.

When it is possible to pass through the trachea, endotracheal intubation can be performed (see Chapter 35). But in situations involving such conditions as edema of the hypopharynx, epiglottis, or glottis; fracture of the larynx; or profound oropharyngeal bleeding that may obstruct the upper airway, surgical opening for ventilation is indicated.

Cricothyroidotomy is also recommended when there is suspicion of injury to the cervical spine, with or without concomitant head and facial injuries.

Materials

- No. 10 and No. 11 scalpel blades and handle
- 7-mm endotracheal or 5-7 mm tracheostomy tube

- 4 x 4-in gauze sponges
- Local anesthetic with syringe and needle
- Povidone-iodine solution (Betadine)
- Adhesive tape and/or twill tape
- Sterile gloves
- Suction machine and catheters
- Hemostats

PROCEDURE

This method of entry is for an adult patient.

1. Place the patient supine with neck neutral. Slight hyperextension may facilitate locating the thyroid notch, but be sure to rule out cervical spine injury if you place the neck in anything but the neutral position. Monitor the patient, have suction available, and have an assistant for sponging and instrument handling whenever possible. Palpate the thyroid notch, cricothyroid space, and sternal notch (see Figure 34-1). Clean the area with povidone-iodine and, if the patient is conscious, inject local anesthetic.

2. Stabilize the thyroid cartilage and, with the belly of the knife blade, make a horizontal skin incision that extends across the cricothyroid membrane (see Figure 34-2,). Incise quickly and deeply to expose the membrane.

3. With the blade point, stab through the membrane into the trachea. If the patient is making a respiratory effort, you will hear air escape when you enter the trachea.

4. You may open the wound with a curved hemostat or by inserting the knife handle and rotating it 90 degrees. The opening must be large enough to accommodate a 7-mm endotracheal tube or a 5-7 mm tracheostomy tube. The standard endotracheal tube is preferred, since it usually is readily available, is easy to use, and can be cut to size (see Figure 34-3).

5. With either tube, inflate the cuff and secure it by ties to prevent dislodging or accidental extubation.

Note: Check ventilation immediately after placing the tube to confirm tracheal cannulation. If the incision is not deep enough to penetrate the trachea, you may unknowingly place the tube in a subcutaneous track created by pressure used to insert the tube. If this happens, you will hear no breath sounds during ventilation, and subcutaneous emphysema may be evident at the cannulation site. If you use an endotracheal tube, be sure it is not placed too deeply into the right mainstem bronchus.

6. Once you secure the airway and note resumed ventilation, provide 100% oxygen by either bag-valve-tube or ventilator. Monitor the patient's arterial blood gases to guide ventilation therapy.

Figure 34-1: Palpate the thyroid notch, cricothyroid space, and sternal notch.

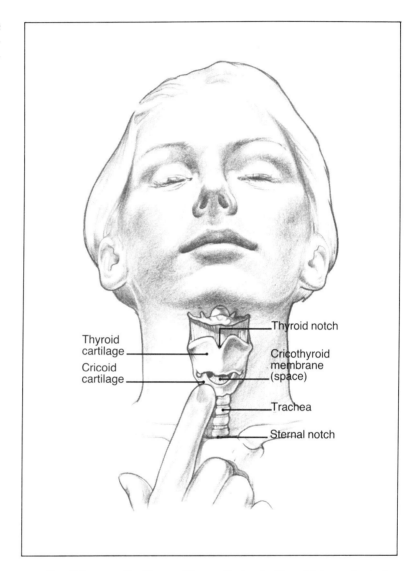

Possible complications with surgical cricothyroidotomy include:
- Asphyxia
- Aspiration
- Hemorrhage
- Hematoma formation
- Stenosis and laceration of the trachea or the esophagus

Emergency cricothyroidotomy is, however, a life-saving procedure intended to secure an airway in a profoundly compromised individual. The alternative to performing the procedure may be death of the patient.

Figure 34-2: With the belly of the knife blade, make a horizontal incision across the cricothyroid membrane. With the blade point, stab through the membrane into the trachea.

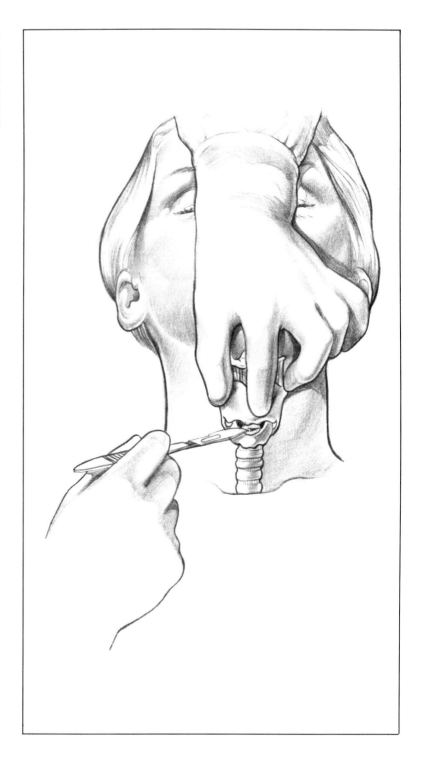

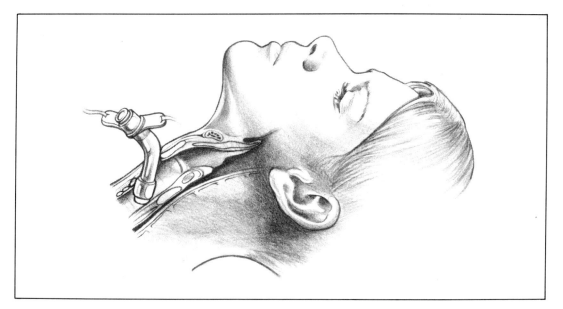

Figure 34-3: After enlarging the opening, insert a 7-mm endotracheal tube. Once ventilation is noted, provide 100% oxygen by either bag-valve-tube or ventilator.

Suggested Readings

American College of Surgeons, Committee on Trauma: *Advanced Trauma Life Support Student Manual.* Chicago, American College of Surgeons, 1984.

American Heart Association: *Advanced Cardiac Life Support Instructor Manual.* Dallas, American Heart Assn Inc, 1983.

Schwartz GR, Safar P, Stone JH, et al (eds): *Principles and Practices of Emergency Medicine,* ed 2. Philadelphia, WB Saunders Co, 1986.

Wilkins EW: *MGH Textbook of Emergency Medicine,* ed 2. Baltimore, Williams & Wilkins Co, 1983.

35

Endotracheal Intubation

Tim Nagel, MD
Charles E. Driscoll, MD

Endotracheal intubation is the definitive procedure for airway management during cardiopulmonary resuscitation (CPR). With the proper equipment and training, you can rapidly establish a patent and protected airway, providing for active and effective regulation of ventilation. It will also guard against aspiration, facilitate suctioning and pulmonary hygiene, and provide a route for the administration of drugs such as atropine, lidocaine, isuprel, epinephrine, and narcan. (Remember these by the mnemonic "ALIEN.")

The procedure should not be undertaken if there is suspicion or evidence of a cervical spine injury, mechanical upper airway obstruction, laryngeal or tracheal trauma, or an inability to open the patient's mouth.

Persons not skilled in passing an endotracheal tube should not try insertion, and those who experience difficulty passing the tube after several attempts should abandon the procedure.

Materials

- Endotracheal tube of proper size (6.5-7.0 mm for women; 7.5-8.0 mm for men) with inflatable cuff
- Laryngoscope with removable curved (McIntosh) or straight (Miller, Guedel) blade
- 10-mL syringe
- Hemostat
- Stylet to stiffen endotracheal tube (optional)
- Bite block or oral airway
- Magill forceps
- Several precut strips of adhesive tape
- Tank or wall source of 100% oxygen
- Bag-valve-mask or pocket mask

PROCEDURE

Note: An intubation attempt should take no longer than 15-20 seconds. Hold your breath when you begin. If the procedure is not

237

completed when you become uncomfortable, remove equipment and ventilate the patient for a few minutes with 100% oxygen, using a tank or wall source and a bag-valve-mask or a pocket mask. Then make another attempt.

1. With the patient supine, place a hand behind the neck and gently pull up to extend it so that the head is tilted slightly backward; avoid hyperextending the neck and take special care to protect the neck if you suspect a cervical spine injury. Place a folded towel or small pillow under the head to keep the mouth, pharynx, and larynx aligned and the neck extended at the atlanto-occipital joint, an alignment commonly called the "sniffing position" (Figure 35-1).

2. Stand at the patient's head with the laryngoscope in your left hand and use your right hand to open the patient's mouth as wide as possible. Gently insert the blade into the mouth along the right side, and let the blade push the tongue gently to the left. Do not allow the tongue to drop back onto the open side of the blade.

3. When the blade is at the midline, exert gentle traction upward at a 45-degree angle to the floor of the mouth, and slowly advance the blade *without* levering against the teeth. If using a straight-blade laryngoscope, place the tip of the blade over the epiglottis to lift it and expose the vocal cords (Figure 35-2). If using a curved-blade laryngoscope, insert the tip between the base of the tongue and the epiglottis to lift them both and visualize the cords (Figure 35-3). If a foreign body obstructs the airway, remove it with the Magill forceps.

4. With the arytenoid cartilages and vocal cords in view, use your

Figure 35-1: A pillow or folded towel placed under the neck keeps the mouth, the pharynx, and the larynx aligned.

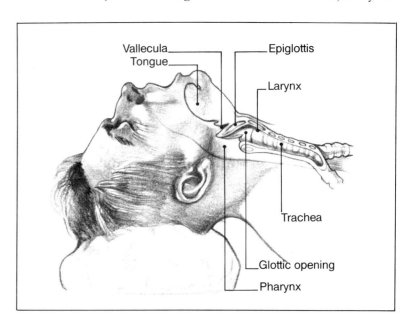

Figure 35-2: When the blade is at the midline, apply gentle traction upward at a 45-degree angle to the floor of the mouth. Slowly advance the blade over the epiglottis to expose the vocal cords.

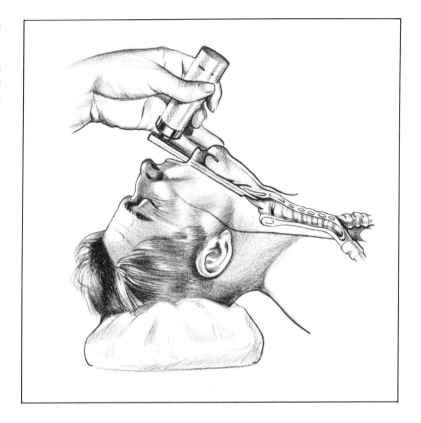

dominant hand to insert the endotracheal tube from the right-hand corner of the mouth, through the vocal cords into the trachea (Figure 35-4). Be sure you see the vocal cords clearly as you move the tube along (Figure 35-5). Pass the cuff about 2.5 cm (1 in) beyond them.

You may want to place a stylet inside the tube before insertion to stiffen the curve. The most likely indications for using a stylet include emesis or blood in the airway, an unusually pliant endotracheal tube, and a narrow or constricted passageway through the vocal cords. When using a stylet, make sure that the end of the stylet rests at least 1 cm (⅜ in) back from the end of the endotracheal tube. Remove the stylet after the tube is passed beyond the vocal cords.

5. Use the 10-mL syringe to inflate the cuff with 5-8 mL of air, and clamp off the inflation line with a hemostat.

6. Make sure the endotracheal tube is placed properly. As a quick assessment, look for symmetric chest rise with ventilation, and auscultate to confirm that breath sounds are equal bilaterally. If breath sounds are absent bilaterally, the cuff is most likely in the esophagus: Deflate it immediately, remove the tube, and ventilate the patient with 100% oxygen for at least three minutes using a tank or wall source and

Figure 35-3: Using a curved-blade laryngoscope. Insert the tip between the base of the tongue and the epiglottis to lift them both and expose the vocal cords.

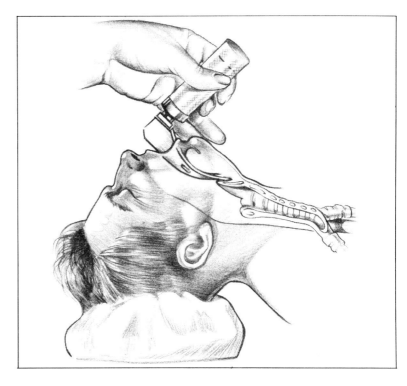

a bag-valve-mask or pocket mask before the next attempt. If you hear breath sounds on one side only (usually the right), the tube has probably entered a main bronchus: Deflate the cuff and very slowly pull the tube back while ventilating, until breath sounds are equally audible on both sides of the chest. Then reinflate the cuff.

7. Use one hand to secure the tube by applying adhesive tape; do not remove your other hand until the tube is taped securely. Once in place, insert a bite block or oral airway to prevent the patient from biting the endotracheal tube and obstructing air flow.

8. With a standard 15-mm adapter on the end of the endotracheal tube, you can attach the tube to a bag-valve device or to a mechanical respirator and continue ventilation with 100% oxygen from a tank or wall source.

9. When intravenous access is delayed, such as occurs when the patient requires CPR, drug administration can be accomplished via endotracheal intubation. The drugs are instilled through the endotracheal tube and ventilation is continued to distribute the drug to the bronchial tree. Absorption into the pulmonary circulation is relatively efficient.

Some complications are common, but they can be avoided or ameliorated by use of the proper equipment and technique:

Figure 35-4: Use right hand to insert the endotracheal tube from the right-hand corner of the patient's mouth.

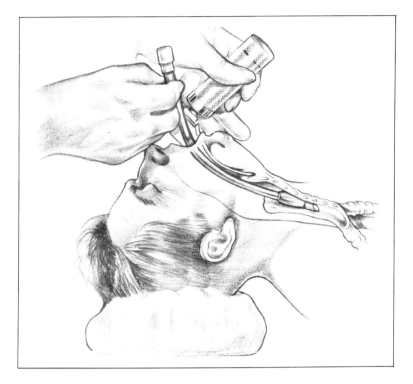

Figure 35-5: Be sure you can see the vocal cords clearly as you advance the tube.

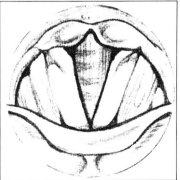

- Cardiopulmonary arrest secondary to hypoxia from a prolonged attempt or improper tube placement.
- Interruption of CPR.
- Aspiration of blood or vomitus during the procedure.
- Endobronchial intubation.
- Vocal cord spasm.
- Teeth fractures.

Suggested Readings

McIntyre KM, Lewis AJ (eds): *Textbook of Advanced Cardiac Life Support.* Dallas, Subcommittee on Emergency Cardiac Care, American Heart Association, 1983.

Raehl C: Endotracheal drug therapy in cardiopulmonary resuscitation. *Clin Pharm* 1986;5:572.

Rosen P, et al: *Emergency Medicine: Concepts and Clinical Practice.* St. Louis, CV Mosby Co, 1983.

Wilkens E, Dineen J, Moncure A, et al: *MGH Textbook of Emergency Medicine,* ed 2. Baltimore, Williams & Wilkins Co, 1983, p. 910.

36

Internal Jugular Vein Catheterization

Ralph Knudson, MD
Gayle Nelson, RN

The medical management of nearly all emergency conditions requires establishing reliable IV access to administer drugs and fluids. Cannulation of a large central vein provides the most versatility and stability; for this procedure, the American Heart Association recommends the internal jugular vein. This vein can also be used to insert an emergency cardiac pacemaker and monitoring catheters (for example, Swan-Ganz).

Cannulation of the internal jugular vein does not require visualization of the vessel, so quick access to central circulation is possible even if peripheral veins are collapsed. But because the internal jugular vein is so close to the carotid and subclavian arteries, the lungs, and the lymphatic ducts and nerves, the risk of damage to these structures is high if the procedure is performed incorrectly. The rate of complications is also higher than for peripheral vein cannulation.

Of contraindication to performing catheterization is acute infection at the site of venipuncture.

Of relative contraindication is the inability to visualize landmarks for any of the following reasons:
- Trauma to the neck
- Hematoma
- Subcutaneous emphysema
- Scarring
- Gross obesity

Materials

- Needle at least 6 cm long with a 16-gauge catheter at least 15-20 cm long; if the catheter is inserted through the needle, a 14-gauge needle is required

- Syringe to attach to the needle as the vein is being located
- IV solution and administration set to attach as soon as the IV line is placed
- Local anesthesia for alert patients (1% lidocaine HCl [Xylocaine HCl]) or normal saline, 5-mL syringe, 25-gauge 1-in needle
- Suture to secure catheter after placement
- Povidone-iodine dressing (Betadine antiseptic gauze pads) and adhesive tape
- Sterile drapes, gloves, mask
- Surgical skin cleanser scrub (Betadine, Hibiclens)

Preparation

Place the patient in a 15-30 degree head-down position to distend the vein and decrease the chance of an air embolus to the cerebral circulation. Work on the right side of the neck because the pleura and dome of the right lung are lower than those of the left, the right atrium is more accessible, and the thoracic duct is not endangered.

The internal jugular vein emerges from the base of the skull, enters the carotid sheath posterior to the internal carotid artery, and lies posterior and lateral to the internal and common carotid artery. Near its termination, the internal jugular vein is lateral and somewhat anterior to the common carotid artery. Posterior, central, or anterior approaches to the jugular can be used. The method described here is the central approach, which is easiest to learn and use.

PROCEDURE

To position the catheter correctly, determine the depth of placement by measuring from the point of insertion to the manubrialsternal junction; this places the catheter at the level of the superior vena cava. Measure 5 cm below that for insertion into the right atrium of the heart. If fluid resuscitation is your major goal, place the catheter in the vena cava above the right atrium.

1. Cleanse the area and prepare with sterile drape. Wear sterile gloves, face mask, and hair cover if possible.

2. If the patient is alert, infiltrate the area with local anesthetic.

3. Palpate the carotid artery, and turn the patient's head to the opposite side of insertion.

4. Insert the needle at the apex of the triangle found by palpating the clavicular (lateral) and sternal (medial) attachments of the sternocleidomastoid muscle (see Figure 36-1). Direct the needle lateral to the carotid pulsation and at a 30-degree angle to the horizontal plane; aim toward the ipsilateral nipple.

Figure 36-1: Insert needle at apex of the triangle found by palpating the lateral and medial attachments of the sternocleidomastoid muscle.

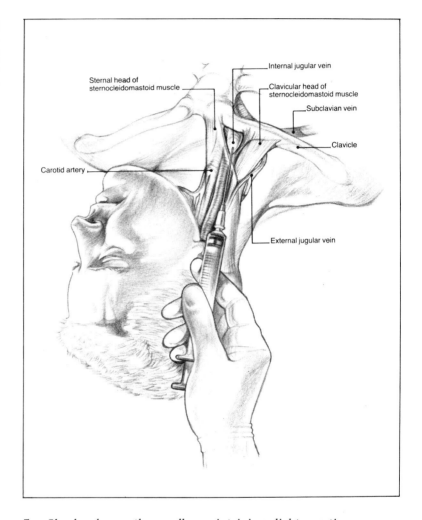

Internal jugular vein

Sternal head of sternocleidomastoid muscle

Clavicular head of sternocleidomastoid muscle

Subclavian vein

Clavicle

Carotid artery

External jugular vein

5. Slowly advance the needle, maintaining slight negative pressure on the syringe until you obtain a blood return (see Figure 36-2). Rapid backward movement of the plunger with the appearance of bright red blood obviously indicates arterial puncture. If this occurs, remove the needle, and apply pressure to the puncture site for at least 10 minutes.

Note: In the event of arterial puncture, do not attempt internal jugular vein cannulation again on either side. This precaution is necessary to avoid a bilateral hematoma that would compromise the patient's airway.

6. Remove the syringe from the hub of the needle, and with gloved finger quickly occlude the needle to prevent air embolization. If the patient is alert, you may have him hold his breath.

Figure 36-2: Slowly advance needle while maintaining slight negative pressure on syringe until you obtain blood return.

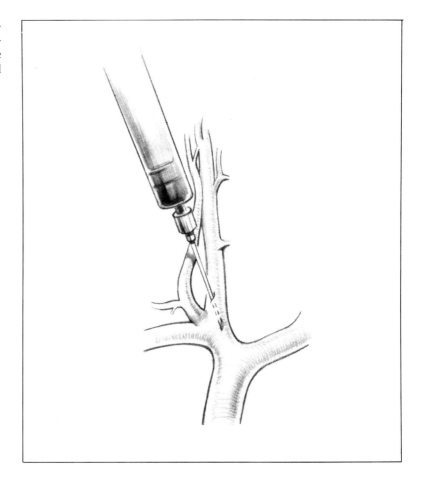

7. Insert the catheter through the needle until it reaches at least the superior vena cava (see Figure 36-3).

Note: If the catheter does not thread easily, remove the entire needle and catheter as a unit to prevent the catheter's shearing and forming a fragment embolus.

8. Affix the catheter to the skin with suture, being careful not to occlude the lumen of the catheter, and attach IV tubing. You may apply a povidone-iodine dressing and tape the catheter IV-line assembly to the skin.

Complications of this procedure include: hematoma, air embolus, pneumothorax, perforation of the right atrium, and puncture of the lung.

A chest X-ray is recommended as soon as possible after completing the procedure to check for proper positioning of the catheter tip, absence of pneumothorax, and inadvertent puncture of the lung.

Figure 36-3: Insert catheter through the needle at least to the depth of the superior vena cava.

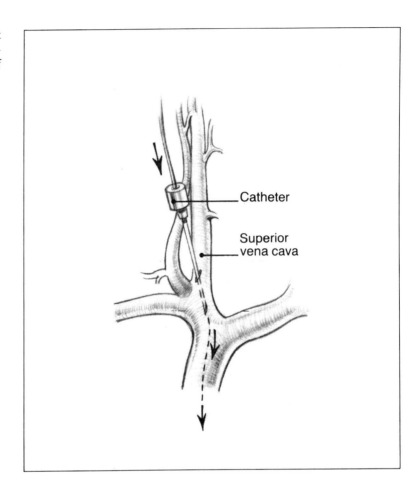

Catheter

Superior vena cava

Suggested Readings

American Heart Association: *Textbook of Advanced Cardiac Life Support.* Dallas, 1983, pp. 157-161.

Schwartz GR: *Principles and Practice of Emergency Medicine,* ed 2. Philadelphia, WB Saunders Co, 1986, vol 1, pp. 430-431.

Standards and guidelines for cardiopulmonary resuscitation (CPR) and emergency cardiac care (ECC). *JAMA* 1986;255:2905-89.

Wilkins EW: *MGH Textbook of Emergency Medicine,* ed 2. Baltimore, Williams & Wilkins Co, 1983, pp. 926-927.

37

Emergency Intraosseous Infusion

Charles E. Driscoll, MD

First developed in the mid-1930s, intraosseous infusion has recently been rediscovered and is recommended for emergency administration of fluids in some cases. The technique is quick and easy to master. It can be performed even in darkness by paramedical personnel as an on-site emergency measure. Complications are minor.

Since bone marrow circulation communicates directly with general circulation, fluids administered into marrow are almost immediately absorbed. The circulation times of intraosseous and IV fluid injections are essentially the same.

With few exceptions, IV access is still preferred, if possible. In situations when venous access is difficult or contraindicated, however, bone marrow infusion should be considered early in resuscitative efforts as an alternative to waiting for central surgical techniques or more sophisticated interventions.

Among its advantages, bone marrow infusion results in a secure access to the circulation that is difficult for an uncooperative patient to dislodge. The technique is preferred over IV infusion in severely burned patients because the small bone-marrow blood vessels act as a filter to prevent pulmonary emboli resulting from embolization of burned epithelial cells into the central circulation. It is also recommended for patients with circulatory collapse, or those in shock.

Intraosseous infusion has been used for administration of blood transfusions, saline, plasma, glucose, Ringer's lactate, thiopental sodium (Pentothal) 5%, dopamine HC1 (Dopastat, Intropin), dobutamine HC1 (Dobutrex), and various antibiotics. Nearly any drug that can be administered by IV infusion can be administered by intraosseous infusion.

The procedure is contraindicated in patients with an underlying infection, bony abnormality, or bone lesion.

249

Materials

- Body or extremity restraints (for small children and uncooperative patients)
- Surgical skin cleanser scrub such as povidone-iodine (Betadine) or chlorhexidine gluconate (Hibiclens)
- Small basin and cotton balls for surgical scrub
- 1% lidocaine HCl (Xylocaine)
- 3-mL syringe with 25-gauge needle for administration of anesthesia
- Sterile rubber gloves
- Sterile towels (if available)
- IV infusion set with drip chamber and tubing
- Adhesive tape for securing intraosseous needle and IV tubing
- 10-mL syringe with 5 mL of sterile normal saline
- No. 11 scalpel blade
- Needles to enter bone marrow: Standard bone marrow needles, special Turkel trephine needles, 18- or 20-gauge short spinal needles, or standard 14-, 16-, or 18-gauge hypodermic needles.

Note: Although the trephine bone needle is preferred, it is rarely available in emergencies, so the standard 16- or 18-gauge hypodermic needle is used more often. Since an open-channel needle may become obstructed with bone chips or marrow during introduction, you may have to introduce a second, smaller-gauge hypodermic needle through the lumen of the first needle to clear the obstruction.

PROCEDURE

1. If the patient is uncooperative or is a small child, apply appropriate restraints.

2. Clean the insertion site thoroughly with surgical scrub and, if convenient, drape the site with sterile towels. Wear a sterile rubber glove on the hand with which you palpate for landmarks.

Recommended insertion sites are the tibia and femur. On the tibia, locate the site in the midline on the flat tibial surface approximately 2 fingerbreadths 2-3 cm (¾-1 in) below the tibial tuberosity (see Figure 37-1). On the femur, locate the site in the inferior third about 3 cm (1 in) above the external condyle in the anterior midline (see Figure 37-2). Less desirable access sites are the iliac crest and the sternum.

3. Anesthetize the insertion site with 1% lidocaine, first raising a wheal in the dermis and then infiltrating the subcutaneous tissues down to and including the periosteum.

4. Make a small nick incision in the skin with a No. 11 blade to facilitate needle insertion.

Figure 37-1: Insertion site on tibia. Find the point in the midline ¾-1 inch below the tibial tuberosity.

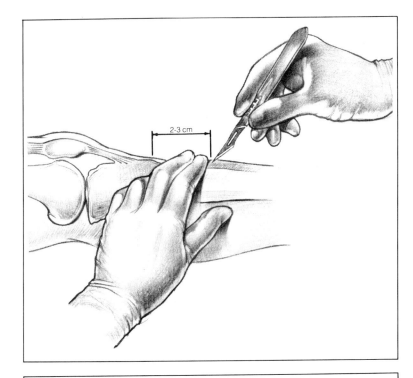

Figure 37-2: On the femur, locate the site in the inferior third approximately 1 inch above the external condyle in the anterior midline.

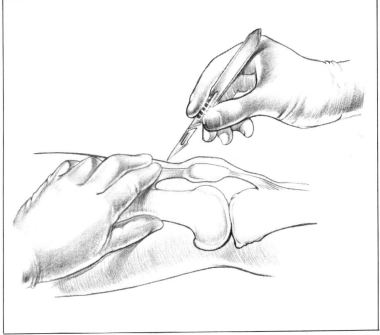

5. Insert a 16- or 18-gauge hypodermic needle (or, if a trephine needle is available, the outer part of the needle with stylet in place) through the incision and down through the subcutaneous tissue until it meets with bone. In the tibia, direct the needle inferiorly, 45-60 degrees above the skin surface (see Figure 37-3); in the femur, direct the needle superiorly at a similar angle (see Figure 37-4).

6. Advance the needle into the marrow space as follows:

Figure 37-3: Through tibial incision, direct needle inferiorly, 45-60 degrees above the skin surface.

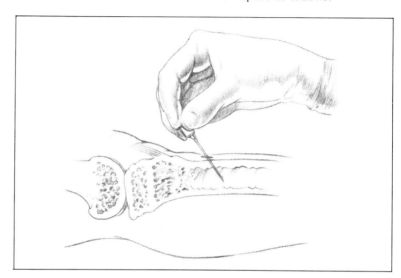

Figure 37-4: In the femur, direct needle superiorly, 45-60 degrees above the skin surface.

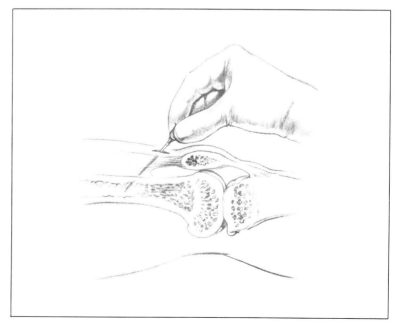

Standard hypodermic needle: Insert the needle well into the medullary cavity. Clean the lumen of the needle by inserting a 14-gauge needle through the larger needle.

Trephine bone needle: Remove the stylet and introduce an inner trephine needle with its stylet through the outer needle. Turn the trephine needle to and fro in a drilling motion with firm downward pressure until sudden lack of resistance signals entry into the medullary cavity. Further advance the trephine needle until it is well within the medullary cavity.

Advance the outer needle through the hole made by the trephine needle. When the outer needle is firmly lodged in the medullary cavity, withdraw the trephine needle.

7. Attach the syringe containing 5 mL of sterile saline to the needle in the bone. Check to be sure marrow is easily aspirated and sterile saline is easily administered into the medullary cavity without significant subcutaneous infiltration.

Other ways to assess needle placement before intramedullary infusion include noting a sudden "give" or lack of resistance as the needle passes through the bony cortex and noting that the needle stands erect without support and feels firmly locked into bone.

8. Detach the syringe, connect the IV line, and infuse sterile saline or other solution as desired. Use strips of adhesive tape to secure the needle and IV tubing to the skin.

Follow-up

Use an intramedullary infusion site for as short a time as possible and for no more than 2-3 days at one site. When infusion is no longer necessary, withdraw the needle and cover the puncture site with a sterile dressing. Observe the puncture site for local inflammation.

Complications are minor but may include:

- Local abscess or cellulitis.
- Subcutaneouos leakage from around the needle.
- Osteomyelitis.
- Small needle-hole defect in the cortex, which may last for several months.
- Sepsis, which can result from improper technique such as failure to observe an aseptic approach, prolonged use of one infusion site, or the infusion of hypertonic solutions.

Suggested Readings

Berg RA: Emergency infusion of catecholamines into bone marrow. *Am J Dis Child* 1984;138:810-1.

Hughes WT, Buescher ES: *Pediatric Procedures,* ed 2. Philadelphia, WB Saunders Co, 1980, pp. 117-119.

Turkel H: Emergency bone marrow infusions. *Am J Dis Child* 1985;139:438-9.

Turkel H: Emergency infusion through the bone. *Milit Med* 1984;149:349-50.

Turkel H: Intraosseous infusion. *Am J Dis Child* 1983;137:706.

38

Emergency Gastric Intubation

Richard W. Niska, MD

There are two diagnostic and three therapeutic reasons for performing gastric intubation on an emergency basis.

When blood is discovered in the stomach, intubation can help diagnose a gastric or esophageal bleed. When a patient is suspected of being poisoned or overdosed with medication, the procedure is recommended to identify the ingested substance.

Therapeutically, gastric intubation provides symptomatic relief from vomiting in a patient to be hospitalized, and prevents aspiration of vomitus into the lungs in a patient whose condition or position makes this likely, especially when the patient has a suspected neck fracture and must be immobilized.

Gastric intubation can be used for lavage, to remove gastric contents, especially ingested poisons or excessive medications, or to instill iced saline to constrict bleeding vessels in gastric hemorrhage. Iced fluid lavage has also been reported as effective in the treatment of heatstroke, as it rapidly reduces the body's core temperature.

During the administration of cardiopulmonary resuscitation (CPR), it can be used to prevent gastric rupture by reducing the air pressure in the stomach, or to improve the effectiveness of ventilation through the reduction of gastric distention and pressure on the lungs.

One other common indication, though seldom an emergency, is insertion of a soft, small lumen tube or intercath for feeding.

While there are a few contraindications, the decision to proceed with the intubation should be made based on the patient's condition, and the risk/benefit ratio involved. In patients with severe otolaryngologic or cranial trauma, the tube can be passed inadvertently into the cranial vault. Avoid this by visualizing the tube in the oropharynx, looking through the mouth.

In cases of esophageal varices, the inserted tube may traumatize a varix and cause hemorrhage. The tube may further traumatize the esophagus of a patient who has swallowed corrosive material.

Figure 38-1: Sump tube (double lumen).

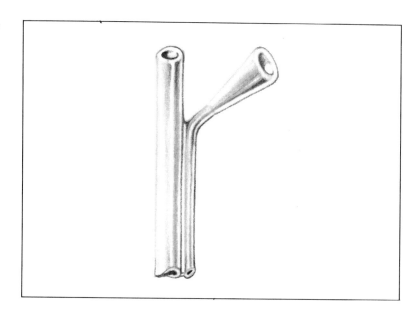

Materials

- *For decompression:* Levin tube (single lumen, with holes in the gastric end), size 10-16 French
- *For aspiration of gastric contents:* Sump tube (double lumen), size 18 French (Figure 38-1)
- *For aspiration of large pills, capsules, or other semi-solid materials:* Ewald tube, size 26-36 French; use a scissors to cut holes in this tube for maximum aspirating capacity if needed; for the conscious patient: diazepam (Valium) injectable
- *General:* 50-mL syringe with catheter tip; drinking water in a glass with a straw; lubricating jelly; adhesive tape; tincture of benzoin (optional)

PROCEDURE

Nasal approach.   This approach is usually used in conscious patients for decompression of the stomach or aspiration of stomach contents other than large pills or capsules.

1.   Examine the nose for septal deviation and select the naris on the side away from deviation to afford more room for passage of the tube.

2.   Have the patient sitting, with neck flexed. (This places the esophagus, rather than the trachea, in a direct line from the oropharynx.)

3.   Lubricate the tube with lubricating jelly.

4.   Advance the tube carefully along the floor of the nasal airway until it encounters the posterior nasopharynx.

Figure 38-2: Firm, steady pressure against the nasopharynx passes the tube downward along the pharyngeal wall.

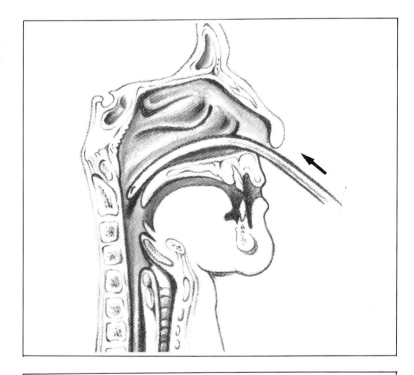

Figure 38-3: Air injected into a tube that has reached the stomach will make a bubbling sound over the epigastrium.

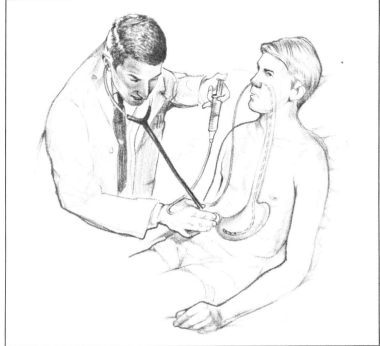

5. Use firm, steady pressure against the nasopharynx to make the tip of the tube slide gradually downward along the pharyngeal wall (Figure 38-2).

6. At this point, have the patient swallow as you advance the tube fairly rapidly. Water sipped through a straw or administered through the tube may facilitate swallowing. *Note:* The patient may regurgitate the tube into his or her mouth. If so, pull the tube back into the nasopharynx, recheck neck flexion, and try again. To avoid passing the tube into the trachea, advance it between the patient's respirations, when the epiglottis is closed.

7. Once the tube is in the esophagus, advance it until the tip is in the stomach. Inject air into the tube with a 50-mL syringe while auscultating over the epigastrium (Figure 38-3), the characteristic bubbling sound of air passing into the stomach will confirm that the tube is in proper position.

Oral approach. This method can be used in unconscious patients when nasal insertion is difficult or in conscious patients when very large-bore tubes must be passed for pill or capsule removal.

1. If the patient is conscious, sedate him with 5-15 mg diazepam IV, administered slowly, determining the dosage by his size and response. Watch for the respiratory depression and cardiac arrest that may occur secondary to injection of diazepam. Be prepared to control the airway or to institute CPR as needed.

2. Place the bite block that comes with the Ewald tube kit into the patient's mouth between the teeth (Figure 38-4).

3. Position the patient's head so that the neck is flexed.

4. Advance the lubricated tube into the oropharynx through the lumen of the bite block. Using the same technique as for nasogastric intubation, advance the tube into the stomach.

Taping. Fasten the nasogastric tube to the patient's nose or cheek with tape. One method is to wrap a long piece of tape around the tube once, leaving two wings of tape that can be used to fasten the tube to the nose (Figure 38-5). Another method is to cut a wide piece of tape down the middle for half its length (Figure 38-6), wrap the uncut end around the tube, and use the split ends for taping to the patient's nose or cheek.

For security, add an extra piece of tape over each wing of tape to keep it down. If you have tape adherence problems, apply tincture of benzoin to the skin and press the tape on when the benzoin has dried enough to be tacky.

Attachment. Connect the external end of the gastric tube to wall suction, syringe, or siphon apparatus as indicated. Whenever possible,

Figure 38-4: Bite block in place. Advance tube into the oropharynx through the lumen.

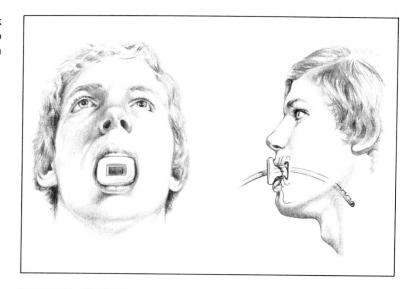

Figure 38-5: Insert is a detail of one taping method. Wrap a length of tape once around the tube, with two wings of tape left hanging to fasten to nose.

use intermittent suction. This allows the tube to fall away from the gastric lining during periods when suction is removed and prevents aspiration of gastric lining into the tube, thereby also helping prevent occlusion.

Figure 38-6: An alternative taping method. Split a wide piece of tape through the center, halfway down its length. Wrap the unslit half around the tube, and afix the flaps to the patient's cheek.

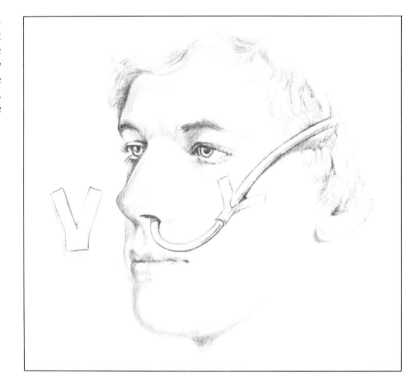

Although nasogastric tube insertion is a routine and safe procedure, certain complications can arise, even when no specific contraindication exists.

Aspiration.   The tube may stimulate vomiting and secondary aspiration. In an obtunded patient without a gag reflex, the airway should be secured with an endotracheal tube, before passage of the NG tube. In a conscious patient, upright positioning will facilitate clearing of vomitus from the airway.

Hematemesis and perforation.   Even in a patient with healthy esophageal and gastric mucosa, passage of an NG tube may traumatize these surfaces. In addition, suction applied to the tube may draw areas of gastric mucosa into the lumen, causing lacerations. A gentle technical approach is the key to minimizing these complications.

Tracheal intubation.   The tube may pass anteriorly towards the trachea, in the hypopharynx, resulting in inadvertent tracheal intubation. Recognition involves the obvious signs of cough and laryngospasm, as well as more subtle signs such as cyclic clouding of the lumen with respirations.

Kinking and lodgement.   The tube may double back on itself in the pharynx or stomach, and become lodged in the esophagus or nasopharynx on retrograde traction. Prevention of injury requires refraining from applying excessive force in removing a lodged tube. Esophagoscopy may be necessary to remove the tube safely. Nasopharyngeal kinks may be managed by oral visualization, grasping the tube with a MacGill forceps, and bringing the kinked section out through the mouth.

Dysrhythmias.   Vagally-mediated bradydysrhythmias, as well as adrenergically-mediated ventricular ectopy, may occur as a result of nasogastric intubation.

Suggested Readings

Askenasi R, et al: Esophageal perforation: An unusual complication of gastric lavage. *Ann Emerg Med* 1984;13:146.

Calvanese JC: Midesophageal kinking and lodgement of a 34-F gastric lavage tube. *Ann Emerg Med* 1985;14:1123.

Syverud SA, et al: Iced gastric lavage for treatment of heatstroke: Efficacy in a canine model. *Ann Emerg Med* 1985;14:424.

Appendix

PRODUCT INFORMATION

Chapter 2   **Starting an IV Line in a Newborn Infant**

[1]Manufactured by Abbott Laboratories Hospital Products Division, Abbott Park, IL 60664.

[2]Manufactured by Critikon Inc., P.O. Box 22800, Tampa, FL 33630.

Chapter 4   **Laryngoscopy**

[1]Dr. Driscoll uses the model ENT-4L Machida fiberoptic flexible nasopharyngolaryngoscope, available from Machida America Inc., 40 Ramland Road, Orangeburg, NY 10962-2698. The scope is 25 cm long (45 cm with control portion) and 4.0 mm in diameter. It weighs 0.2 kg. Angulation is controlled by thumb movement of control knob. Similar instruments are now also available from Olympus Corporation of America, 4 Nevada Drive, Lake Success, NY 11042, and Pentax Precision Instruments, 30 Ramland Road, Orangeburg, NY 10962.

[2]Dr. Driscoll uses the Cavitron Burton LarynxVue, available from Cavitron Burton Medical Products, 7922 Haskell Avenue, Van Nuys, CA 91406. It focuses down to 0.5″ with 3X magnification.

Chapter 5   **Skinfold Measurements**

[1]Two reliable metal calipers are recommended: Lange Skinfold Calipers, Cambridge Scientific Industries, P.O. Box 265, Cambridge, MD 21613, telephone (301) 228-5111 or (800) 638-9566; and Harpenden Skinfold Calipers, British Indicators Ltd., St. Albans, Hertfordshire, England. Fairly reliable plastic calipers are available from Ross Laboratories, 625 Cleveland Avenue, Dept. 441, Columbus, OH 43216, telephone (614) 227-3333.

Chapter 8   Inserting an Intrauterine Device

[1]Source of IUD described: Progestasert, Alza Corporation, 950 Page Mill Road, Palo Alto, CA 94304.

Chapter 9   Newborn Circumcision with the Gomco Clamp

[1]For further information about the Gomco circumcision clamp, write or call Gomco Division of Allied Health Care Products, 828 East Ferry Street, Buffalo, NY 14211, telephone (716) 894-6678; for information about the Plastibell circumcision device, write or call the Customer Services Department, Hollister Inc., 2000 Hollister Drive, P.O. Box 250, Libertyville, IL 60048, telephone (312) 680-1000.

Chapter 14   Flexible Fiberoptic Sigmoidoscopy

[1]Manufacturers of flexible sigmoidoscopes include: American ACMI Division of American Hospital Supply Corporation, 300 Stillwater Avenue, P.O. Box 1971, Stamford, CT 06904; AO Reichert Scientific Instruments, 122 Charlton Street, Southbridge, MA 01550; Fujinon Inc., 672 White Plains Road, Scarsdale, NY 10583; Olympus Corporation, 4 Nevada Drive, Lake Success, NY 11042-1179; Pentax Precision Instruments, 30 Ramland Road, Orangeburg, NY 10962.

Chapter 16   Fine-Needle Aspiration of the Breast

[1]The Cameco syringe pistol is available from Precision Dynamics Company, 3031 Thornton Avenue, Burbank, CA 91504. The Asp Gun is available from Everest Company, 5 Sherman Street, Linden, NJ 07036.